Legal Scholarship in International and Comparative Law

Thomas Groß (ed.)

# Legal Scholarship in International and Comparative Law

PETER LANG
Frankfurt am Main · Berlin · Bern · Bruxelles · New York · Oxford · Wien

**Bibliographic Information published by Die Deutsche Bibliothek**
Die Deutsche Bibliothek lists this publication in the Deutsche Nationalbibliografie; detailed bibliographic data is available in the internet at <http://dnb.ddb.de>.

ISBN 3-631-50895-6
US-ISBN 0-8204-6439-2



Printed in Germany 1 2 3 4 6 7

www.peterlang.de

# Foreword

*Prof. Dr. Thomas Groß, Universität Gießen*

The essays collected in this volume have been presented to the Gießen-Warwick-Lódź-Colloquium at Rauischholzhausen castle in September 2002. The partnership between the law faculties of Gießen and Warwick, going back to the year 1986, has always included a close scientific collaboration of the teaching staff. In that context a colloquium on contemporary topics of general interest in the legal cultures of Germany and Britain takes place every two or three years. In 2002, for the first time, another close partner, the law faculty of the Polish University of Lódź, has joined the colloquium in order to widen up the perspective to the most important eastern neighbour of Germany which will soon accede to the European Union.

The special occasion of this colloquium was the 65th birthday and the "Emeritierung" of Professor Dr. Günter Weick who for a long time has been in charge of the partnership with Warwick. His devotion to the international relations of the Gießen law faculty and his scientific work in comparative and international private law has been highlighted in the inaugural speech by the dean, Professor Dr. Walter Gropp. With kind permission I cite a part of that laudatio:

"It is no coincidence at all that you, dear Mr. Weick, have always been committed to the field of international law. Due to your venia legendi in comparative law the former chair of your predecessor, Prof. Rödig, Bürgerliches Recht, Zivilprozessrecht, Rechtstheorie und Rechtsinformatik was renamed into Bürgerliches Recht, Handelsrecht, Rechtsvergleichung und Internationales Privatrecht only shortly after you received your call to the Justus-Liebig-University. With your commitment it was possible to introduce the two international oriented courses of studies Magister Legum as well as Magister Juris Internationalis. In addition to that you took over the co-ordination of the exchange programmes with the universities of Warwick, Nottingham and Keele. You were responsible for the evaluation of foreign exams and diplomas of LL.M. students, a task that has to be handled with enormous sensitivity and care. I would not be surprised if this task had caused occasional stomach ache to you, dear colleague.

In your scientific publications the international element has always been predominant: Your monograph of your university lecturing qualification published in 1981 is entitled "Vereinbarte Standardbedingungen im deutschen und englischen Bauvertragsrecht". I now know why you carried out your job on construction purposes for our faculty with so much passion. My attraction was also drawn to another publication of 1981: a comparison between the (now former) AGB law and the Unfair Contract Terms Act. The emphasis on terms of business is the thread that is running through your publication. This has also played an important role in several Warwick colloquiums and recently in edition 9 of the Juristenzeitung 2002 in a contribution on the reform of the German law of obligations that contains humour and irony. In 1982 you contributed to the publication in honour of Helmut Coing with your article "Prevention and solution of conflicts in international contracts", a contribution that nowadays is more helpful than ever. Another focus seems to me of hermeneutic nature: "Some problems of interpretation of international legal texts", published in 1991. However, I must admit that I do not know whether "interpretation" means translation rather than interpretation, it might also mean both. You will know better than me what I am talking about, since legal terminology is one of your main subjects as a teacher and as a legal scholar."

The title of the colloquium, "Legal Scholarship in International and Comparative Law", has been chosen to contribute to the special fields of interest of Günter Weick. Scholars of all disciplines of legal science have given presentations on various contemporary problems of common interest. Also guests from other universities with special personal relations to Günter Weick have participated in the colloquium. Some of the contributors are at the beginning of an academic career, others can look back to long and fruitful work as a scholar. Therefore not only the topics but also the participants represent the diversity of European legal cultures.

As vice dean and responsible person for the European relations of the Gießen law faculty I have been in charge to organise the colloquium and collect the contributions for publication. The authors have been free to present either the original version given in the colloquium or an enlarged article. I thank Günter Weick who has always been helpful and willing to share his long experience in the collaboration with Warwick. I am very grateful that the colloquium and the publication have been supported by generous grants of the Gießener Hochschulgesellschaft e.V. and the Verein zur Förderung des Fachbereichs Rechtswissenschaft der Justus-Liebig-Universität e.V. Import assistance during the preparation of the publication has been rendered by Brunhilde Glock and Felicitas Riedel.

## Table of Contents

# Comparative Law and the Past

*Prof. Dr. Dr. h.c. Geoffrey Wilson, University of Warwick*

My contribution to this colloquium breaks a number of rules and traditions of legal scholarship in general, and of the comparative study of law in particular. One is that legal scholars should work from primary sources. To impose this requirement in this case would be to defeat a major object of the exercise. The primary sources are in ancient Mesopotamian languages, mostly Sumerian and Akkadian, written in the script known as cuneiform (Keilschrift). The circle of legal scholars equipped and dedicated enough to read them will, it seems to me, never be adequate to give the subject matter the publicity, accessibility and taken for grantedness it deserves, for it is one of my contentions that ancient Mesopotamian law and culture should be part of the common culture of all legal scholars and particularly of European legal scholars. I would fall at the first hurdle if an ability to read the original texts was a necessary condition. This means, of course, that what I have to say is more in the nature of a foray or exploration than an authoritative exposition that one would expect from an expert in the field.

My contribution also departs from some at least of the traditions of comparative legal scholarship. In spite of its international aura, the comparative study of law has long had a heavily national orientation. We look at other systems to see what we can learn from them, directly for the benefit of our own national systems, or indirectly, by improving our understanding of our own, or we do our best to explain our system to others so that they can do the same.

Of course there is a large body of comparative work that has a truly international character, which has, for example, the aim of harmonising the laws and approaches of different legal systems in the interest of international trade, international public order, international human rights and the reduction of conflicts of laws. From these my contribution differs for another reason. It has no immediate and obvious practical purpose. Here too it is more in the nature of an exploration, this time to see what point there is, what benefit is to be derived, from looking at ancient Mesopotamian civilisation and, because we are legal scholars, the law it produced.

The third departure from tradition is its starting point. It has long been my view that the starting point for the study of law, indeed the sources of its meaning and significance, are to be found outside of the law and, in particular, outside legal rules. The rules and the legal systems themselves are all instrumental. However powerful their internal logic and however autonomous they are or seem or even ought to be, their importance and the relative importance of their different parts, and of the activities that go on inside them, are to be measured by reference to what goes on outside of them in the larger community and culture.

Given the expectations that legal scholarship should be useful and seek to make an impact on contemporary law and society, it was natural in the 1960s when applying this philosophy and looking for points of reference outside the law from which to approach the tasks of reorienting legal scholarship and the wider legal culture of which it is a part, to choose in the first instance common problems facing individuals and the community at large in daily life, individuals as citizens, employers, workers, out-of-workers, businessmen, consumers, householders, and members of families or of minority or disadvantaged groups, which at a community level became problems of constitutional and administrative structures, of the workplace, of commercial activities, housing, families and the environment, many of which cut across the traditional internal classifications of many legal systems, and then to ask what was law doing or could law do about them, alone or in partnership with other agencies and instruments.

My starting point today is completely different. It is the Pergamon Museum in Berlin, which I visited for the first time in 1973 at a time when the city was still divided and the accident of boundary drawing had put the Museumsinsel, and with it the Pergamon Museum, in the eastern sector. The museum is named, of course, after the Hellenistic altar from Pergamon which it houses. But it not only contains the altar. It also contains the Roman market gate from Miletus, and, even more unexpectedly, and far more impressively, a reconstruction of the Processional Way and Ishtar Gate from the ancient Mesopotamian city of Babylon, discovered by Robert Koldewey (1855-1925) in the early years of the twentieth century though not brought to Berlin till 1926, by boat, all the way to the doors of the museum.[1]

The Ishtar Gate was the main gate of at least eight double gates, each dedicated to a different god or goddess, set into some eighteen kilometres of the double outer walls of the city, which also had towers set in them every seventeen metres or so. The Processional Way was the main street. It led from the Esagila temple dedicated to Marduk patron god of the city, round the palace, through the Ishtar Gate, to the Akitu temple outside the walls. It was the route of the annual procession at the New Year festival when the images of the gods were carried along it.

Babylon was generally a highly coloured city and the Processional Way and the Ishtar Gate were typical. For some two hundred metres the Way passed between high walls which were covered in blue glazed bricks decorated with two rows of lions, the symbol of the goddess Ishtar, made of moulded glazed bricks, either white with yellow manes or yellow with red manes. The Gate itself was covered in blue bricks decorated with moulded glazed bricks of dragons and

1 G. Leick, Mesopotamia, The Invention of the City, London, 2001, p. 247.

bulls, the symbols of the gods Marduk and Adad, alternating in white and yellow.[2] It is the combination of monumentality and colour which create such a striking effect in the museum, even though the reconstructed Processional Way itself is only one third of its original width and the Gate itself consists of only the smaller outer gate flanked by two towers. It was, in fact, the coloured tiles, which he said were of "singular beauty and art-historical value",[3] that had attracted Koldewey when he was looking for a site for a major German exploration on behalf of the Berlin royal museums in 1882.

The Pergamon museum is not unique in its possession of impressive and monumental artefacts from ancient Mesopotamia. Koldewey in fact came somewhat late to the task of rediscovering the ancient sites. As early as 1811 to 1817 the English Resident of the East India Company in Baghdad, Claudius Rich, had done some digging at Babylon and sent some objects back to the British Museum in London.[4] But it was in the 1840s that the first major discoveries came, and then not in southern Mesopotamia, the land of Babylon, but further north in the heartland of the Assyrian Empire.[5] And it was the Louvre in Paris and the British Museum in London who were the major beneficiaries.

Up till the nineteenth century knowledge of the area was sparse and uncertain. It came from the Bible, Greek historians such as Herodotus (484-420), medieval Arab geographies and the reports of occasional travellers over the centuries.[6] Herodotus had actually visited the site of the ruins of Babylon. The city in his view surpassed the splendour of all the cities of the known world.[7] The Bible was less enthusiastic. Both Babylonia and Assyria had attacked Jerusalem and deported its leading inhabitants.[8] It presented the Tower of Babel as a symbol of

---

2 Nebuchadnezzar himself wrote of the gate "I caused (the gate) to be firmly set forth with bricks of blue enamel on which wild oxen and dragons were pictured ... lusty wild oxen of bronze and raging dragons I placed at the thresholds. The gateways I caused to be made glorious for the amazement of all peoples." R. Koldewey, The Excavations of Babylon, translated A.S. Johns, 1914, p. 44.

3 R. Koldewey, Das wiederentstandene Babylon, 9th edition, Munich, 1990, p. 7.

4 He also published the first detailed study of the site in 1815.

5 Mesopotamia means the land between the rivers Tigris and Euphrates. Southern Mesopotamia was divided into Akkad in the north and Sumer in the south. Assyria occupied much of Northern Mesopotamia. It is therefore the area covered today by Iraq, northern Syria and parts of south-eastern Turkey.

6 Although some ruins were above ground the bulk of the traces of these ancient cities and civilisations lay beneath large mounds of debris, in what was then part of the Ottoman Empire, waiting to be discovered.

7 He was particularly impressed by the outer walls, wide enough to allow a four-horse chariot to turn, with, he said, one hundred bronze gates, and inside them a tower, a palace, a temple and three-storey houses.

8 "By the waters of Babylon we sat down and wept, when we remembered thee O Zion", Psalm 137. "In the ninth year of Hoshea the king of Assyria took Samaria and carried Is-

man's folly and arrogance and Babylonian rulers such as Nebuchadnezzar and Belshazzar as tyrants. In the New Testament Babylon was the symbol of decadence, "mother of harlots and abominations of the earth".[9]

It was not until the nineteenth century that reliable knowledge of the area began to accumulate as a result of extensive excavations in the area. In March 1843 that Emile Botta, the French Consul at Mosul, discovered the palace of the Assyrian king Sargon II at Khorsabad (Dur-Sharrukin)[10] and shortly afterwards in 1845 that Austen Layard found the palace of Ashurnasirpal II (883-859) at Tell Nimrod (Nimrud) and in 1846 the palace of Sennacherib (705-681) at Tell Kuyunjik (Nineveh).[11] And in 1853 his former assistant Hormuzd Rassam discovered the palace and library of Ashurbanipal at Nineveh. The objects they found, colossal statues and reliefs, formed the basis of the Mesopotamian collections at the Louvre and the British Museum. And further French and English discoveries elsewhere in Mesopotamia followed those of Koldewey. In 1902 French archaeologists at Susa, capital city of the Elamites, found the stela on which the laws of Hammurabi were written and in the 1920's the Englishman Leonard Woolley discovered the royal tombs of Ur, one of the earliest Sumerian cities.[12] Both discoveries served further to enrich the museums of Paris and London.

But spectacular statues, reliefs, buildings and objets d'art were only a part of what was discovered by the diggers of Mesopotamia. Even more spectacular were the thousands of clay tablets (Tontafeln) covered in writing that were also

---

rael away into Assyria ... And the king of Assyria brought men from Babylon, and from Cuthah and from Ava and from Hamath and from Sepharvaim and placed them in the cities of Samaria instead of the children of Israel", 2 Kings 17: 6 and 24.

9 Revelation 17:5.

10 He sent sculptures back to the Louvre. Henry Rawlinson for the British Museum acquired some he had left behind because they were too heavy to move, including two large winged bulls with human heads. He solved the problem of transportation by sawing them into pieces.

11 "I opened ... not less than seventy-one halls, chambers, passages, whose walls, almost without exception, had been pannelled with slabs of sculptured alabaster, recording the triumphs and great deeds of the Assyrian kings. By a rough calculation ... nearly two miles of bas-reliefs, with twenty-seven portals formed by colossal winged bulls, lion sphinxes, were uncovered in that part alone", A. Layard, Discoveries in the ruins of Nineveh and Babylon, London 1853, p. 589, cited Leick p. 219.

12 Leonard Woolley's discoveries at Ur rivalled those of Howard Carter a few years earlier in Tutankamun's tomb in Egypt. The Royal Graves of Ur contained members of the royal family buried with their retinues and spectacular objects. One grave had sixty-eight skeletons of women with gold and silver headdresses together with soldiers armed with spears and two ox-drawn wagons. The Royal Standard of Ur had scenes of war, chariots and footsoldiers fighting a naked enemy, and of peace, a royal feast with figures in sheepskin kilts.

found. Many of them were found stacked together in archives created for administrative purposes such as the records of the administration of a palace or temple. Others were collections of texts and exercises used in schools for the education and training of scribes, some even containing the mistakes and repetitions one would expect of someone engaged in a learning exercise. Others had been collected together as booty or brought together in libraries. And it was not only the clay tablets that contained writing. There were inscriptions on foundation stones, stelae, boundary stones, even on some of the reliefs and statues themselves, as well as on smaller objects such as cylinder seals. Some of the clay tablets themselves were contained in sealed envelopes with the text on the tablets inside repeated on the envelopes outside. Vast quantities ended up in the major European and, later, American and Iraqi museums, as well as in the hands of private collectors.

Many of the tablets are originals but there are also many copies, made later. Scribes in the Old Babylonian period c1800-1660 copied many older texts including royal inscriptions as did scribes employed by the Assyrian ruler Ashurbanipal in the seventh century.[13] Some of the copies were made for practical reasons as a means of preserving or publishing their contents, collections of laws for example, or standard legal procedures. Others were made for and by scribes in the course of their training which included training in the drafting of legal transactions.

The earliest written tablets came from Uruk (the Biblical Erech) and the writing was largely pictographic, like Egyptian hieroglyphs and early Chinese characters, where the symbols picture the object they are meant to represent, cattle, fish and barley, for example.

Later the signs lost their pictographic character and came to represent words, sounds and even syllables. There were changes too in the writing method, at first to a pointed stylus used to scratch the symbols on wet clay, and, from the beginning of the third millennium BC, to an instrument which impressed the wedge shaped marks known as cuneiform, which continued to be used as the standard script throughout the Near East till the first centuries A.D. The original language used was Sumerian but this was gradually replaced by Akkadian in official

[13] Ashurbanipal wrote that "I wrote this tablet ... following the contents of clay and wood tablets, exemplars from Assyria, Sumer and Akkad, checked and collated it and placed it in my palace for myself to read." H. Hunger, Babylonische und Assyrische Kolophone, 1968, p. 97. This is the same Ashurbanipal who is shown on a relief from his palace at Nineveh having a picnic while the head of his defeated enemy, the Elamite king, hangs from a nearby tree.

documents. The laws of Ur-Nammu, for example, are in Sumerian, the laws of Hammurabi are in Akkadian.[14]

Even without writing the reliefs and statues convey messages, record events and provide information about Mesopotamian civilisation as a whole. The graphic Assyrian reliefs in particular illustrate, with greater realism than their Egyptian equivalents, details of battles and victories as well as lion hunts, with the kings shooting from moving chariots. But quite often the statues and reliefs do have captions. In addition boundary stones record land transactions as well as boundaries. Cones set in walls of temples and palaces and foundation stones record who built or restored them and why. But it is above all the many thousand of inscribed clay tablets that provide the basis of most of our information.

This does not mean that we know all we may want to know. There is both a randomness and possible bias in what we know. The randomness is the result of our dependence on what has survived and what has been discovered. Some ancient sites now lie below new towns which cannot be disturbed. The location of others still remains a mystery. Some remains are below the water level. Some unbaked clay tablets dissolved as soon as they were exposed to the air. And any generalisation from what we know can easily be upset by new discoveries. The possible bias is the result of archaeologists' preoccupation with public buildings, in particular temples and palaces, and as a result the more likely discovery of official records and archives, rather than the records of private individuals.

The earliest tablets were simple accounts, recording the movement of cattle or the distribution of rations. Then there are lists of all kinds, the names of animals, cities, professions, and most important of all, lists of kings. Later come letters, diplomatic letters between rulers,[15] letters between rulers and their subordinates and from subordinates to one another,[16] letters between rulers and their

---

14 Cuneiform script was deciphered in 1850 by Henry Rawlinson (1810-1895) using a three language inscription of Darius of Persia (521-486) carved on to a mountain side in Behistun in Persia.

15 Diplomatic letters from Babylonian and Assyrian rulers to the Egyptian pharoah were found in Tel-el Amarna which Akhenaton (Amenophis IV) built as his new capital. Ashur-uballit I of Assyria (1353-1310) wrote to him "Gold in your country is dirt; one simply gathers it up. Why are you so sparing of it? I am engaged in building a new palace. Send me as much gold as is needed for its adornment .... If your purpose is graciously one of friendship, send me much gold." W.L. Moran, The Armarna letters, Baltimore, 1992, p. 39.

16 "Say to my lord ... the troops are well. The city is safe. The garrison ... is strong. Even if the Amorites should make war for ten years and bring ten battering rams, ten siege towers (and) twenty ladders (?) I will remain strong in my city. My lord should not worry." A letter from Eshnunna in Old Babylonian Times. R. Whiting, Old Babylonian Letters from Tell Asmar, Chicago, 1987.

families,[17] letters between merchants and their agents.[18] There are myths and legends,[19] proverbs and wise sayings,[20] mathematical and astronomical texts and, of course, records of laws, legal transactions and judicial decisions.

The general history that the tablets, inscriptions, letters, archaeological finds, and the Bible, reveal is one of the rise and fall of a number of cities and city states, and of some empires, in particular the Babylonian and Assyrian empires, stretching from the 4th millennium BC when Sumerians settled in the area to the defeat of Belshazzar of Babylon by Cyrus of Persia in 539 BC.[21]

But the points of this paper can be made without looking at the whole history. It is enough to concentrate on the period up to the time of Hammurabi (c1792-1750 BC) and the first, Old Babylonian empire. And, though it mentions Assyria on the way, it does not discuss Assyrian laws[22] or those of powerful neighbours such as the Hittites. It focuses in particular on the sources of infor-

---

17 Yashmah-Addu governor of Mari writes to his father Samshi-Addu governor of Ashur "I read the letter you sent to me Daddy, in which you said: '... You are a child, not a grown man, you have no hair on your chest. How much longer will you fail to direct your own household properly? Don't you see that your own brother is directing vast armies? ...'. I am coming to you right away now to have it out with (you) Daddy about my unhappiness", G. Dossin, Archives royales de Mari I. Correspondence de Samshi-Addu et ses fils, transcrite et traduite, Paris, 1950, p. 183.

18 The best examples are letters between merchant principals in Ashur and their agents in Kanesh in Anatolia which throw a good deal of light on business practices and relationships. J. N. Postgate, Early Mesopotamia, London, 1992, p. 213; Leick, p. 201.

19 E.g. the Epic of Gilgamesh, the legendary king of Uruk, and the Flood Myth or Epic of Utnapishtim who built an ark to save his family and animals from the Great Flood. There is also a reference to a Great Flood in the Sumerian king list which distinguishes the kings "before the flood swept over the land" from those who came after. Cp. The legend of Sargon of Akkad who was floated as a child in a reed basket sealed with bitumen on the river Euphrates, was found and brought up as a gardener. "While I was still a gardener" he recalled "Ishtar grew fond of me", J.G. Westenholz, Legends of the Kings of Akkade, 1997, p. 41.

20 "A millstone will float for a righteous man." "A thriftless woman living in the house is worse than all diseases." "What has been spoken in secret will be revealed in the women's quarters"; B. Alster, Proverbs of Ancient Sumer, Bethesda Md., 1993, vol. 1 pp. 20, 204 & 220. "Do not loiter when there is a dispute. For ... they will have you as an observer. Then you will be made a witness ... and they will involve you in a lawsuit to affirm something that does not concern you." J.B. Pritchard, Ancient Near Eastern Texts, Princeton, 1969, p. 595.

21 As foretold by Daniel in his interpretations of the mysterious writing which appeared on the wall at Belshazzar's feast, "Thy kingdom is divided and given to the Medes and Persians", Book of Daniel, 5.28.

22 Even though this means excluding e.g. the collection of Middle Assyrian Palace devices of c1076 BC which regulated behaviour in the royal harem and provide an attractive diversion from the normal subject matter of land sales and the liabilities of neighbours, boatmen and shepherds.

mation we have about law in the city states of Ur, Isin, Eshnunna and the first empire of Babylon.

### Law in ancient Mesopotamia

There are four major sources of our knowledge of law in ancient Mesopotamia, the royal law collections, in particular those made by Ur-Nammu of Ur, Lipit-Ishtar of Isin, an unknown king of Eshnunna and by Hammurabi of Babylon; records of judicial decisions, particularly a collection found at Girsu from the time of the Third Dynasty of Ur; numerous records of legal transactions; and the many copies, collections of texts and of standard provisions used by and for the training of scribes, prominent among which is the series known as Ana Ittishu,[23] a collection of legal terms and formulae set out in Sumerian with their Akkadian equivalents, and a similar series known as Harra-Hubullu.[24]

In addition of course administrative and economic texts, letters, and royal inscriptions can offer clues, if not directly to the laws and legal systems themselves, at least to the background against which and the framework within which the laws and systems worked, family and business relations, for example, or the roles of different groups within the community, such as the women, dedicated to a god, known as naditu, who were active in the commercial field.

## THE LAW COLLECTIONS

### The king and the administration of justice

Much of what we know about ancient Mesopotamia comes from royal inscriptions. They may not always reveal the truth but they do reveal what it is that rulers wanted people to know about them, and the same goes for the reliefs with which they decorated their palaces.

In conducting their activities the rulers do not simply claim to be acting in their own names but on behalf of the gods who have given them their "kingships" and legitimacy but are also presented as a source of authority for their activities.

Among their claims to fame there is no shortage of victories and defeated enemies, both dead and paying tribute. This is especially true of the Assyrian rulers. "I filled the caves and ravines with their corpses" wrote Tukulti-Ninurta I (c1244-1208), son of Shalmaneser I. "I made heaps of their corpses (like piles of grain) beside their gates. Their cities I ravaged (and) I turned them into hills of

---

23 The name seems to be derived from the records of loans where the repayment date was to be notified. The collections were made in Neo-Assyrian times but their contents seem to go back as far as the Third Dynasty of Isin (c2302-2076) and include provisions one would expect to find in Old Akkadian and Old Babylonian contracts.

24 These are the Sumerian and Akkadian words for a debt or loan.

ruins".[25] And we are not spared the detail. Reliefs on the walls of Sennacherib's palace in Nineveh include Judaean captives being impaled on stakes outside the walls of Lachish.[26] A relief in the palace of Ashurbanipal shows the decapitation of the king of the Elamites and another shows his severed head hanging from the tree while Ashurbanipal and his queen enjoy a feast in the open air.[27]

But victorious campaigns are not the only things in which Mesopotamian rulers express pride. Building and buildings came high on their lists of achievements especially restoring old and building new temples, and building grand palaces.[28]

High on the divine and royal agenda of rulers is the well-being of their people and it is not surprising to see some of them at least calling themselves the shepherds of their people.[29] And these general claims are supported by reference to specific acts, the introduction of a system of weights and measures, fixing prices and wages, fixing the rates of hire of basic animals such as oxen or donkeys, fixing rates of interests, fixing the exchange rates of silver and barley.[30] The Prologue to the laws of Ur-Nammu, King of Ur from 2112-2095, includes the fact that he had among other things regulated the river traffic on the Tigris, the Euphrates and other rivers. Rimsin I of the city state of Larsa (1822-1763) recorded that "Enlil ... gave me the great mission of digging a canal to bring abundant waters to Sumer and Akkad, to make their extensive fields grow the dappled barley, to let the orchard wells increase the [ ] of honey and wine, and to let their marshes joyfully provide fish... The towns and villages, the numerous people Enlil has given me, having assembled them from top to bottom (of the land) I fashioned the (canal's) two banks like awe-inspiring mountains .... I called the canal Tugmat-Erra and thus restored the eternal waters of the Tigris and the Euphrates".[31]

---

25 A.K. Grayson, Royal Inscriptions of Mesopotamia, Toronto, 1987, vol. 1, p. 234.

26 See M. Roaf, Cultural Atlas of Mesopotamia, 1990, p. 185.

27 E. Strommenger, and M. Hirmer, The art of Mesopotamia, London, 1964, p. 1, 241.

28 "I assembled the kings of the Hittites and of the other bank of the Euphrates, in all twenty two kings" wrote the Assyrian king Esarhaddon (c680-669). "I gave them my orders; beams, columns, cedar and cypress boards. Winged bulls and stone colossi, stone covering slabs, baked bricks, marbles, stones from the mountains, for the needs of my palace they had brought to Nineveh, my royal city, with difficulty and trouble.... Gates with pleasantly perfumed cypress wood I had covered with silver and copper", L. Laroche, p. 72.

29 A king of the city state of Isin writes "In Nippur I sought out nourishment for them like sheep and fed them with fresh grass", Postgate, p. 239, citing F.R. Kraus, Königliche Verfügungen in altbabylonischer Zeit, Leiden, 1984, p. 29.

30 The laws of Eshnunna, below, do this extensively, p. 18.

31 E. Sollberger and J.R. Kupper, Inscriptions royales sumeriennes et akkadiennes, Paris, 1971, p. 206.

Part of the well being of the people was freedom from oppression both as a people and as individuals. And one of the explicit duties and functions accepted by Mesopotamian rulers as being imposed on them by the gods was the provision of justice to the people. The Prologue to the Laws of Lipit Ishtar king of Isin (r1934-1924) is typical. "(T)he gods An and Enlil called Lipit-Ishtar to the princeship of the land – Lipit-Ishtar, the wise shepherd, ... in order to establish justice in the land, to eliminate the cries for justice, to eradicate enmity and armed violence, to bring well-being to the lands of Sumer and Akkad."

The role of the king in this respect took a variety of forms. He was both a source of social justice and justice in the community at large and of justice in individual cases. He removed abuses. Urukagina of the city state of Lagash (r c2378-2371) said he had tried to restore the golden age of Sumer before the gods had introduced pain and misery. He had stopped palace officials extorting goods and he had extended royal ownership over much of the land.[32] The king protected his merchants and citizens when they were abroad, negotiating agreements with other rulers to protect each others' citizens.[33] He issued decrees from time to time to cancel debts and obligations and to free existing debt slaves,[34] not only debts and obligations owed to the palace but generally, and even cancelled

32 When he had come to power, he said, "the oxen of the gods were used to plough the garlic plots of the ensi (the secular ruler) and the best fields of the gods became the garlic and cucumber plots of the ensi ... (T)he grain of the temple administration was distributed by the personnel of the ruler. These were the practices of former times. When Ningirsu, warrior of Enlil granted the kingship of Lagash to Urukagina ... he replaced the customs of former times, carrying out the commands Ningirsu had given him", J.S. Cooper, Sumerian and Akkadian royal inscriptions, 1986, 71. A king of Isin wrote "I turned the palace livestock out of their ploughed fields and banished the people's cries "O Shamash", F.R. Kraus, Königliche Verfügungen in altbabylonischer Zeit, Leiden, 1984, 29-30, cited Postgate, p. 239.

33 Postgate, p. 256, for a treaty between the rulers of Sadlas and Neribtum. There is also a letter from the Hittite king Hattusili to king Kadashman-Enlil of Babylonia c1270 in which he apologises for the murder of some Babylonian merchants, says that compensation had been paid, but adds that it was not Hittite practice to execute murderers. "They do not kill (as punishment) in Hatti ... If the king hears about it they pursue that matter. They apprehend the murderer, deliver him to the relatives of the dead man, but they allow the murderer to live. If his relatives will not accept the compensating silver they will make the murderer their slave." G. Beckman, Hittite Diplomatic Texts, 1996, p. 133.

34 E.g. the decree of Ammi-Saduqa (c1646-1626) last but one king of the Old Babylonian dynasty, who cancelled debts and freed debt slaves. Leick, p. 187, citing F.R. Kraus, Ein Edikt des Konigs Ammi-Saduqa von Babylon, Leiden, 1958. Enmetana of Lagash said he had "annulled debts for Lagash, restoring mother to child and child to mother", Postgate, p. 196, citing J.S. Cooper, Sumerian and Akkadian royal inscriptions, vol. 2, New Haven, 1986, p. 58. It seem that the decrees of debt relief were often of particular benefit to foreign debt slaves.

sales made under the pressure of poverty.[35] He acted as judge in the more serious cases.[36] He heard appeals for justice when the law did not provide it.[37] And occasionally he made at least some laws, both individual laws, and in the grander of cases, collections of laws.

**The law collections**

Although the law collection of Hammurabi is the most heard of (it seems too much to say best known) it is not the only collection of laws that has survived from ancient Mesopotamia. At least three earlier collections are known, the laws attributed to Ur Nammu, king of Ur, the laws attributed to Lipit-Ishtar, king of Isin, and the laws of Eshnunna.

It is probably too late to stop calling the law collections "codes", especially when we come to the "code" of Hammurabi. But it is nonetheless misleading. They certainly do not have the characteristics of modern European law codes. They are not comprehensive. It is clear that the legal provisions themselves must be seen as part of a wider customary tradition which is often more directly revealed in records of actual legal transactions and of judicial decisions or even in letters and administrative texts. They are not organised on the basis of any general concepts or principles or even on any obvious plan, even on the basis of subject matter though similar situations do sometimes come in a block – a group of provisions dealing with physical injury, or husbands and wives, or inheritance, for example, but one cannot rely on this. They are not authoritative in the sense that we find judges referring to them or relying on them explicitly as the basis of their decisions. In many ways the provisions resemble legal rulings

---

35 Cp. The laws of Eshnunna s134, below p. 24.

36 The Laws of Eshnunna (below pp. 24) for example, explicitly provide (s48) that capital cases are to be heard by the king. Some of the judgments from Ur (below pp. 38) record that they were heard before the king.

37 Postgate, p. 197, cites the appeal of a creditor whose tablets had been destroyed in purported implementation of a royal decree cancelling a number of obligations. He says judges were appointed to examine cases arising in Sippar. They looked at the tablets recording purchases of fields houses and orchards and broke the tablets of those affected by the decree. He had taken his tablets to the Assembly. "Rish-Shamash, a resident of Sippar, Kudiya, the stool bearer, and Sin-nadin-shumi the survey scribe, examined the tablets, sealed them and had them transferred to Salim-tehhusa, the Overseer of the Barbers, … for him to examine. Salim-tehhusa, … without even hearing my statement, broke my tablets … I took the fragments and showed them to Rish-Shamash, Kudiya and Sin-nadin-shumi. They said "What can we say to the Overseer of the Barbers? So now I have come to you, (as to) a god. May my lord judge for me the case of the tablets, which are broken without the knowledge of the judges or the principal party, and so all Sippar will see that before my lord the weak is not given over to the strong and the strong (are not allowed) to oppress the weak", Postgate, p. 197, citing J.J. Finkelstein, Some new misharum material and its implications, in Studies in honor of Benno Landsberger, Chicago, 1965, p. 236.

rather than legal rules, something more than decisions in individual cases, but something less than a rule, in particular a rule that might be developed or applied by analogy. And the collections contain provisions that one would not expect to find in a modern code of private law, such as the fixing of prices and wages, of the exchange values of silver and barley, and rates for the hire of various things and people. One should not perhaps be surprised at the inclusion of such regulations. Many of the other provisions resemble these regulatory provisions which fix prices or wages by having as their primary function the setting of the compensation or penalty due for some stated infringement of the law, or fixing what is to happen on divorce or a death, what does the wife get, what do the heirs get, or what is to happen if a wife becomes severely ill. None of the situations is itself problematic and the provisions do not look as if they are there to establish liability. It is simply a question of making clear what is to happen when they occur or fixing a tariff for the payment of compensation. Other provisions may simply determine on whom the burden of proof lies, when a written document may be needed, who is to take what oath. And this becomes even clearer when we come to look at legal decisions. They are not solving questions of law. They are about the facts and often not even about these but about who should bring what evidence or in the final analysis who should be called on to take an oath that his version of the facts is the correct one.[38]

We do not know the exact nature and purpose of the laws, the extent to which they modify or simply confirm or clarify questions which have arisen in the customary traditions. It is Hammurabi's collection that most clearly states a purpose. In the Epilogue to his laws he writes "In order that the mighty not wrong the weak, to provide just ways for the waif and widow, I have inscribed my precious pronouncements upon my stela and set it out before the statue of me, the king of justice, in the city of Babylon, within the Esagil; in order to render the judgments of the land, to give the verdicts of the land, and provide just ways for the wronged.... Let any wronged man who has a law suit ... have my inscribed stela read aloud to him. Thus may he hear my precious pronouncements and let my stela reveal the lawsuit for him; may he examine his case, may he calm his (troubled) heart ... and may he praise me".

38 In some cases it is left to the gods to determine by way of the River Ordeal.

## The laws of Ur-Nammu of Ur[39]

Ur, on the Euphrates, the Biblical Ur of the Chaldees, from which Abraham set out for Canaan, was already an important city state in the early part of the Third Millenium B.C. It was later incorporated into the Akkadian empire founded by Sargon (2340-2284). It revived under its Third Dynasty after the defeat of that empire by the Gutians, and the Gutians defeat by Utu-hegal of Uruk. Under Ur-Nammu (r2112-2095) Ur came to dominate the whole of Southern Mesopotamia for just over one hundred years.

The laws, which are in Sumerian, were discovered in Nippur, a centre for the training of scribes, and in Ur, on tablets written in the Old Babylonian period, some two hundred years after they were first published. None of the texts is complete. Together they contain a limited number of provisions and a Prologue, though it has been suggested that another fragment known simply as the Laws of X, which contains a few more provisions and an Epilogue may originally have been a part of them.[40]

*Causing physical injury*

The provisions include penalties for physical injury and assault, the death penalty for murder or for "deflowering of the virgin wife of a young man", though if it is the wife who initiated the liaison it is she who is killed and the man goes free (ss6-7). If the victim is a slave woman there is a payment of 5 shekels of silver (s8). Monetary compensation is fixed for cutting off someone's foot (10 shekels), or knocking out his tooth (2 shekels). False imprisonment is punished with imprisonment and a payment (15 shekels) (s3).

*Duties of neighbours and tenants*

A man who floods his neighbour's field must give grain based on the acreage affected, as must a tenant who takes land to cultivate but fails to do so, so that it becomes wasteland (ss31-32).

*Slaves*

A reward is fixed for someone who returns a fugitive slave (s17). A slave woman who curses someone in authority over her is to have her mouth washed out with salt – the only example of a symbolic penalty in the laws (s25).

---

39 Although attributed to Ur-Nammu they may have been the work of his son and successor Shulgi (r2094-2047) who was known to have been active as an administrator and reformer. For the sources and provenances of all the collections see M. Roth, Law Collections from Mesopotamia and Asia Minor, Atlanta, 1995, from which quotations from them are taken. The laws of Ur-Nammu are at p. 13. The numbering of the provisions in the collections is the work of modern editors and is not in the original texts.

40 M. Roth, p. 36.

*Family matters*

A man who divorces his wife must pay her 60 shekels, or 30 if she was a widow (ss9-10), but only if there has been a formal written contract – the only implicit requirement of a formal record in the laws (s11). A father who gives the daughter he has promised to one man to another must pay him double the value of the property he brought with him into the father's house (s15).

*The legal process*

And there are provisions dealing with the protection of the legal process itself. A perjurer must pay 15 shekels (s28). A witness who refuses to take an oath must pay compensation equivalent to the subject matter of the case (s29). If as the result of an accusation someone is put to the River Ordeal and survives the accuser pays 3 shekels; if it is a wife accused of sexual promiscuity 20 shekels (ss13-14).

*Regulatory provisions*

The Laws of X fix the fees for various services performed by a doctor (f-i), the rates of hire for female weavers (j), the prices of land and houses (q-r), the rates of interest on loans of silver and barley (m-n), the amount of grain a woman innkeeper is to receive at harvest for giving beer on credit (l).

*The Epilogue*

The laws have an Epilogue with a traditional curse on any ruler who attempts to deface or alter the text. "May his city be a city despised by the god Enlil; may the main gate of his city be left open (and undefended). May the young men of his city be blind; may the young maidens of his city be barren."

## The laws of Lipit-Ishtar

The laws of Lipit-Ishtar, (r1934-1924),[41] fifth ruler of the First Dynasty of Isin, which was founded after the collapse of the Third Dynasty of Ur, were also found on tablets discovered in Nippur, probably copies made by scribes in Old Babylonian times. They are in Sumerian. Their Prologue says they were originally written on a stela. Some of the Prologue and of the early provisions are missing and the Epilogue is fragmented. As a result a good number of the provisions are incomplete and others unclear. But the territory they cover is becoming familiar.

41 M. Roth, p. 23.

*Causing physical injury*

The provisions dealing with physical injury are quite specific. There are financial penalties for striking a woman and causing a miscarriage – 30 shekels for a free woman, 5 shekels for a slave woman. If the woman dies the penalty is death (ss d-f).

*Regulatory provisions*

The amount of grain for the hire of oxen is fixed (s9), so is compensation for a man who hires an ox and causes it to lose an eye (one half its value), or severs its hoof tendon (one third), or breaks its horn or tail (one quarter) (ss34-37). A gardener who takes an orchard to plant it is to get dates from one-tenth of the palm trees (s7).

*Personal liabilities*

The man who hires a boat and departs from the agreed route must replace the boat if it is lost, as well as paying its hire (s5).

*Protection of property*

The man who is found in another man's orchard with intent to steal must pay 10 shekels (s9). A man who cuts down a tree in someone else's orchard also pays 10 shekels (s10).

*Duties of neighbours*

The man whose neighbour has warned him that the state of his land has made his neighbour's land more vulnerable to a break-in has a duty to compensate the neighbour for any loss he has suffered as the result of a break-in if he failed to take action (s11).

*Slaves*

A man who harbours a fugitive slave for a month must compensate the owner (s12).

*Family matters*

And there are extensive provisions on family matters which is an important feature of other collections of laws. The concern for wives appears as one of the most distinctive and attractive features of Mesopotamian law.

The father who gives his daughter promised to one man to the man's friend must hand back the bridewealth. This time it is expressly provided that the friend may not marry the girl (s29).

If a man's first ranking wife loses her attractiveness or becomes paralyzed, she is not to be evicted from the house. Her husband may marry a healthy wife, but the second wife is to support the first ranking wife (s28).

If a man's wife does not bear him a child but a prostitute does then he is to provide grain, oil and clothing rations for the prostitute and the child will become his heir. But as long as his wife is alive the prostitute is not to live in the house with the wife (s27).

If a young married man has sexual relations with a prostitute and the judges order him not to see her again but he then divorces his wife he still may not marry the prostitute, even though he makes a divorce settlement for his wife (s30).

And there are provisions on inheritance. Children of two wives share in the father's estate. The children of each wife share in her dowry. A man's children by a slave woman do not inherit unless he marries her subsequently, but the man is to give the woman and her children their freedom (s24-25).

If a man gives his favourite son a gift and records the fact in a sealed document, again one of the few references to the requirement of a record in writing, then the gift is not to be included as part of his share of the inheritance (s31). If a man's daughter becomes an ugbabtu, naditu or qadishtu – all categories of women dedicated to the gods - she shares equally with her brothers in the inheritance (s22).

*The legal process*

There is one provision dealing with the legal process. The man who makes a false accusation suffers the penalty prescribed for the wrongdoing charged (s17).

One provision that does not seem to be repeated elsewhere provides that if the owner of land fails to pay taxes and someone else assumes the responsibility for paying them s/he can keep the land after three years (s18).

## The laws of Eshnunna

Eshnunna – Tel Asmar - a city on the Diyala river in the southern outskirts of Baghdad, was the first city to rebel against Ibbi-sin the last ruler of the Third Dynasty of Ur. It was conquered by Hammurabi c1764. Two tablets were found in 1945 and 1947 and a third in the early 1980s. The first two tablets are almost complete. The third which contains extracts, looks like a student exercise. The laws were probably published between the fall of the Third Dynasty of Ur and the time of Hammurabi (r1792-1750) perhaps by king Dadusha. They are in Akkadian. There is no Prologue or Epilogue.[42]

*Regulatory provisions*

The laws begin with a large number of provisions fixing prices in silver and barley for a number of basic commodities including oil, lard, bitumen, wool,

---

42 M. Roth, p. 57.

salt, potash and copper, and in silver for barley itself. The rates for hiring a wagon with oxen and driver, donkey and driver, boat and boatman are fixed, as are the wages of a harvester,[43] winnower and fuller, and the rates of interest on loans of silver and barley (ss1-4, 7-11, 14).

*Causing physical injury*

Compensation is set for a variety of physical injuries such as biting off someone's nose, or causing the loss of an eye (60 shekels), an ear (30 shekels) or slapping him on the cheek (10 shekels), cutting off a finger (20 shekels), breaking a hand (20 shekels), and breaking a foot (30 shekels). There is still a financial penalty (40 shekels) for causing a death in the course of a brawl (ss42-47A).[44] But it is a capital offence to take another man's betrothed and deflower her (s26). So it seems is adultery (s28). If the victim is a slave woman 20 shekels is the penalty (s31).

If a man[45] is killed by a collapsing wall after the local authorities have warned the owner of its dangerous state the penalty is death (s58). By contrast a man who has been warned that his ox is a gorer or that his dog is vicious and who fails to keep them in check is to pay 40 shekels, or, if the victim is a slave 15 shekels (ss54—57).

*Protection of property*

Property is protected by a number of provisions. Where someone buys a slave, ox, donkey, or anything else and cannot identify the seller he will be treated as a thief (s40).[46] A similar presumption is made in the case of a public official who has seized a lost slave, ox or donkey and has not returned it within a week. He too is to be prosecuted for theft (s50). A merchant or a woman inn-keeper is not to accept silver, grain, wool, oil or anything else from a slave (s15).

When property is deposited and is then lost and there is no sign of a break-in the depositee must make good the loss. If, however, the depositee has also suffered loss and is prepared to swear an oath at the gate of the temple of Tishpak "Together with your property my property was lost. I have done nothing im-

---

43 There is also a penalty for the harvester who does not appear (s9). The waggon driver and boatman are to work one whole day (ss3-4).

44 s47 describes the victim as a member of the awilu class, i.e. a member of the upper class.

45 The text speaks of a awilu which usually refers to a member of the upper class.

46 This is one of a number of provisions in Mesopotamian law which without actually requiring it makes it highly desirable to conduct important transactions in the presence of witnesses whose names are then recorded along with details of the transaction on a written tablet. As we shall see when we come to some of the judicial decisions that have come down to us, written tablets are not necessarily conclusive, but they are often essential if a claim or defence is to be sustained.

proper or fraudulent", then he will not have to pay (ss36-37), a good example of the reliance on oaths to settle questions of fact and liability which is another important feature of Mesopotamian law in general.

Another provision relevant to the protection of property is the prescription of the death penalty for someone found in another's house or field by night. If he is found there by day the price is 10 shekels (s12-13). And the guard whose negligence has allowed a break-in to occur will be put to death, with the added humiliation that it will be on the spot where the break-in occurred and he will not be given a grave (s60).

*Professional liabilities*

Where a boatman is hired and his negligence causes the loss of the boat he is responsible for all the resulting loss (s5).

*Debts and debtors*

There are a number of provisions dealing with debt, debt slavery and distraint for debt. Neither a son who has not received his inheritance nor a slave is to be given credit (s16). A debtor who is forced to sell his property because of his poverty is entitled to buy it back if the purchaser decides to sell it (s39). If a man's slave woman is distrained for debt the distrainor will have to pay the slave's value as compensation if her owner is prepared to swear an oath that the distrainor has no claim against him. If the distrainor causes the slave's death he must hand over two slave women by way of compensation. If the distrainor distrains a wife or child without a valid claim and causes their death the penalty is death (ss22-4).

*Business relations*

And there are traces of more complex business relationships e.g. the provision that when a partner wishes to sell his share in the partnership and another partner wishes to buy it he must match any outside offer (s38).

*Family matters*

The father who goes back on his word and gives his daughter to another man must pay back double the bride price (s25). Abducting someone else's bride is punishable with death. Marrying a woman without her parents' consent does not make her his wife if there has been no nuptial feast or written contract even if she has been in his house a full year (ss26-27).

Wives are protected by a provision that a man who divorces his wife after they have had children and marries another woman must leave his house and his possessions (s59).

The man who gave his child to be nursed and then failed to provide barley, oil and wool for three years must pay 10 shekels and take back the child (s32).[47]

*Special categories*

There are special provisions for the man who is doing his military service, an important and protected category of person in Mesopotamian law where much of the land was held in return for obligation to undertake royal service of one kind or another. If he is captured he can get back his wife when he is released even if by then she is living with someone else and has had a child by him. It is different if he has "repudiated his city and his master and then flees" (ss29-30).

*The legal process*

s48 provides that cases in which the penalty is between 20 and 60 shekels are to be heard by the judges. Capital cases are for the king.

**The Laws of Hammurabi**

Looking at these earlier collections makes it clear that when Hammurabi (r1792-1750) drafted his laws he had a good deal to build on. And this is quite apart from the oral and customary traditions which clearly made up the background against which all these laws must be seen.

Many of the topics and even some of the particular rules will be familiar to readers of the earlier collections. The most noticeable difference is the harshness of the penalties. In Hammurabi's laws they are more retributive and deterrent. Gone is the heavy reliance on financial penalties with the death penalty a rare exception. Now we have death, the loss of a hand, the tit-for-tat loss of an eye, limb or son for causing the loss of an eye, limb or the death of a son, and symbolic penalties such as casting into the fire if someone who takes the opportunity of a fire to rob the victim of his goods.

The laws of Hammurabi were discovered by French archaeologists in three fragments in 1901-2 at Susa, the capital of the Kingdom of the Elamites. When put together the fragments were found to make up a stela of black diorite some 2.25m high, with a circumference 1.9m at the bottom and 1.65m at the top. At its top is a relief showing the god Shamash, the sun-god and therefore the god of Justice, seated on a throne, with Hammurabi standing before him. The laws themselves are inscribed below and at the back of the stela. They are in cuneiform script. The language is Akkadian. Although the stela, which is now in the Louvre, is complete, some of the writing has been removed. The stela had been taken to Susa by the Elamite king Shutruk-Nahhunte I in the twelfth century,

---

[47] It is provisions like these which sound like rulings in particular cases.

probably from Sippar,[48] along with other booty, and it seems to have been his intention to record the fact on the blanked out space, as he had done with other booty taken to Susa, but he had not got round to doing it.

Some of the missing parts have been filled in from later copies of the laws on clay tablets. The British Museum already had four fragments of a much later date taken from the library of the Assyrian ruler Ashurbanipal (c668-626) which had not till then been identified, though there had been suggestions in the 1890s both that they contained legal provisions and that these might be the work of Hammurabi.

The laws consist of a Prologue, the legal provisions and an Epilogue. There are more provisions, 282 in all, than in any other surviving text. The style of the Prologue and the Epilogue is said to be more literary. The Prologue makes the familiar claims that the ruler has divine authority and that his collection of laws is a fulfilment of his obligation to the gods to bring justice to the land. "The gods Enu and Enlil, for the enhancement of the well being of the people, named me, Hammurabi, to make justice prevail in the land." It also recites his achievements, particularly those which show his piety, restoring the sacred sites of Eridu and Nippur, for example, and contributing to the restoration, adornment and the rituals in temples in the various cities of the land, Ur, Sippar, Uruk, Lagash, Girsu, Akkad, Assur, Nineveh and others.

*Regulatory provisions*

Like earlier royal pronouncements the laws fix wages, prices, rates of interest and rates of hire, not in a single set of sections, but throughout the collection. So we find the appropriate rates of interest on loans of silver or barley (ss t-u), the amount of grain a woman wine seller is to receive at harvest for giving wine on credit (s111). Fees for doctors are prescribed, varying according to whether it is a major operation which saves a life or an eye, or something less such as setting a bone or healing an injured muscle and depending on the status of the patient, awilu, commoner or slave (s215-217). Fees for vets are also fixed (s224). Rates are fixed for building a building (s229), storing grain (s121), for the for the hire of boats of different sizes (s275-7) and a boatman (s239), and for caulking a boat (s234); for the hire of oxen (s268-270); and ox-drivers (s258), of waggons and waggon drivers (s271-2), of shepherds, herdsmen, agricultural labourers (ss257, 261, 273), leatherworkers, artisans, bricklayers, linen weavers, seal cutters, smiths, basketmakers and carpenters (s274).

[48] The Epilogue to the laws Hammurabi stated that he had put up the stela in the Esagil, the temple in Babylon dedicated to Marduk, but he also refers to the setting up of a stela in the temple E. Babbara. This suggests Sippar.

*Causing physical injury*

It is in relation to causing physical injury in particular, that the harshness, tit-for-tat and symbolic nature of some of the penalties, and the variation of penalty according to the status of the victim stand out. The provisions distinguish the awilu (a member of the higher class of freeman), the commoner, and the slave.

If an awilu blinds another he is to lose his eye, if he breaks a bone his bone is broken, if he knocks out a tooth, his tooth is knocked out (ss196-7, 200). If an awilu strikes another during a brawl and causes an injury but swears that it was not deliberate he has only to pay the doctor's fees (s206). If the victim dies he pays 30 shekels, or if the victim is a commoner, 20 shekels (ss206-208). If it is a commoner who loses an eye or whose bone is broken the penalty is 60 shekels or if a tooth is lost 20 (s198, 201). If the victim is a slave whose eye is lost or bone broken half his value is to be paid (s199).

An awilu who strikes the cheek of another of a higher status is to be flogged in the public assembly. If he is of equal status he pays 60 shekels. A commoner who strikes a commoner pays 10 shekels (ss202-204). If a child strikes his father his hand is to be cut off (s195). If a slave strikes an awilu he loses an ear (s205). An awilu who strikes an awilu woman and causes a miscarriage pays 10 shekels. If she dies, his own daughter is killed. If the victim was a commoner he pays 30 shekels for death and 5 for a miscarriage. If the victim is a slave the sums are 20 and 2 shekels (ss209-214).

If a man's ox gores a man to death in the street there is no liability unless he has been warned by the local authorities that his ox is a gorer. If he has, and he has failed to blunt its horns or control it then he has to pay 30 shekels if the victim is an awilu, 20 if he is a slave (ss250-252).

*Professional liabilities*

With the receipt of fees come duties and liabilities. The doctor whose carelessness or incompetence causes an awilu patient to lose his life or an eye is to have his hand cut off (s218). If it is a slave who dies he pays his full value, if the slave loses an eye he pays a half (ss219-220). The vet who causes the death of an ox or donkey pays a quarter of its value (s225).

The builder who builds an unsound house which collapses and kills the owner will himself be killed. If the owner's son is killed the builder's son is killed. If a slave is killed he must replace him. He must also make good any property that is lost as a result as well as rebuild the house. He must similarly replace a wall which has not been properly built (ss229-233).

If a boatman hires a boat and his negligence leads to its loss he must replace it (s236). If a man has hired a boat and boatman and loaded it with grain, wool, oil, dates or any other goods and as a result of the boatman's negligence the boat and goods are lost the boatman must replace them (s237). A boatman who does not caulk a boat properly so that it springs a leak within a year must make the boat sound (s235). If an upstream boat collides with a downstream boat and sinks it the master of the upstream boat must replace the boat and any goods which the owner swears were lost (s240).

Shepherds have to make good oxen or sheep entrusted to them which are lost unless they swear an oath that they were lost as a result of illness or a lion taking them, though not if the illness spread because of their negligence (ss266-267). It is also a shepherd's duty to maintain the size of the flock. If he does not he is to pay compensation "in accordance with the terms of his contract" (s264).

A shepherd who alters the brand on the cattle or sheep entrusted to him and sells them pays a tenfold penalty (s265).

A shepherd must pay compensation based on the size of the field, if he grazes his animals on someone's land without his permission (s57). He must pay three times this if, it is "after the sheep and goats come up from the common irrigation area when the pennants announcing the termination of pasturing are wound round the city gate" (s58).

A woman wine-seller who overcharges is to be drowned. One who fails to arrest criminals who meet in her bar and take them to the palace is to be killed (ss108-109).

*The protection of property*

Robbery is punishable with death. So is being found on someone's land or field by night, housebreaking, stealing goods from a palace or temple or receiving such goods (ss21-22, 6). A man who goes to assist in putting out a fire and steals property is to be put on to the fire (s25). In the case of a robbery, if the thief is not caught, and the victim states on oath what he has lost, the city or governor in whose jurisdiction the robbery occurred must compensate him. If the victim was killed they must pay his relatives 60 shekels. If the local authority proves that his claim is false he must pay twice the value he claimed (ss23-24, 126).

There are financial penalties for other thefts. A man who steals an ox, sheep, donkey, pig or a boat must pay 30 times its value if it belonged to the palace or temple, 10 times if it belonged to a private person. If he cannot pay he is to be killed (s8). Stealing a plough from the common irrigation area attracts a penalty of 5 shekels, theft of a harrow 3 shekels (ss259, 260).

There are special provisions for carriers. A carrier who fails to deliver silver, gold, precious stones or other goods entrusted to him and who appropriates them for himself pays five fold.

There are also a number of provisions designed to facilitate the settlement of property disputes, which emphasise the importance of witnesses and written records of transactions.

If a man finds his property in the possession of someone else and says he has witnesses to prove it is his, but the possessor equally claims he has witnesses to the fact that he had bought it, then the witnesses of both sides are to be examined by the judges. If the witnesses swear an oath that what each party says is true then the seller is to be treated as a thief and killed and the buyer will receive the purchase price from his estate. If only the owner can produce his witnesses then it is the present possessor who will be killed and the owner will recover his property. If the owner cannot produce his witnesses he will be killed for making a false accusation. The provisions also take into account practicalities. If the possessors' witnesses are not readily available the judges are to give him six months to produce them. If he fails to do so the judges will impose the death penalty (ss9-11, 13).

It is provided that, generally, when a deposit is made for safekeeping of gold, silver or anything else it should be done before witnesses and recorded in writing. Otherwise there will be no claim. If the proper procedure has been followed and the depositee denies receiving the property he has to pay double its value. If any of the property is lost as the result of a break in the depositee who was careless must compensate for the loss even if he has lost some of his own property. If grain has been deposited for storage and some is lost or the depositee takes some of it, or denies having received it, he will have to pay double in value if the owner swears an oath as to the true facts (ss122-5, 120).

Anyone who buys or accepts for safekeeping gold, silver, a slave, ox, sheep, donkey or any other thing from the son or slave of the owner without witnesses or a written tablet will be treated as a thief and killed (s7).

*Landlords and tenants*

A number of provisions deal with the duties of tenants and others who have been given land for a specific purpose. A landlord cannot evict a tenant. If he attempts to do so he forfeits the rent due (g). A tenant who steals the grain intended for the use of the cattle and the cultivation of the land is to lose his hand. If as a result of taking the grain the cattle are weakened he must pay twice the value of the grain he received. If he hires out the cattle or if there is no crop because he stole the seed then at harvest time he must pay 18,000 silas of grain for every 18 ikus of land.[49] If he cannot do this he will be dragged round the field by the cattle (ss253-256). A tenant who fails to plant any grain is to compensate the owner for the loss of his share of the harvest on the basis of the yield of neighbouring fields. If he failed even to plough and harrow it then he is to do this before handing back the land. If it is a three year lease of land that has never been cultivated and he fails to cultivate it then he must do so in the fourth year and pay the owner 3000 silas of grain for each 18 ikus of land (ss42-44).

If, however, the reason for a crop failure is a storm or a flood the loss falls on the tenant if he has already paid the rent. If rent has not been paid in full then

[49] A sila is equivalent to about one litre. An iku is about 3600 square metres. Roth, p. xvi.

the owner and tenant are to share the loss in whatever proportions they had agreed on for the harvest. It seems that if in the first year the crops failed and the tenant did not recover his expenses the lease can be extended for a year and the owner and tenant will then share the next harvest in the proportions agreed (ss45-47). Where it is an orchard that has been given to a gardener to plant date palms he has four years in which to cultivate them. In the fifth year he and the owner are to have equal shares of the harvest with the owner having first choice. If the gardener fails to plant the whole orchard the uncultivated part is counted against his share. If he fails to plant at all then, if it was arable land, he must cultivate it and compensate the owner on the basis of the yields of neighbouring land. If it has not been cultivated he must cultivate it and pay 3000 silas of grain per 18 ikus (ss60-63). Where a man gives an orchard to a gardener to pollinate he gets two-thirds of the yield. If the gardener fails to pollinate he must compensate the owner on the basis of neighbouring yields (ss64-65).

*Debts and debtors*

The laws fix interest rates. A creditor who demands more forfeits the debt. If a creditor fails to deduct interest paid from what is due or fails to write a new tablet setting out the amount due he must pay twice the amount paid. If a debtor has borrowed silver but does not have silver to repay he may repay in grain at the rate of exchange set by the laws. Once a loan is repaid the tablet recording the loan is to be destroyed (ss f-w).

A creditor who helps himself to the debtor's grain to meet a debt will forfeit the debt. A person who distrains a member of a household or slave of someone against whom he has no valid claim must pay 20 shekels. If there is a valid claim and the person distrained dies of natural causes the creditor is not liable but if he dies as a result of beating or other physical abuse then if it is a son, the son of the distrainor will be killed, if it is a slave the distrainor must pay 20 shekels. In each case he forfeits the debt (ss113-116).

If a debtor sells his wife, son or daughter or gives them into debt slavery they are to serve for three years. If it is a slave that is handed over the creditor may keep them longer and may even sell them but the owner of a slave woman with whom he has had children can recover the slave by repaying the loan (ss117-119).

A number of provisions seem designed to protect tenants in particular from oppressive creditors. If a debtor agrees to let his creditor have land which has been prepared for planting with grain or sesame for the creditor to cultivate, he may not agree to let the creditor take the whole harvest to meet the debt. The harvest remains the debtor's and it is for him to pay from it what he owes, plus interest and the costs of cultivation. And the same applies if the land is already planted or it is an orchard of pollinated date palms that are handed over (ss49-50 and a). In the case of the planted field it is provided that if the tenant does not have the silver to repay a loan of silver he may repay in grain or sesame "in accordance with the royal edict ... according to their market price" (s51).

An obligation to repay a debt will be suspended if the tenant's field has been devastated by a storm or the crops destroyed by a flood or if the crops have failed as the result of lack of water. Interest will not have to be paid for that year (s48).

*Business relations*

There are a number of provisions dealing with the relationship between a merchant and his trading agent. Not all of them are clear. What is clear is that if enemy forces make him abandon the goods he has taken he will not be liable if he swears that this is what happened; that if the merchant gives an agent grain, wool, oil or any other commodity for sale the agent is to return silver for each transaction and is to obtain a sealed receipt for each payment. If he is negligent and does not do this the payment will not be taken into account. A trading agent who denies having received any silver from a merchant will have to pay three-fold the amount if the merchant can prove "before god and witnesses" that he did. A merchant who denies having received back everything he had given the agent will have to pay six fold their value if the agent can prove "before god and witnesses" that he had[50] (ss104-107).

*The duties of neighbours*

If a man has told his neighbour before witnesses that he should repair his wall or cultivate his land to reduce the risk of a break-in and the neighbour does nothing and there is a break-in the neighbour must replace everything that was taken (e).

A farmer who fails to keep his dyke and embankment in good repair must compensate his neighbours for any loss that results from water breaking through and damaging the common irrigated area. If necessary he and his goods will be sold and the proceeds divided to compensate the victims. And the same applies if the loss is due to his opening up his canal for irrigation purposes and negligently allowing water to carry away his neighbour's field (ss53-55).

*Slaves*

If a slave develops epilepsy within a month of his purchase he can be given back. The seller is also responsible for any claims made in relation to the slave

[50] More obscure are provisions relating to what is to happen if an agent fails to make a profit. It is said both that if the agent has been given silver and makes no profit he is to give the merchant twice what he received, and that if he incurs a loss he is to return the merchant the sum he received. Clearly there is a difference in nature between the two ventures but it is not clear what the difference is (ss101-102). Where one man gives another silver for a partnership venture they share the profit and loss (cc).

(ss270-279). If a man recognises his slave in another man's possession and the latter says he bought him abroad he is entitled to have him back without payment if the slave is a native of his country. If he is not then the owner will have to compensate the purchaser for the price he swears he paid for him (ss280-281).

Helping a slave to escape from the city, harbouring a fugitive slave or failing to produce a slave whom the herald has declared is missing are punishable with death (ss15-16). If someone finds a slave in open country and returns him to his owner he is to be given 2 shekels. If a slave refuses to say who he is he is to be taken to the palace to be examined (ss15-20). Removing the hairlock which identifies slaves is punishable with loss of a hand unless the person doing it swears that he did not do it knowingly but had been deceived by someone who pretended to be the slave's owner. Then it is that person who is put to death and hanged in his own doorway (ss226-227).

*Family matters*

There are provisions about breach of promise of marriage. A future son-in-law loses any bridewealth he has brought. A future father-in-law returns twice what he has received. If it is the result of a comrade slandering the future son-in-law, the comrade cannot marry the daughter himself (ss159-161). A father who is caught sleeping with his daughter-in-law is to be drowned. If his son has not yet slept with her he must pay 30 shekels, give her back whatever she has brought into the marriage and she is free to marry someone else (ss155-6). Incest is punished with banishment (father and daughter) or burning (son and mother) (s154, 157).

Marriage requires a formal contract (s128).

If a man decides to divorce his wife who has had no children he can divorce her after giving her her bridewealth in silver and her dowry, or if there is no bridewealth, 60 shekels, or, if he is a commoner, 20 shekels (ss138-140). But a man cannot divorce his wife because she has become seriously ill. He can take a second wife but must continue to support the first though if the first wife wants to leave she can, taking her dowry with her (ss148-149). If a wife decides to leave her husband and she is shown to have taken goods, squandered possessions or disparaged her husband the husband can divorce her without making any settlement on her and without even giving her her travel expenses. If he decides not to divorce her he can marry someone else and his first wife stays on as a slave (s141). If a wife tells her husband that she no longer wants to have marital relations with him the local authorities are to look into the matter. If they conclude that she is a careful wife who does not disparage her husband, while he is wayward and disparages her, she can leave him, taking her dowry with her. If on the other hand she is not careful but is wayward and squanders her possessions and disparages him she is to be thrown into the water (and presumably drowned) (ss142-143).

If a wife is caught committing adultery both parties will be drowned. But if the husband decides to forgive his wife then the king must spare the man (s129). If her husband accuses her of adultery without catching her in the act she can return to the house if she swears an oath that she is innocent. A wife who is accused by someone else of adultery is put to the River Ordeal (ss131-132). A wife who has her husband killed because she is having an affair is to be impaled (s153).

A husband and wife can make an agreement that the wife cannot be seized for the husband's debts and this apparently is binding on creditors who cannot seize either wife or husband for debts incurred before the marriage, but only for debts incurred subsequently (ss151-152).

The provisions on inheritance mostly deal with variations from the normal rule that on death the heirs inherit equally. If a man has children by a slave-woman and acknowledges them as his children they are to have a share in his estate (s170). If a husband gives his wife a field, orchard or house or moveable property, then provided the gift is recorded in a sealed tablet the heirs have no claim to them after his death. She can give the property on to any of her children though not to an outsider. The same applies to a gift to a son (ss150, 165). If a father has provided wives for all his sons except the youngest then the cost of a bride purchase for him is deducted from the inheritance before it is shared (s166).

A man will not be allowed to disinherit his son if the judges find that the son has not been guilty of some serious offence which merits disinheritance. They may also pardon him for a first offence (ss168-9).

On the death of her husband the wife will keep her dowry and any marriage settlement made by her husband in writing and may continue to live in the matrimonial home but may not sell it. If there has been no marriage settlement she will have the share of an heir. If her children try to pressure her to leave the house the judges will investigate and impose a penalty on them (ss171-172). If the widow decides to leave the house she takes her dowry but leaves her marriage settlement for her children. She can remarry (s172). A widow with young children can only enter another man's house with the approval of the judges who are to make a written inventory of the first husband's estate before handing it to her new husband. The new couple are to use it to raise the children. They may not sell the household goods. Any sale is invalid and the purchaser loses the purchase price (s177).

A wife's dowry goes to her children and not to her husband on his death. If she has no children her father gets it provided he returns the bride price. If he does not the husband can deduct it from the dowry (ss163-164).

There are also rules dealing with adoption.

*Special categories*

There are special rules dealing with those who hold land in return for royal service and as regards women dedicated to the gods, in particular the naditu. Land held with a service obligation cannot be sold, exchanged or assigned in connection with a debt. If the tenant is captured while on military service and his land is given to someone else he can recover it when he returns (s27). If his son is old enough to perform the service obligations then he should do so. If he is not then one third of the orchard and field is to be handed over to his mother for his support (s29).

Although the normal rule is that when a ransom has been paid to secure the release of a prisoner-of-war the latter must repay the sum paid, his house, field or orchard cannot be taken to meet the payment. If he does not have the funds his local temple is to pay and if the temple cannot, the palace will (s32).

Anyone performing his military service is also given a number of other protections. The death penalty is prescribed for an officer who takes a soldier's goods, oppresses him, hires him out or "delivers him to the power of an influential person in a lawsuit" (s34).

While he is a prisoner his wife may not go and live with someone else provided there is enough to live on in the house. If she does she will be drowned. If there is no adequate provision for her she can move in with someone else, but, if she does, and even if she has children by her new partner, the prisoner will get her back when he returns, though the new children will not be his heirs. As in earlier laws it is expressly provided that this does not apply to someone who has simply fled from the city (ss133-136).

The naditu had a special status in the community and a good deal of economic independence. Tablets that have come down to us from the religious centre of Sippar show them engaged in a wide variety of business enterprises.[51] Provided he records it in writing a man can give his daughter who is a naditu, ugbabtu or a sekretu a dowry, and freedom to give her estate to whomever she wishes. If he records the gift but not the authority to deal with it as she pleases then her brothers will take the property though they must provide her with food, oil and clothing equivalent to a share in the inheritance. If they fail to do so, she

[51] See e.g. Leick, p. 175, citing R. Harris, "The naditu women", in E. Reiner (ed.), Studies presented to Leo A. Oppenheim, Chicago, 1964, and V. Jeyes "The Naditu women of Sippar", in A. Cameron and A. Kuhrt, Images of women in antiquity, London, 1983, pp. 260-72.

can lease her property to a tenant in return for the support she needs, though she cannot sell it. It belongs to her brothers. If the father makes no provision she has a life interest in the equivalent of an heir's share (ss178-181).

*The legal process*[52]

Anyone who accuses another of homicide and is unable to prove it is himself to be killed. This applies to all capital offences. If it is not a capital offence he must pay whatever penalty is prescribed for the offence. If however the charge is witchcraft the person accused is put to the River Ordeal. If s/he escapes, the accuser will be killed and his estate will go to the person accused. If a man makes an accusation against a man's wife of promiscuity and cannot prove it he is to be flogged before the judges and half his hair is to be shaven (ss1-4, 127).

*Epilogue*

Hammurabi's laws have a lengthy Epilogue in which he draws attention to his achievements in looking after his people. "I am indeed the shepherd who brings peace, whose sceptre is just"." "In order that the mighty not wrong the weak, to provide just ways for the waif and the widow, I have inscribed by precious pronouncements upon my stela and set it up … in the city of Babylon … within the Esagil …." "May any king who will appear in the land in the future … observe the pronouncements of justice that I inscribed upon my stela. May he not alter the judgments that I rendered and the verdicts that I gave."

The Epilogue ends with a whole catalogue of curses on any ruler who fails to follow his pronouncements, or who removes his name and replaces it with his own. Hammurabi calls on the gods one by one to wreak havoc and destruction on him and his people.[53]

## JUDICIAL AND OTHER RECORDS

Postgate, writing as a non-lawyer, notes that the law collections "are a poor mirror of the role of law in society" and "are likely to give a distorted picture of conditions, being either atypical or unreal".[54] And if it is true that the collections give a limited view of the law it is even more true, of course, that they say even less about the context of the law. This is the reason why records of individual decided cases and even more of individual legal transactions and more generally of records which provide evidence of the political, commercial, family and domestic environment are so important.

---

52 These provisions in fact come right at the beginning of the laws.

53 E.g. "May the goddess Ninkarrak … cause a grievous malady to break out upon his limbs, … a serious carbuncle which cannot be soothed … which he cannot ease with bandages … may he bewail his lost virility until his life comes to an end."

54 Postgate, p. 275.

## Judgments and legal decisions

It is from the time of the Third Dynasty of Ur (c2060-1955) that we have the largest collection of judicial decisions. Most of them (183) were found in archives in Girsu (modern Telloh) in the province of Lagash, the rest (3) in Umma. The judgments from Girsu include decisions taken in the nearby town of Nina, but they were decided by the same judges. Most of the decisions describe themselves as di-til-la, final judgments, though the word is also used to describe formal transactions conducted before the judges, such as declarations of marriage, divorce, divorce settlements, disinheritance and the emancipation of slaves. In addition there are a number of records not described as di-til-la from Girsu, and other cities such as Ur (2) and Nippur (1). The most comprehensive publication of the records is that of Adam Falkenstein in "Die neu-sumerische Gerichtsurkunden"[55] on which what follows relies. They cover a period of about forty nine years between the reigns of Shulgi, son of Ur-Nammu, to Ibbisin, the last ruler of the Third Dynasty. Although Falkenstein warns that Girsu and Nina were provincial towns and there might be differences between what happened there and what happened elsewhere, particularly in larger cities such as Ur, Nippur and Uruk, these decisions are one of the main sources of our knowledge of the workings of the Mesopotamian legal system. Most of them are dated either by a year reference or a reference to the governors, judges or commissioners who were recorded as being present. Judgment 107 is typical. "Ti-Emahta was the commissioner, Lusara (and ) Urstatama were the judges. The year was the year after the year (in which) Siman(um) was destroyed".[56] They are all in cuneiform. The language is Sumerian.

So far as the personnel are concerned judges play a central role, but cases may also be heard by the provincial governor or even the king. In addition most cases involved a commissioner whose main function seems to have been to conduct a preliminary investigation of the case, though we also see commissioners being called on in later cases to give evidence of what happened in earlier related litigation in which they were involved.

The number of people recorded as being present could be quite large. Judgment 69, for example, says "Akalla, the inspector, Urigata, the inspector, Sigbu, the mayor, Nidamu, Dati, Urnanse, the kings' messenger, and Aza, his supervisor, were the people present".

The judgments tell us little about the law that we cannot learn from the law collections. The judges are not concerned with questions of law. They are concerned primarily with questions of fact.

---

55 Munich, 1977.

56 Cp. Judgment I "the year (in which) Susin, king of Ur, put up the high stela for Enlil (and) Ninlil" or Judgment 11 "the year in which Susin became king".

There are three ways in which a party can support his case, by producing a written tablet, by producing witnesses or by swearing an oath. In practice, tablets and witnesses are not really distinct means of supporting a case. They go together. One of the primary purposes of recording a transaction was to record the names of the witnesses to it so that they could be called upon to give evidence should a query arise later, just as one of the reasons for recording the name of the commissioner in the case in the judgment was to have someone to refer to if what happened in earlier litigation became relevant in a later case.

All these means of supporting a case are reflected in the judgments from Ur. In some cases the presence or absence of a tablet is treated as conclusive. In Judgment 16, for example, a creditor claimed that a slave was due to him under an agreement that the debtor was to hand her over if he had not repaid the debt within two years. The creditor produced the tablet which recorded the promise and was awarded the slave. In Judgment 109 the widow and heirs of Dudu(m) gave the defendant seven days to produce a tablet to show he had bought a garden from Dudu(m) which they said was theirs by inheritance. He failed to do so and the case was decided in their favour.

But neither a tablet nor witnesses were necessarily conclusive. In some cases witnesses are called to supplement a tablet, to give evidence that the full price was paid, or that a wife made the purchase with her own money and not that of her husband. The possibility of people making false accusations or giving false evidence is recognised by provisions in the law collections making this an offence. And in the di-til-la there are examples of evidence being rejected both by the judges and the other party. Judgment 84 is a case in which a man had given two slaves to his daughter but after his death her brother claimed they had been given to him. Two witnesses supported his claim by saying that they had seen him at the gift giving. But their evidence was rejected. Even the evidence of a commissioner might be rejected. In Judgment 138 the plaintiff claimed that the defendant had 180 of his sheep. The defendant admitted to only 30 and he was supported by two witnesses. It then emerged that the commissioner appointed to look into the case had received 15 sheep from the defendant, some of which belonged to the plaintiff. The commissioner's explanation that these were his sheep, which he had entrusted to the defendant to look after, was rejected and a penalty was imposed on him.

And a party may not accept the evidence whether documentary or oral.

Cases like these are not decided by the judges making a finding of fact. Instead they will call on one or other of the parties to take an oath either at the local temple or before a symbol of the god brought to the locality (more rarely the oath was made in the name of the king). It is the oath which determines the case.

Taking the oath is accepted as validating a claim or defence. Refusing to take the oath is an admission of defeat.[57]

So in Judgment 107 Akalla and Utansi-Anni appeared as witnesses to the sale of twelve fully laden date palms by Lunanna, the father of Urabba, to Kaku for three shekels of silver. Urabba, however, rejected their evidence. But Kaku supported his claim with an oath and won the case. In Judgment 42 the wife, daughters and slave of a man convicted of robbery had been handed over to his victim. The wife later denied this and rejected the evidence of the governor and commissioner who had been present at the handing over. An oath by the victim settled the matter. Even an oath by a slave was, it seems, conclusive. In Judgment 126 Luhuwawa, a slave of Urbaba, when accused of stealing clothes from Bazi, claimed that they had been given to her by Lugaldurdu, one of Bazi's slaves. But Lugeldurdu swore that he had not given the clothes to her and the judges ordered Luhuwawa to be handed over to Bazi.

Oaths were also used as a guarantee that a judgment or settlement made in court will be observed.[58]

The various weights given to different kinds of evidence and the way a case unravels before the court can be seen in the record of Judgment 99. After the death of Dudu his sons as his heirs claimed land and a slave and his children from their mother Innasaga. Although while Dudu was alive one of the sons had cultivated the land, Innasaga produced a tablet of purchase by her of the land and supported this with an oath that she had bought it with her own money and not her husband's. She said that the slave had been given to her as a gift by her husband and she supported this with the evidence of three witnesses before the governor and the Grand Vizier. The record says that the witnesses were not called on to swear an oath because at that point the heirs withdrew their claims. The wife then freed the slave, who was the son of free parents whom her husband had bought, before the judges. Her sons swore an oath that they would no nothing to reverse this.[59]

---

57 And it is clear oaths are taken seriously by the participants. Pritchard, p. 220, cites a striking example from the time of the Akkadian empire. A father had given his unmarried son a slave woman to marry but after his death his brothers claimed her. The judges examined witnesses for the son and then told his brothers "Go and take the oath of the gods against the witnesses of Tarmiya (the son). Shukkiya and Kula-hupi (the brothers) shrank from the gods, so that Tarmiya prevailed on the lawsuit".

58 E.g. in Judgment 5 which resembles s148 of the laws of Hammurabi. When Lugulla became seriously ill she told her husband Urigalina "Marry Gemebaba, the daughter of Lukazala … and I will keep the provision of barley and wool". Urigalina then swore before the judges that he would not change this arrangement.

59 Cp. The record cited by Pritchard, p. 218. "Nur-Shamash, Illima-ashi, Palatum and Humurum, divided the property of their father. On no account will they file claim against

All these methods of supporting a claim are found later in the laws of Hammurabi. He makes a written contract necessary for a valid marriage (s128). Anyone making a deposit of silver or gold for safekeeping must do it in front of witnesses and have it recorded or he will have no claim for its return (ss122-123). The trading agent who fails to get a written receipt for payments he makes to his principal will not have them included in the final account (ss104-105). A person who claims to have bought or received a deposit from a son or slave of another man should make a written record if he is to avoid being treated as a thief (s7). A man who wishes to give his wife or his son a gift which will not then be included in his inheritance needs to do so in writing (ss150 and 165) as must a man who wishes to give nis naditu daughter freedom to deal with her share of the inheritance as her own (s179).

And as we have seen there are also cases in which the laws of Hammurabi specify that an oath is to be sworn. A shepherd who claims sheep have been lost as a result of illness or the attack of a lion must swear an oath that this is what happened if he is to escape liability (s266). An awilu who strikes or kills a man in a brawl can swear he did not do it deliberately (ss206-207). The man who has shaved off the insignia of a slave can swear he did not do it deliberately and was deceived (s227). A wife accused of adultery by her husband can take an oath as to her innocence (s131).[60]

## LEGAL TRANSACTIONS

If the records of legal decisions give a greater sense of immediacy and liveliness to the laws of ancient Mesopotamia than the collections this is even more true of the records of legal transactions.

They not only give a far wider range of examples of law in action but also provide evidence of the traditional customary law that the law collections assume and also of the variations and developments that occur at the level of individual transactions. One certainly gets the impression that there is both greater freedom and greater complexity and sophistication possible in day to day arrangements of e.g. business and family life than appears from simply reading the provisions of the law collections. It is also clear that given there is no evident master mind or master plan behind those collections which provide a framework for the law as a whole, any generalisations about Mesopotamian law much rest largely on the contents of the records of individual legal transactions which have survived, supplemented by the draft standard provisions preserved in the working documents and exercises of the scribes, legal decisions and finally the law collections themselves.

---

one another. By Shamash, Aya, Marduk and Hammurabi they swore". Four witnesses were also named.

60 Cp. The laws of Eshnunna ss22 and 7 above, p. 26.

The records of legal transactions are too numerous to sum up or even consider in a short general paper. Three examples must suffice to give a small window on what is available.

> "One female slave ... bought from Damiq-Marduk ... her owner. As her full price he weighed out 5/6 mina 1 shekel of silver as extra payment. Three days are allowed for investigation [and] one month for epilepsy, in order to clear her, in accordance with the ordinance of the king". Five persons and the scribe are named as witnesses.[61]
>
> "92 ewes, 20 wethers, 22 young sheep, 24 lambs, 33 nanny goats, 4 billy goats, 27 kids. - total 158 sheep; 64 goats, which Sin-Samuh has entrusted to Dada, the shepherd. He takes liability for them and will replace any lost animal. If Nidnatum, his shepherd boy makes off, he shall be responsible for the loss. Dada will pay (the boy) 5 gur of grain." Three witnesses are named. [62]
>
> "Five shekels of silver, at the usual rate of interest, loaned by the temple of Shamash and by the I company to Idin and his wife, are payable with interest on sight of the payers at the market place to the bearer of this instrument." [63]

## ADMINISTRATIVE TEXTS, LETTERS AND OTHER READINGS

Here we come to the richest sources of all. Even the administrative texts often go into considerable detail and the letters provide descriptions and evidence of e.g. daily commercial and family life, not available from any other source.

"During the hundred years of Ur III, an enormous amount of written documentation was produced, with even the most mundane transactions, such as the purchase of a single sheep, being recorded.... The tablets record incoming and outgoing produce and livestock, details of contract labour, of work done and rations paid, projections of future agricultural yields as well as the actual harvest gain, allocations of seed grain and, of course, computations and receipts for taxes. The personal names of thousands of people employed by, or enslaved to, the large institutions, are preserved, and at least occasionally the tablets contain information about family size and residential customs."[64]

Another very large number of tablets were found in Mari where Zimri-Lim ruled as the last king before Mari was taken over by Hammurabi in 1757BC. "Life in Zimri-Lim's palace was recorded in great detail, as the king engaged in long correspondence with his officials on all manner of subjects; a lion is cap-

---

[61] c1669-1582. Cited Pritchard, p. 218, from M. Schorr, Urkunden des altbabylonischen Zivil- und Prozessrechts, 1913, No. 84.

[62] Postgate, p. 160, from J.J. Finkelstein, An old Babylonian trading contract, and Genesis, 88 *Jo. Am. Or. Studies*, 130, 1968.

[63] c2100. Cited H. Wigmore, Panorama of the worlds' legal systems, p. 69, from M. Schorr, Urkunden des altbabylonische Zivil- und Prozessrechts, 1913, no. 58, p. 88.

[64] G. Leick, pp. 123-4.

tured on the roof of a house and sent in a wooden cage to Zimri-Lim; the banks of a canal were in need of repair; a horde of locusts arrived in Terqa and the local governor collected them and sent them to the king."[65]

And the information we have is not limited to life in the palace and temple. One of the texts used for the training of scribes records:

> "What did you do in school? ... I recited my tablet, ate my lunch, prepared my (new) tablet, wrote it, finished it; then they assigned me my oral work, and in the afternoon they assigned me my written work. When school was dismissed, I went home, ... and found my father sitting there. I told my father of my written work, then recited my tablet to him, and my father was delighted."[66]

## THE QUESTION

This paper has been intended to provide a glimpse of what is available in the way of information about Mesopotamian law and the civilisation of which it was a part. It has reached the point at which in some crime thrillers the author tells the readers that they have enough information before them to reach a solution. In this case the solution is to the question what should our reactions be?

In preparing this contribution I came across two extremes. In England Driver and Miles, two pioneers in the publication of translations and commentaries on Babylonian and Assyrian laws, apologised because, they wrote in 1952, the subject was "not one of general interest and few readers can be expected". Their only excuse, they said, was "the pleasure of satisfying what the Master of Trinity College calls "disinterested intellectual curiosity".[67] At the other extreme two German pioneers, J. Kohler and F.E. Peiser in their "Aus dem babylonischen Rechtsleben" had written in 1890, "Die Hauptaufgabe der babylonischen Rechtsforschung besteht heutzutage unzweifelhaft darin, das massenhafte Urkunden-material juristisch zu analysiren und die in dieser Analyse zu Tage tretenden Rechtserscheinungen zu einem System des Rechts zu verarbeiten".

One of the purposes of this paper is to suggest that this does not exhaust the range of possibilities either as regards the attraction or the purpose of looking at Mesopotamian law and the civilisation of which it was a part.

Some possibilities may be excluded. It is not suggested that Mesopotamian law was as developed and sophisticated as Roman law, quite apart from the question of their relative influence on the development of European legal systems. Nor is it suggested that our understanding of modern European systems

65 M. Roaf, Cultural Atlas of Mesopotamia, p. 117.

66 Cited S.N. Kramer, History begins at Sumer, 1959, p. 8, from a scribal exercise tablet, c2000 BC.

67 G.R. Driver and J.C. Miles, The Babylonian Laws, Vol. I, Oxford, 1952, p. 56.

will be improved by looking at Mesopotamian law in the way that the claim is still made for the study of Roman law.

Nor is the claim for a more general awareness of Mesopotamian law and the civilisation which it served concerned with the question what should or should not be the subject matter of legal scholarship. It is far more about the intellectual and cultural environment in which legal scholars work and, in particular, the scope and content of their shared and taken-for-granted scholarly legal culture.

So far as the claim for Mesopotamian law in particular is concerned, at the moment European legal scholars, in so far as they look back at all, tend rarely to go beyond Roman law. And even Roman law for some two hundred years or so has claimed attention largely because it has been seen as the source of concepts used in modern European legal systems, culminating in the BGB. Rome itself, the Colosseum, the Arch of Titus, the insulae and villas in which the Romans lived, Leptis Magna, the rhetoric of Cicero and even Caesar's campaigns have largely disappeared from view. One of the stepping stones towards a case for Mesopotamian law and its civilisation is the suggestion that, at least for those who do not specialise in the study of Roman law, and even for some who do, it is the Colosseum which provides a more appropriate starting point, an Ishtar Gate to Roman law and civilisation, than the BGB.

In some ways, the specific case for Mesopotamia is strengthened, or at least paralleled, by the experience of museums. Until the nineteenth century both private collectors and museums emphasised the preeminence of the art and artefacts of Greece and Rome as the classical roots of European civilisation. One of the results of the acquisition by European museums of works of art from ancient Mesopotamia was that, after an initial hesitation, they came to be accepted not only as part of the cultural heritage of the countries whose museums acquired them, but as part of general European culture. And this was not simply because of an appreciation of their biblical connexions or of some proven links or influences that emerged between Mesopotamian civilisation and modern Europe, though there clearly are some. It was because the development and contents of a culture are not simply a question of historical cause and effect. They are a question of choice and of what may make a culture richer than it was before.

And what is true of European culture generally is also true of European legal culture. We speak of legal scholarship as a discipline and we use that discipline to distinguish the subject matter of our studies, to differentiate it from other disciplines and to mark out the relevant from the irrelevant. Even when we speak of legal scholarship as a discipline we are apt to forget that it is a self discipline and that much of what we say and do is a matter of choice. But it is also true that the strength of that discipline in any event weakens the further we move from legal scholarship in a strict sense to the wider legal culture of which it is a part and the range of choice extends as we move from our day to day working practices with their associated pressure and constraints to considerations of the wider legal culture in which we want to work.

And there is a more general case for taking a broader view that goes beyond the specific merits of Mesopotamian law and civilisation's claim to be seen as part of our wider shared European legal culture. They are only an example. It is my view that we could do much more generally to break down the barriers and strengthen the links between European legal culture and the wider general European culture of which it is part and to be far more ambitious and daring in our willingness to use that general culture as a source of starting points for the creation of wider European legal culture. In fact I would go further and suggest that we should not only use it to expand the subject matter of our legal culture but that we should also be tempted to use it to enlarge the range of responses and satisfactions that we can expect to get from the study of law to include those we expect and get when we look at objects like the Ishtar Gate and the Processional Way, by attempting to make legal scholarship itself similarly impressive and colourful.

# Some Problems of a European Legal Methodology

*Privatdozent Dr. Wolfgang Schur, Universität Gießen*

## I. Introduction

As a legal scholar there might be no bigger mistake than to talk about legal methodology to lawyers from different countries. Anyhow some think that legal methodology is nothing but the instrument of judges, that makes it possible for them to justify their decisions they have apparently achieved in another way. Others regard legal methodology more than the law itself as expression of the cultural characteristic of national legal scholarship, which is basically from the outside inscrutable. Nevertheless I would like to deal with some problems of legal methodology, especially since I think that legal methodology can guide us even if we are not aware of it. Above all I am convinced that without any mutual understanding for basic questions of legal methodology an approximation of laws in Europe is in the long term problematical, maybe even impossible. Discussing these questions it seems to me less important to achieve agreement. Even within the national discussion of such questions is that a rare case. Actually the aim of discussing problems of legal methodology should be that lawyers of different countries are able to come in this field to an understanding with each other. Only such an understanding makes it possible to get a deeper understanding of foreign law, which is not restricted to find identical legal conclusions in foreign law.

In the following I can only give some reflections of a German lawyer who tries to make clear the problems and perspectives of German legal methodology, which arise from European legal unification. It might be useful to point out that I understand myself as a lawyer who mainly works on private law. Such a focus is probably not without significance for a lawyer's view on methodical questions. A lawyer, who is more focused on public law or criminal law, might stress other points. Finally I make my contribution as a lawyer whose main focus lies in national law, not in international law. The idea to deal with questions of a European legal methodology, although I am not working on international law, rests upon the experience of the reform of the German law of obligations, which is in force since January 1st of 2002. It is probably common knowledge that the German government has used the necessity to implement different Directives of the European Union to reform central parts of the German civil code from January 1st 1900. Since this reform is in force no German lawyer, who works on private law, can restrict himself any longer on the national legal frame. Although this reform brings a lot of problems along, it has made clear for German legal scholarship in private law that it is unavoidable to open to European law, that national legal scholarship can only last as European legal scholarship. That requires in a further step of European unification that lawyers who focus their attention on national law take part in the European process of discussion, in order that the pioneers of European, international and comparative law do not longer stand alone.

Referring to my law teacher Jan Schapp,[1] who has pointed out the Greek origin of this word, I would like to comprehend legal methodology as the way like lawyers understand and apply law. What European legal methodology means is everything else than clear. At bottom this question is the reflected image of the complex relations of the states in the frame of the European Union and total Europe. Certainly a European legal methodology is related to the understanding and applying of community law itself. A central subject of a European legal methodology might be further the handling of the relation between national and European law. Finally a European legal methodology has to raise the question whether there are uniform basics of understanding and applying law in the different European states.

In the centre of my following reflections I would like to move by the example of interpretation in accordance with Directives the relation of national and European law (or more exactly the law of the European Union). That means I concentrate my attention on the problems arising from the impact of European law to national law. From this starting point follow necessarily views on other scopes of a European legal methodology.

## II. Some problems of the impact of European law to national law

### 1. The example of interpretation in accordance with the Directives

I suppose the most important instrument of the European Union to establish uniform living conditions is the Directive. By a Directive each addressed state is according to Art. 249 III EC Treaty bound to implement the Directive's standards. The instrument of Directives is based on the idea that it should be left to national legislation how to put the required statutes into the whole of the national legal order. With regard to this proceeding in Germany more and more frequently the problem is posed to go back upon the Directive in order to interpret the implemented law. So far the principle is effective to apply national law in accordance with the Directive. That means, if there are according to the standards of national law different interpretations possible, the interpretation takes precedence that fits best to the aims of the Directive. The principle to interpret national law in accordance with the Directives seems to be a copy of the princi-

1 *Schapp*, Die juristische Methode als der Weg zum Verstehen und Anwenden des Rechts, Jura 2001, p. 217 sq.; *idem*, Methodenlehre, Allgemeine Lehren des Rechts und Fall-Lösung, Rechtstheorie 2001, p. 305 sq.

ple to interpret law in accordance with the constitution, which is in Germany a generally accepted method to interpret law.[2]

Interpretation in accordance with Directives poses a lot of problems that spin around the question, how national and European law work together. A fundamental point concerns the question, why national courts are bound to take Directives into consideration when they interpret national law.[3] Until now this question has found no clear answer. Of course, similar to the constitution Directives seem to be superior law from the conception of a legal order as a hierarchical object. But first of all Directives are addressed to the national legislator, although the state as such is bound. Indeed, Directives which are not implemented by a state can have direct effects between the state and an individual, so that the judge is bound by the Directive. But still uncertain is the relationship between direct effects of Directives and interpretation in accordance with Directives.[4] Are the principles concerning direct effects of Directives only valid in cases of non-implementation? Are these principles also valid in cases of incorrect implementation? Or has the Directive always direct effects, so that interpretation in accordance with the Directive is only a result of the direct effects of Directives?

As far as I can see the opinion is predominant, that the binding effect of a Directive refers to all national authorities including the courts.[5] However, due to some ambiguous statements of the European Court of Justice[6] increasingly it is stated clearly that national courts are only bound by Directives in the frame of the national distribution of powers, so that a German judge cannot apply a Directive's content against national law.[7] Under these conditions interpretation in accordance with Directives seems to fit without bigger problems into the national legal methodology of Germany. This also seems to be the very aim of a

---

2 For interpretation in accordance with the constitution see only *Larenz*, Methodenlehre der Rechtswissenschaft, 6th. ed., 1991, p. 339 sq. For some parallels between interpretation in accordance with Directives and interpretation in accordance with the constitution see *Müller/Christensen*, Juristische Methodik, vol. I, 2002, at margin no. 428 b (p. 328 sq.).

3 For this problem I only mention from the German discussion *Canaris*, Die richtlinienkonforme Auslegung und Rechtsfortbildung im System der juristischen Methodenlehre, Festschrift für Franz Bydlinski, 2002, p. 47 sq.; *Franzen*, Privatrechtsangleichung durch die Europäische Gemeinschaft, 1999, p. 291 sq.; *Müller/Christensen*, op. cit. (Fn. 2), at margin no. 428 c.

4 Cf. *Müller/Christensen*, op. cit. (Fn. 2), at margin no. 428 a (p. 327); *Ruffert*, in: Calliess/Ruffert (eds.), Kommentar zu EU-Vertrag und EG-Vertrag, 2nd ed., 2002, at Art. 149 EGV margin no. 111; *Biervert*, in: Schwarze (ed.), EU-Kommentar, 2002, at Art. 249 EGV margin no. 30.

5 Cf. *Canaris*, op. cit. (Fn. 3), p. 55 sq.; *Müller/Christensen*, op. cit. (Fn. 2), at margin no. 428 c.

6 Marleasing SA v. La Commercial International de Alimentatión SA – Case C – 106/89 of 13.11.1990 ECR I-4135.

7 *Canaris*, op. cit. (Fn. 3), p. 56 sq.; *Müller/Christensen*, op. cit. (Fn. 2), at margin no. 428 b (p. 331), 428 e (p. 359).

view in the German discussion, that doesn't found the requirement of interpretation in accordance with Directives in European law, but with the argument, that there is a presumption the national legislator has intended to implement the Directives in a correct manner.[8] From this point of view interpretation in accordance with Directives is some kind of historical interpretation to find out the will of the legislator in the frame of the classical German doctrine of interpretation (that includes grammatical interpretation, systematic-logical interpretation, historical interpretation and objective-teleological interpretation).

I am far away from the idea to try to answer the question what the reasons are for the validity of interpretation in accordance with Directives with more shrewd arguments that have already been delivered in this discussion. Instead I would like to move the attention to some conditions of interpretation in accordance with Directives.

(1) Interpretation in accordance with Directives means interpretation of national law and interpretation of a Directive. It is not always clearly recognized that there are own standards for the interpretation of Directives. Taking up a methodical idea of private international law we can qualify this kind of interpretation as autonomous interpretation.[9] That means, legal rules of Directives and the terms used in them have to be interpreted in the light of the Community law itself and not simply from the point of national law. With that the requirement of autonomous interpretation leads to the not very much convincing coexistence of two different levels of interpretation.

(2) Interpretation in accordance with Directives by a national judge requires that he knows the relevant Directive. However, this is increasingly a problematical requirement. When a German judge had to do with special enactments like the Statute on the Protection of Consumers in Respect of Contracts Negotiated Away from Business Premises or the Consumer Credit Act, he had in mind that some of these rules were caused by European Directives.[10] But since the German legislator has put all these rules in the German Civil Code and you can't withdraw from the usually used textbooks of the Code which rule serves for the implementation of which Directive, it is becoming more difficult to take the European background of national rules into consideration. This is getting even more complicated by the fact that interpretation in accordance with Directives doesn't only refer to implemented law, but – what is widely accepted – to the entire national law and with that also to the rules that were already existing before the legislator implemented the Directive.

8 See for example *Schnorbus*, Die richtlinienkonforme Rechtsfortbildung im nationalen Privatrecht, Archiv für die civilistische Praxis, vol. 201 (2001), p. 860, 880 sq.

9 Cf. *Franzen*, op. cit. (Fn. 3), p. 475 sq.

10 For the European background of these enactments see *Ulmer*, Münchener Kommentar zum Bürgerlichen Gesetzbuch, 3rd. ed., 1995, at Vor § 1 VerbKrG margin no. 11 sq. and HausTWG at Vor § 1 margin no. 6 sq.

The question, whether or not the national judge who interprets national law knows the relevant Directives, shows also a difference between interpretation in accordance with Directives and interpretation in accordance with the Constitution. It corresponds to the importance of the constitution that we can expect of each lawyer to interpret rules in accordance with the Constitution. Under this point of view a similar expectation concerning interpretation in accordance with a lot of dispersed Directives might be a little bit exaggerated.

(3) If we take it seriously that interpretation in accordance with Directives has to take care of the distribution of powers in the state, at least in Germany it cannot simply mean that the national judge – in difference to the European judge – interprets the Directive like he think it is correct. We know from German constitutional law that in fulfilling superior law there is something like a prerogative in interpretation of the legislator. This means from my point of view that the national judge who interprets a Directive has to do that in reference to the understanding of the national legislator, that is expressed in the implementation act, and that he is not empowered to put his understanding instead of the legislator's understanding.

(4) Recently the European Court of Justice has stated in the Case Commission of the European Communities versus Kingdom of the Netherlands from 2001 that the implementation of Directives requires that the legal status must be clear and unambiguous for those who can confer upon these Directives specific rights.[11] In Germany this decision for example has lead to an explicit rule concerning the check of standard terms for transparency, where as before this check was only accepted by judicial interpretation. If we take the argument seriously the legal status has to be clear and unambiguous the role of interpretation in accordance with Directives is getting doubtful. This kind of interpretation is just based on the idea that the sense of a national rule has to be developed in accordance with the Directive and that means from the national point of view the national rule is anything else than clear and unambiguous.

## 2. Some reasons for the unsufficient coordination between European law and national law

The problem developed by the example of interpretation in accordance with Directives for the difficult relationship between European and national law easily leads to the result of an insufficient harmonization of both legal spheres. This understanding is not new, but corresponds to the wide-spread impression of European legislation in a so-called pointilistic way, that means it is a kind of

[11] Commission of the European Communities v. Kingdom of the Netherlands, of 10.5.2001 – C-144/99, published e.g. Neue Juristische Wochenschrift 2001, 2244 sq.

legislation that picks out a lot of points which are in no inner connection.[12] Such statements suggest the question what the methodical consequences might be. Recently Axel Flessner, in Germany a well-known comparative lawyer, has given some reflections on this question.[13] His starting point is that he characterises German legal methodology as a doctrine of statutes. The law in the form of statutes is considered as an expression of national sovereignity for the legal order within the territory. That makes it possible for the legal order to orientate itself to the ideas of unity, completeness and consistency. But – so Flessner's thesis – the unity of national legal order is irretrievable lost and gone. For that reason he argues for a new legal methodology that gives up to focus on the unity of national law and instead of that prepares for the plurality of different sources of law and relativity of different parts of a legal order.

But first of all it might be wise to analyse more exactly what is insufficient of the national legal methodology in handling the impact of European law to the national law before raising the demand for a new orientation of the national legal methodology. For the German point of view the ideas of unity, completeness and consistency of a legal order are tightly connected with the idea of codification. A codification like the German civil code is ideally a complete regulation of legal questions in private law.[14] The proceeding to implement a Directive into private law makes it more or less necessary to adjust anew the entire codification and maybe even the entire written law. This can be recognized on the face of it that the modification of a single rule can lead to the modification of a whole lot of other rules. The task to adapt a new rule to the whole of a legal order is first of all a task of legislation, but after that as well of legal scholarship and the courts. The necessity of such an adaptation of new rules is nothing peculiar within a codified law system that arises from the implementation of Directives. More or less this is for every legislative act necessary. In this connection the Directive is an instrument that makes it even possible for a legal order to keep to the idea of unity and completeness of this order, while giving the national legislator the task to implement the Directive in a manner that preserves the unity of national law. Nevertheless, the implementation of Directives causes more and more problems. Therefore it is a significant question what the reasons might be for these problems. From my point of view the following points are important:

---

12 See *Kötz*, Rechtsvereinheitlichung – Nutzen, Kosten, Methoden, Ziele, Rabels Zeitschrift für ausländisches und internationales Privatrecht, vol. 50 (1986), p. 1, 5; *Rittner*, Das Gemeinschaftsprivatrecht und die europäische Integration, Juristenzeitung 1995, p. 849, 851; *Basedow*, Anforderungen an eine europäische Zivilrechtsdogmatik, in: Rechtsgeschichte und Privatrechtsdogmatik, ed. by Zimmermann/Knütel/Meincke, 1999, p. 79, 82.

13 *Flessner*, Juristische Methode und europäisches Privatrecht, Juristenzeitung 2002, p. 14 sq.

14 *Wieacker*, Privatrechtsgeschichte der Neuzeit, 2nd ed., 1967, p. 475.

(1) The first point is obvious. At least in Germany the quality of national legislation is rather bad. That is exactly also true in respect to legal methodology. More and more frequently the German legislator ignores essential methodical contexts that he wisely can't have at his disposal. I don't even mean the integration of the provisions concerning standard terms into the general part of the law of obligations which was effected in the cause of the reform of the law of obligations and remained controversial.[15] But I mean for example a rule like § 241a of the German Civil Code (BGB) that is add to the general part of the law of obligations, although it is just related to rights arising from property as well.[16] Slips like this make it more and more difficult to impart to young lawyers the necessity to apply law according to methodical standards. Beyond that in the course of the reform of the law of obligations one could get the impression that the German legislator neglected his actual task to fit in the European Directives into the systematical order of national law in favour of the efforts he made under the headword "competition of codifications" to bring the national law nearer to some imaginary European law.

(2) A further important reason for the insufficient results which are caused by the implementation of Directives can increasingly be put down to the content of the Directives itself. As long as Directives only refer to side-issues of a national legal order the implementation leads usually to no problems. But as soon as a Directive touches an essential part of the national legal order, it is possible that the entire order of this area is beginning to rock. That is the underlying reason why the German legislation didn't leave it at a simple implementation of the Directive on certain aspects of the sale of consumer goods and associated guarantees of 1999, but felt urged to redesign the entire law of sales (and something more than that). And from what you can hear is that such effects of the implementation of Directives are absolutely desired.

Maybe one could object, the problem whether a Directive refers to an essential part of a national legal order is posed for each national legal order in a different way. Nevertheless, in my opinion it is obvious that someone who regulates questions of sales contracts has to realize that this can cause a lot of serious interventions into the national legal order.

The outlined problem suggests the question for the limits of Directives. I think no one would expect a European codification of private law – of what kind however – by enacting a Directive. Evidently the Directive can only be a limited means of legal harmonization. It seems to me that these limits arise essentially from the fact that Directives must leave the opportunity to implement them by preserving the peculiarity of a national legal order. However, what we can actu-

---

15 *Cf.* only *Wolf/Pfeiffer*, Der richtige Standort des AGB-Rechts innerhalb des BGB, Zeitschrift für Rechtspolitik 2001, p. 303 sq.

16 Cf. *Heinrichs*, in: Palandt, Bürgerliches Gesetzbuch, 61st ed., 2002, at § 241a margin no. 4.

ally experience, if we take these standards, is a tightrope walk between European standards, which are suitable for fitting them into the different national legal orders, and those, which can only be implemented by redesigning the existing legal order.

(3) Finally a third point concerns the concentration of legal harmonization upon legislation by Directives and by national law that is created to implement these Directives. By giving these means such an importance a positivistic stamped legal understanding appears that in Germany is overcome since a lot of years. By legal positivism I would like to understand the idea, that legal rules can be understood of their own accord and applied in the way of mathematics. This idea is even in a legal order, which is like the German one based on codified law, too limited. Even such a legal order is not only constituted by the text of statutes. The statutes are rather a short mark for the intellectual system behind them, even if this system certainly has to be proved by the wording of these statutes.[17] Above all applying law means from this point of view to pick out a rule and to show off the intellectual system behind that rule for a particular case. This explains as well the remarkable importance of teleological interpretation in Germany, which is directed to discover the purpose of a rule in the frame of a more comprehensive systematical context.

By the way, I would not deny that all legislative acts are marked by a positivistic feature, because legal rules demand for validity regardless of the reasons for them. But this doesn't exclude to distinguish between a successful legislative act, which makes it possible to combine the rules together to an intellectual system, and a less successful legislative act.

Against this background one of the most important reasons for the problems of the contemporary process of European legal harmonization is that there is no sufficient intellectual European frame of reference visible for the different national legislators. The European Union creates standards for rules which the national legislator has to integrate in a national legal order without having the opportunity to orientate himself on an intellectual system standing behind these Directives. From a methodical point of view the Directives are situated in an abstract sphere, which national legislation can more and more frequently only fill by changing the statutes faster and faster.

Altogether the result of this analysis leads me to the estimation that the essential reasons for the insufficient managing of the impact of European law to national law is less the result of an insufficient national legal methodology, but more of an insufficient looking after the tasks and the instruments of European legal harmonization. That is why I think as well that national legal methodology, which is in Germany in its essentials anchored in constitutional law, doesn't

---

17 See *Schapp*, Grundlagen des bürgerlichen Rechts, 2nd ed., 1996, at margin no. 9, 35.

have to be replaced by an original European legal methodology. But certainly there is a need for supplementary perspectives of national legal methodology.

At this point I don't want to presume my thoughts further with regard to the future process of European legal harmonization. From my point of view I think it is even clear to everyone that at least the process of legal harmonization by means of directives has come to an end.

## III. Legal methodology and comparative law

At the end of my reflections let me take a brief glance at the relationship between legal methodology and comparative law. According to an opinion already hold in France at the beginning of the 20$^{th}$ century comparative law is an own kind of legal interpretation.[18] In Germany especially Konrad Zweigert had argued in favour of comparative law as an universal method of interpretation.[19] For a long time this view hasn't attract much attention, since it met – as far as I can see – in legal methodology with almost no response. But in the course of the implementation of the German reform of the law of obligations again the opinion is expressed to take the results of comparative law much more into consideration for the interpretation of national law.[20] Indeed, it can't be denied the significance of comparative law for national and European legislation as well as for the interpretation of such law. For difficult problems like for example damages in cases of wrongful birth the German judge as well looks with pleasure at the insights and thoughts of his foreign colleagues. Nevertheless I have not the impression that the function of comparative law is accurately characterized as method of interpretation. Comparative law stands in a line with basic subjects like history of law, philosophy of law or sociology of law. These subjects open horizons up to us for a better understanding of law. But we shouldn't believe that this kind of understanding the law is identical with the understanding of statutes.

---

18 *Raymond Saleilles*, Conception et objet de la science du droit comparé, in: Congrès international de droit comparé, Procès-verbaux des seances et documents t. 1, 1905, p. 167, 182 sq.

19 *Zweigert*, Rechtsvergleichung als universale Interpretationsmethode, Rabels Zeitschrift für ausländisches und internationales Privatrecht, vol. 15 (1949/50), 5 sq.

20 *Gruber*, Zur Rolle der Rechtsvergleichung nach der Schuldrechtsreform, Zeitschrift für Vergleichende Rechtswissenschaft, vol. 101 (2002), p. 38 sq.

# Change, Culture and the Future: Public Law in Transition

*Prof. Dr. John McEldowney, University of Warwick*

## Introduction

Until quite recently, constitutional arrangements in the United Kingdom have exemplified continuity. A strong historical tradition has ensured that constitutional change when it occurs has been incremental in preference to any radical or revolutionary break with the past. Britain is one of the few countries in the world without a formal written constitution. In fact there has always been cultural resistance to changing in any fundamental way the role and function of key institutions or the constitution itself. Notwithstanding this traditional reluctance, new and unprecedented reforms have been introduced to modernize many of the institutions and organizations under the constitution. The process of change is slow and recent changes may be traced back to policies begun in the 1980s with Mrs Thatcher's privatization of the major utilities, and reforms to the civil service through the introduction of "next step" agencies that exemplified a new public management style. Such developments dramatically altered the relationship between the citizen and the state. Since the 1980s the system of public management and administration[1] has undergone rapid and diverse change. The traditional approach to public life, based on stewardship and public duty, has been replaced by a market-orientated approach to the delivery of public goods and services. This provides new terminology and a new way of describing the relationship between service provider and client: the principal, namely the purchaser or consumer of services, is distinguished from the provider, the public body or agency that provides the service. The latter may be part of the pre-existing public service or form a new competitive element whereby private and voluntary sectors may bid to provide goods and services. The provider is then engaged in the award of the contract, including negotiation of various conditions for performance. Set against this background of fundamental change in the way the public sector behaves is the development of standards and ethics in public life.

The election of a new Labour Government in 1997 has brought significant constitutional reforms. These include, in 1998, devolution to Scotland, Wales and Northern Ireland and, later, creation of the new position of elected mayor for London. Fundamental constitutional reforms have embraced changes to the electoral system, a more independent Bank of England with the responsibility for adjusting interest rates removed from the government of the day, reforms to the House of Lords, and strategies to modernize almost every aspect of govern-

---

1 D. Oliver and G. Drewry, *Public Service Reforms*, 1996.

ment institutions and procedures. There is also a new Freedom of Information Act 2000 and a new Terrorism Act 2000. There are significant changes to the criminal justice system, tribunals and inquiries, and to the management of the courts system. The most celebrated and acclaimed innovation is the Human Rights Act 1998, which came fully into force in October 2000. The 1998 Act is having an impact on how rights are construed with a steady increase the use of judicial review[2] resulting in the potential to shift decision-making in public law matters from elected ministers to the courts under the direction of increased judicial controls.

The focus of this paper is on the role of change within the culture and tradition of the British constitution. The paper outlines the nature of constitutional change in the " culture" of the United Kingdom and attempts to define culture in terms of understanding how beliefs and perceptions in society may influence law and legal thinking. The main constitutional reforms introduced since 1997 are explained. Particular attention is given to the role of the judges and the compatibility of the office of Lord Chancellor with the Human Rights Act 1998 and the need for a separate Supreme Court from the existing constitutional arrangements for the Appellate Committee in the House of Lords. Finally, some conclusions are offered as to the future direction of public law.

## Constitutional change and culture

Tinkering with Britain's constitution is a fine art developed through centuries of incremental changes.[3] There has always been cultural resistance to changing the role and function of major institutions or the constitution itself. The word "culture" is used to refer to the ideas, customs or manners that characterise a people.[4] Reference to culture has a long anthropological history.[5] In the 16$^{th}$ and 17$^{th}$ centuries the term is found as part of the physical world referring to cultivation as in agriculture. The intellectual refinement that came at the end of the 17$^{th}$ century links culture to an intellectual movement, inclusive of human manners, and the characteristics of civilised society. In the late 18$^{th}$ and 19$^{th}$ centuries the German[6] term "Kultur" emerged as referring to the complex set of beliefs and

---

2 *Practice Statement* [2002] 1 All ER 633. It is noted that from 2$^{nd}$ October to 31$^{st}$ December 2001 some 19% of judicial review cases raised an issue of human rights. In numerical terms judicial review receipts for 2001 showed an overall increase of 11% on 2000.

3 See: S.F.C. Milsom, *Historical Foundations of the Common Law* second edition London: Butterworths, 1981.

4 See: Tessa Morris-Suzuki, "The Invention and Reinvention of "Japanese Culture". *The Journal of Asian Studies* 54 no. 3 (August, 1995) pp. 759-80.

5 Fernand Braudel, *A History of Civilizations* translated Richard Mayne London: Allen Lane, 1994.

6 A.L. Kroeber and C. Kluckhohn, *Culture: A Critical Review of Concepts and Definitions* New York: Vintage Books, 1963.

customs that are part of a particular society.[7] The *Oxford English Dictionary* takes up the idea of society and refers to the civilization of a people in a particular stage of their development. There is a shift in the meaning given to the word culture from its early origins to refer to mental and moral cultivation, to its newer form of referring to the practices or beliefs in a particular society. It is in this newer form of interpretation may be found the meaning of the word that best describes attitudes to constitutional change and reform. English culture found in legal education and training has generally ideologically resisted fundamental constitutional change. Cultural constraints have impeded the development of administrative law in the nineteenth century as well as inhibited codification and a written constitution.

The Englishness[8] of the idea of the nation is found embedded in the common law. By the middle of the nineteenth century, as Colls points out[9]:

> The case for the freeborn Englishman went deeper and wider than the case for the supremacy of Parliament. Parliament, after all, was only virtual representation. At the hustings, most people were not entitled to vote. Common-law doctrine, on the other hand, held that the law embodies nothing less than the historic nature of the English people.

Writing in the 1867 Waler Bagehot identified how the English constitution owed much to the fact that[10] "... the mass of the people yield obedience to the select few", a sign that the decision makers were an elite and following the development of a new industrial society, composed of middle class politicians. Bound together through popular monarchy and nationalism the Englishness of the constitution was linked with Scotland, Wales and Ireland through a series of union treaties which deterred popular nationalism and allowed representation rather than democratic government. As Colls identifies the cornerstone of political power owes much to the way the constitution was shaped[11]:

> the constitution has been far more interested in giving politicians the freedom to rule with the minimum of interference.

---

7 F.C. Gamst and E. Norbeck, *Ideas of Culture: Sources and Uses* New York: Holt, Reinhart and Winston, 1976.

8 Simon Schama, *A History of Britain* London: BBC 2000-2; Adrian Hastings, *The Construction of Nationhood: Ethnicity, Religion and Nationalism* Cambridge: Cambridge University Press, 1997; Colin Kidd, *British Identities before Nationalism* Cambridge: Cambridge University, 1995.

9 R. Colls, *Identity of England* Oxford: Oxford University Press, 2002 p. 23; J.G.A. Pocock, *The Ancient Constitution and Feudal Law* Cambridge: Cambridge University Press, 1957; Michael Lobban, *The Common Law and English Jurisprudence 1760-1850* Oxford: Oxford University Press, 1991.

10 W. Bagehot, *The English Constitution* London: 1867 p. 248.

11 Colls, *op. cit.*, p. 54.

The cultural reticence to embrace change of a fundamental kind finds support in the fear that change may lead to revolution.

It is a mistake, however, to regard such cultural inhibitions about change as inimical to good government. In fact for a number of reasons the values that underpinned some of the resistance to change came from identifying different strands of government and distinguishing political from legal elements. Milsom warns of the dangers of adopting too rigid a model of how change is actually accomplished. He makes the following observations[12]:

It is not only lawyers and legal historians who work to models: how people think and act depends partly on their vision of their own society.

The cultural resistance to changing the role and function of major institutions or the constitution itself appears to be founded on a number of reasons.

One simple reason for this is flexibility: elected governments come and go, but once elected, the government of the day is relatively free to govern with "... no institutional restraints on a legally sovereign legislature and a politically sovereign electorate".[13] The essence of political power is its legitimacy. The democratic will of the majority, exercised at a general election under the first past the post (FPP) electoral system, elects governments with a mandate to govern for up to five years largely free from restraints on their political decision-making or their legal powers to execute their policies.

Another reason for resisting change is that the common law is largely problem-centred. Unlike the civilian tradition concerned about the application of legal or constitutional principles, the common law rarely involves points of constitutional principle. Drawing on a mixture of past experience, case law or past precedent, pragmatic solutions to problems are often invented to fit the circumstances of the time. Much effort is given to making things work and ensuring where appropriate that the necessary repairs are made before any attempt to develop new structures. As McCrudden has observed:

> A number of the principles which are said to describe, inform, and underpin the British constitution (majoritarian democracy, parliamentary supremacy, and constitutional conventions) may be seen as the embodiment of this tradition, concentrating as they do on " the authority of experience and the continuity of practice" and ensuring the flexibility of the process by which decisions are made. In this tradition, authoritative constitutional structures *evolve*, they are seldom *made*.[14]

Cultural resistance to constitutional change may come from the pragmatic qualities of the English character and approach to problem solving. The legacy

---

12 S.F.C. Milsom, *op. cit.*, p. 150.

13 K.D. Ewing, "The Unbalanced Constitution" in *Sceptical Essays on Human Rights*, T. Campbell, K.D. Ewing and A. Tomkins (eds), 2001, p. 104.

14 C. McCrudden, "Northern Ireland" in *The Changing Constitution*, J. Jowell and D. Oliver (eds) 3rd ed., 1994, p. 325.

today is that the constitution is sufficiently flexible to accommodate major political differences through changes in the party in power. Political power, its loss and acquisition have led the way in shaping modern Britain largely free from much judicial or legal restraint. Incremental constitutional change has occurred over centuries in tandem with Britain's economic development and changing role in the world. At the end of the nineteenth century Britain was a major industrial country with a large empire and equipped to legislate for many countries in the world. The grant of independence to the colonies developed the art of constitutional drafting, as many countries adopted the Westminster model of government in their constitutional arrangements. Gradually, after the Second World War, Britain began coming to terms with its new position in the world, without the British Empire and with the creation of the Commonwealth. The country has come under new influences, particularly since 1972 and its membership of the European Union: perhaps the greatest change is the impact of the European civil law tradition and the European Union on the United Kingdom's constitution.

In the fundamental shift to accommodate Europe, with its civil law tradition, the way Britain is governed has changed. At the same time, the new "value for money" focus has brought modest but significant changes in the way government is able to govern. Such changes have been incremental, part of the general progression towards an "organic change", rather than any revolutionary or radical break with past tradition, but nonetheless may have significant effects. One example is the development of various agencies to conduct the work of the civil service. Nearly 80 per cent of the civil service may be found in such an agency arrangement. Yet the doctrine of ministerial responsibility remains virtually unchanged to meet the demands of the complex relationship between civil servant and minister.

Another example of organic change is in the gradual evolution of the role of select committees in Parliament. Reforms introduced since 1979 created 14 departmental select committees. Today there are 24 such committees that range across government departments, with the remit to scrutinize the departments' financial, policy, administrative and operational decisions. Ministers and, under their guidance, civil servants may be required to attend to give evidence. The doyen of select committees is the Public Accounts Committee (PAC) charged with holding to account government expenditure, including value for money. The PAC is aided by the National Audit Office (NAO), an independent public audit office under the Comptroller and Auditor General, an officer of the House of Commons, and responsible to Parliament for the scrutiny of public money and departmental accounts. Building on nineteenth-century practice and convention, the twin elements of specialist expertise through the NAO and political accountability under the PAC provide a modern and effective means to scrutinize government. The substance of the work of the Comptroller and Auditor General is carried out by the National Audit Office under statutory authority (the National Audit Act 1983) but influenced by conventions and rules that may be traced back to the nineteenth century.

Although the select committees are subject to party political influence and party whips' influence in the selection of members, the committees have the potential to affect the culture of government. The government of the day may ultimately have to comply with a select committee's requests for information that has been withheld. In a recent example, the Foreign Affairs Select Committee in their investigation of arms exports to Sierra Leone (1997–1998) were initially prevented from receiving information on Sierra Leone. Through the select committee's publication of critical reports,[15] the government eventually compromised and made more information available.

## The essential characteristics of the United Kingdom's Constitution

It may not be unreasonable to ask whether Britain has a constitution. The question arises from the notable absence of a formal written constitution and the difficulties of clearly defining the powers of the executive and the roles of the legislature and judiciary. The constitution may be described as unwritten, as opposed to written; flexible, as opposed to rigid; unitary, rather than federal; and institutional and practical, as opposed to theoretical and doctrinal. The contemporary monarchy maintains a largely symbolic role and continuity of tradition. Bagehot aptly described the monarch's formal powers as "the right to be consulted, the right to encourage, the right to warn".[16] The monarch retains the power to grant a dissolution of Parliament on the advice of the government. There is also the power to invite the leader of the political party with the majority of seats (the Prime Minister elect) to form an administration. In the case of a hung parliament this might be not just symbolic but decisive in the choice of the party to form the government.

The absence of a single codified or written constitution leaves the working out of the practicalities of the constitution to the system of laws, conventions and customs that are the hallmark of the medieval inheritance. A notable feature is the use of conventions — essential norms of political behaviour, difficult to categorize in any strictly legal or constitutional sense, that comprise the common practices and workings of government and that link the modern with the ancient, medieval constitution. Dicey's influence since the nineteenth century has led constitutional lawyers to believe that conventions serve the purpose of examining past practices to determine future conduct. Unlike rules or laws such as statute law, conventions are not enforceable by the courts but often help explain the political workings of the constitution.

---

15 HC 760 (1997–98) and HC 852 (1997–98).

16 Walter Bagehot, *The English Constitution* London, 1867 reprinted and edited by G. Phillipson Sussex Academic Press, Sussex: 1997 p. 42.

Conventions have grown historically as unwritten rules, and may adapt to the changing methods of modern government. That is their enduring quality. They are not the product of either judicial or legislative intervention, but rather of custom, usage, habit, and common practice. The most formative period for their development was probably in the eighteenth and towards the end of the nineteenth century. Conventions have the shortcoming that they reflect the values of mid-Victorian Government and, perhaps, fail to take account of modern party-political realities. The increasing complexity of the machinery of government may make accountability through conventions more of a myth than a reality. Many important practices are part of the internal working of government, and it is difficult to give internal working practices special value or elevation to the status of a convention. In essence, conventions are "the morality of the constitution". They may be relied on to alter with the political circumstances of the time.

The constitution essentially consists of the sovereignty of parliament and the rule of law. With Britain's membership of the European Union, and the Human Rights Act 1998, both these traditional aspects of constitutional law have recently come under debate and scrutiny as part of the process of fundamental reform. Another unique feature of the constitution that has been questioned is the absence of a formal or rigid doctrine of the separation of powers. This remains a gap in the United Kingdom's constitutional arrangements which is difficult to fill. Montesquieu's philosophy of the separation of powers has influenced the creation of a constitutional doctrine or principle that is commonly found in most written constitutions, notably that of the USA. However, the idea of separation of the three functions — the legislature, the executive and the judiciary — is hard to conceive of as applying to the United Kingdom. For example, the Lord Chancellor is head of the Lord Chancellor's Department, Speaker of the House of Lords, and head of the judiciary. Defining separation may mean that one organ of government should not exercise the functions of another; or that no one element of the three should dominate the other; or that the same person should not occupy a position in all three organs of government — which the Lord Chancellor clearly does. While the separation of powers is fine in principle, it is hard to operate in practice. The need for a distinction between the three functions is at the heart of the doctrine. A recent example of the lack of clear separation in practice is when the government attempted to act in a judicial fashion when exercising legislative powers. Lord Templeman, in the House of Lords in *M v Home Office*,[17] considered the question of the courts' contempt powers when the Home Secretary appeared to be in breach of his undertaking not to deport a citizen of Zaire. In anticipation of any judicial decision the citizen was deported despite assurances that this would not happen until the judges had de-

17 [1993] 3 WLR 433.

termined the legality of any deportation order. The House of Lords found that the deportation had taken place and that technically the Home Secretary was in contempt of court. The fundamental principle was that the Home Secretary should obey the law like any other citizen. As Lord Templeman noted, "Parliament makes the law, the executive carry the law into effect and the judiciary enforce the law."[18] It is the role of the Lord Chancellor and the function of the Law Lords that will be considered in further detail below.

It might be concluded that there is no formal separation of powers in the United Kingdom and that the formalities of such a doctrine are unlikely to be observed until there is a written constitution. However, the doctrine is important, and has influenced the United Kingdom. The separation of powers doctrine seeks to apply checks and balances in the way powers are exercised, and may have guided the way the three organs of government have developed. The rule of law, which Dicey defined in terms of preventing " arbitrary decision making", rests on the wisdom of convention and relies on good sense and judgement to prevail. The sovereignty of Parliament could on a whim curtail the rule of law, but Parliament has, with certain exceptions, limited its own powers to interfere with it, and thus ensured its survival. Arguably, the test of the rule of law is at times of emergency or threat, when it is at its most vulnerable. Exceptional measures may always appear justifiable to meet a specific emergency. Posterity may not with hindsight see such powers as so clearly justified when evaluated in a more objective way than at the time they were invoked. Safeguards may be fragile and weak, but without them the values of a liberal democracy appear vulnerable. Authoritarian states are capable of usurping the democratic system and it is all too easy to slide into elected dictatorships — a danger that is ever present in the life-cycle of any system.

Since the 1980s the United Kingdom has experienced fundamental constitutional change, beginning with Mrs Thatcher's Government and culminating in the modernization strategy of the new Labour Government in 1997. As noted above, the sovereignty of Parliament, at the apex of the constitution, traditionally defined the authority of Parliament over the courts of law. Sovereignty provides Parliament with the final say and the authority to change any law. The supremacy of legislation gives ultimate political power and authority to the majority over the minority. However, a number of fundamental constitutional reforms affect the traditional doctrine of Parliamentary sovereignty.

The Human Rights Act 1998 provides that legislation may be examined as to its compatibility[19] with rights under the European Convention, but this falls short of allowing the courts to strike down any law as unconstitutional. Nevertheless, the courts are free to say when Parliament has acted in a way that is incompati-

---

18 At p. 437.

19 R (On the application of Holding and Barnes plc) v Secretary of State for the Environment, Transport and the Regions [2000] All ER (D) 2264.

ble with Convention rights. This represents a potential shift in power from the political to the legal, and provides the greatest potential for changing how decisions are made. The second fundamental reform is membership of the European Community; this has a direct impact on the legal system and the substantive law of the United Kingdom, and is therefore a contentious issue.

### The Europeanization of UK law

British membership of the European Community since 1973 has had long-term consequences for Britain's constitutional arrangements. At the apex of the Community is the Court of Justice of the European Communities with its absolute power to ensure that the body of European law is maintained throughout all the member states. The Court of Justice has had a considerable influence over the development of judicial thinking in the United Kingdom and also over the authority of Parliament. Parliamentary sovereignty, long held by the courts to be the bedrock of constitutional principles, appears considerably weakened in the context of what is now the European Union. The coming into force of the single European currency from January 2002 and the development of a unified system of central banks are but two of the institutional changes that confront the United Kingdom. More significant is the realization that the English common law is now part of a shared inheritance with the civil law tradition. The two traditions have long been contrasted as "codified" and "uncodified", but their differences are more profound and far-reaching in terms of the cultural adjustment needed to understand both of them.

Membership of the European Union creates a possible challenge to the doctrine of the sovereignty of Parliament. Traditionalists insist that the doctrine asserting that an Act of Parliament is free from being struck down by the courts would prevail in spite of Britain's membership of the European Union. The traditionalist view is compelling when it is remembered that Parliament carries through the wishes of the majority of the electorate, through the government which carries out its election manifesto. In this way parliamentary sovereignty translates into the wishes of the people, as opposed to the decisions of unelected judges. However, the issue that arises is whether the traditional view is capable of accommodating membership of the European Union. Tensions between UK and EC law inevitably lead to the question of which might prevail in the event of a conflict that is not resolved by Parliament or the political system but is left to the courts to decide. One example of the need for judicial decision-making arose from a series of cases[20] that centred around the dispute involving Spanish fishing

[20] R v Secretary of State for Transport ex parte Factortame Ltd (No.3) [1991] 2 Lloyd's Reports 648, R v Secretary of State for Transport ex parte Factortame Ltd (No 2) [1991] 1 AC 603, R v Secretary of State for Transport ex parte Factortame Ltd [1999] 4 All ER 906, R v Secretary of State for Transport ex parte Factortame Ltd [1990] 2 AC 85.

boats operating within the United Kingdom's fishing quota. The Spanish boats formed companies and registered in the United Kingdom. The Merchant Shipping Act 1988 introduced various requirements such as nationality and domicile in an attempt to restrict the use of UK fishing quotas to only the UK-based fishing fleet. The Spanish fishermen went to court in the United Kingdom and sought interim relief from the English courts restraining the application of the 1988 Act as a first step in challenging its compatibility with Community law. The supremacy of Community law, long acknowledged in the case law of the Community, appeared at odds with the doctrine of the supremacy of United Kingdom legislation. The House of Lords in a number of key decisions arising out of the dispute resolved:

- that the United Kingdom courts must give way to European Community law even if this means acknowledging that part of an Act of Parliament is incompatible with community law;
- that in general the United Kingdom courts must not apply United Kingdom statutes whenever there is a potential conflict with Community law;
- that the courts are required to ensure that United Kingdom law is consistent with Community law;
- that national courts are required to ensure that the government complies with the requirements of Community law, and may provide compensation in the event of any failure to do so.

It is possible to see the *Factortame*[21] set of cases as evolutionary as well as revolutionary. In terms of evolving principles it is clear that United Kingdom law must be held to be compatible with Community law. More revolutionary is the idea that integrating common law and civil law approaches requires the courts of the United Kingdom to be seen as part of a single unified court system. The European Court of Justice stands at the apex of judicial powers while the House of Lords, as part of the domestic judiciary, is there to implement changes. On that analysis, the United Kingdom has unwittingly developed a Supreme Court system, composed of the House of Lords and the European Court of Justice, with inherent jurisdiction over community law in the United Kingdom. In a pragmatic and case-by-case approach it is possible to see the beginnings of a common law shared throughout the Community.[22]

### The asymmetrical constitution

Devolution has also brought about fundamental constitutional changes. It is clear that, historically, a remarkable feature of Parliamentary power has been its centralization in the hands of government. This gives central government ulti-

---

21 Ibid.

22 P. Craig, "Public Law, Political Theory and Legal Theory" [2000] *Public Law* 211.

mate legal authority over local government. In the absence of any federal system offering local government an entrenched protection, local government may be amended or modified at the whim of central government. Similarly, newly devolved government to Wales, Scotland and Northern Ireland are subject to Parliamentary authority. In strict constitutional theory devolution may be retracted, modified, suspended or amended. In practical and political terms it is unlikely that the unitary nature of the United Kingdom will be restored. The term asymmetrical seems appropriate. Centralized and ultimate sovereignty continues to rest with the United Kingdom Parliament, with subordinate law-making powers delegated to Scotland, Wales, Northern Ireland and the London mayor.

Devolution[23] was first experienced under the Government of Ireland Act 1920[24] and the creation of a devolved parliament for Northern Ireland. The experiment proved unsuccessful, and direct rule by the United Kingdom Parliament was imposed on Northern Ireland again in 1972. Nevertheless, devolution as a principle of providing local community government has endured. The attempt by a previous Labour Government to introduce devolution to Scotland and Wales failed in 1978. In September 1997 referendums were held in Scotland and Wales. The result was that in Scotland 75 per cent of the voters were in favour, on a 60 per cent turnout. In Wales support for devolution was more marginal, and on a turnout of around 50 per cent the majority were in favour but by the narrowest of margins (0.6 per cent). The new Labour Government with a secure Parliamentary majority at Westminster could afford to be radical and proceeded to introduce devolution for Scotland, Wales and Northern Ireland and London.

The Scotland Act 1998 creates a new Scottish Parliament, elected for four years, with defined legislative powers to pass Acts (Schedule 5 of the 1998 Act) and a limited tax-raising authority. There is a Scottish First Minister, and an appointment process for ministers nominated by the first Minister from members of the Scottish Parliament but requiring the agreement of that Parliament. The United Kingdom Parliament maintains overall legislative competence over matters relating to foreign affairs, including the European Union, the Crown, defence, and economic and monetary matters. Over the first few years with a devolved Parliament, Scotland has developed a distinctive style and content in governing its own affairs.

The Government of Wales Act 1998 creates a Welsh Assembly, more limited in powers and scope than the Scottish Parliament. The Assembly is unable to legislate in terms of passing Acts, but may exercise the functions of the Secretary of State for Wales that have been transferred to the Assembly. This power

---

23 John F. McEldowney, "Legal Aspects of Relations between the United Kingdom and Scottish Parliaments" in *The Law and Parliament*, D. Oliver and G. Drewry (eds), 1998, p. 192.

24 The Government of Ireland Act 1920 incorporated many ideas from the British North America Act 1867 c. 3.

includes subordinate legislative powers under Part III of the Government of Wales Act 1998. There is a First Minister, and the Assembly operates cabinet-style committees for decision making. It is possible that under political influence the powers of the Welsh Assembly could be increased beyond the modest powers it already has. Most notably unlike the Scottish Parliament, it does not have power to raise taxes. However, the Secretary of State for Wales may be forced to concede additional powers under pressure from the Welsh Assembly. This may not have been envisaged in the legislation, but this is in practical terms how the Welsh form of devolution may result in more autonomy for Wales than originally planned. However, it is conceded that the Assembly does not have powers to adopt primary legislation. As a result as Burrows has pointed out[25]:

> In Wales there is the anomaly that an Assembly deriving its legitimacy from the will of the people demonstrated in elections lacks the power to carry out the functions associated elsewhere within the United Kingdom with such a body.

Finally, in the case of Northern Ireland, devolution is part of an ongoing peace process and as such has a number of unique qualities. There is an assembly, elected for a four-year term, and a power-sharing executive unlike any other, with a requirement to address divisions between Nationalists and Unionists. There is a First and a deputy First Minister who must satisfy the requirements of a majority vote in the Assembly and a majority of both Unionists and Nationalist members of the Assembly. There is then a complex set of powers that may be devolved to the Assembly once it is up and running, with excepted matters listed in the Act as most likely never to be devolved. This leaves reserved matters which might be transferred under an Order in Council, and transferred matters that are devolved. The essence of devolution is that the constitutional order may create, but not impose, a system of government. Under the Northern Ireland Act 2000 devolution was suspended in May 2000 and then later restored, an indication of the fragility of the peace process underpinning devolution.

It may be concluded that devolution has an organic quality. Self-reliance and a desire to be distinctive from the history of English influence are potent forces that will pull in the direction of greater independence. Nationalism may claim a stake in drawing together distinct and different groups as an elected subordinate body grows in confidence and legitimacy. These are potent forces that have the potential to develop in opposition to the centralizing tendencies of the past. Most significant are the features common to the devolution arrangements: four-year instead of five-year terms; unicameral assemblies or parliaments as distinct from the Westminster bicameral system; forms of proportional representation for elections, rather than the existing FPP system for Westminster elections; and the

25 N. Burrows, *Devolution* London: Sweet and Maxwell, 2000 p. 186.

continuation of United Kingdom sovereignty, rather than any settlement resolved around federalism. This leaves unanswered the question of the future role and functioning of the United Kingdom's Parliament and the possibility of its reform.

## Reform of the House of Lords

The United Kingdom's Parliament has a bicameral system, with the House of Lords forming the second chamber to the Commons. The Parliament Acts 1911 and 1949 made the Lords subsidiary to the pre-eminent House of Commons. The Lords have only a limited power to delay most legislation, and a money bill may be passed by the Commons acting alone. Long-standing questions are what is the role of the Lords, and how should this House be composed to reflect its role and function? These questions have been consistently fudged by successive governments. An inter-party conference in 1948 reached limited agreement that the Lords should be complementary to the Commons. In 1967 another all-party conference was held with limited success. The new Labour Government in 1997 determined to tackle the problem of composition first. The House of Lords Act 1999 abolished hereditary peers but allowed for 92 to be retained through election from existing hereditary peers. The abolition of the hereditary element is a big step. It abolishes the potential Conservative in-built majority and moves the House of Lords to the position of having only life members, some of whom have the unique distinction, of having been elected from the hereditary peers and thus a legitimacy to their standing. This transitional House is as much as has yet been achieved, but the past history of the House as a revising and debating chamber is retained. There is a sense of renewal permeating the work of the revised House of Lords. There is also a growing self-confidence to speak out and criticize government Bills and introduce amendments both on technical matters and on substantive points.

The future reform of the Lords is problematic. In March 1999 a Royal Commission[26] under the chairmanship of Lord Wakeham was set up with limited terms of reference to recommend reforms. The terms of reference were set in the context of maintaining the existing powers of the Lords as follows:

> Having regard to the need to maintain the position of the House of Commons as the pre-eminent chamber of Parliament and taking particular account of the constitutional settlement, including the newly devolved institutions, the impact of the Human Rights Act and developing relations with the European Union:

---

[26] *A House for the Future* Cm 4534, January 2000.

- To consider and make recommendations on the role and functions of a second chamber;
- To make recommendations on the method or combination of methods of composition required to constitute a second chamber fit for that role and those functions;
- To report by $31^{st}$ December 1999.

The Wakeham Commission reported in January 2000 and made various proposals about the future of the Lords. Three characteristics were identified for the Lords:

- it should be authoritative, capable of holding the executive to account and scrutinizing government;
- it should be sufficiently confident to use its powers and act effectively;
- ideally it should be representative of British society as a whole.

The Wakeham Commission recommended lengthy terms of non-renewable membership of up to 15 years, salaries for members, and an independent commission with the ultimate right to decide which party nominees are suitable for membership. Wakeham also recommended that there should be an elected element of up to 35 per cent of members and the continuation of appointed members. Thus he rejected making a straight choice between elected or appointed members by recommending a compromise. It was suggested that a regional list system might assist in ensuring local representation. The present House of Lords consists of about 750 members including the 15 Law Lords and 26 Lords Spiritual. Wakeham recommended a smaller House composed of up to 550 members.

Recently the Government published a White Paper on Lords reform.[27] While the main recommendations of the Wakeham Commission were accepted, it is clear that there are serious points of difference between the White Paper and Wakeham. The government appears to favour only 20 per cent elected members, and that the nominees of the party leaders should be put forward in consultation with the appointments commission but with the final say to the party leaders. Instead of the 15-year non-renewable terms proposed by Wakeham, the White paper considers shorter renewable terms of 5–10 years. The size of the House is to be capped at 600, but the present 750 will remain for the next 10 years or so.

The dilemma about Lords reform is a symptom of the dilemma that faces the constitution under modernization. Legitimacy is best conferred through elections, and this is a strong argument for having a wholly elected House of Lords. The concern is that such a House might behave along party political lines and mirror the behaviour and activities of the Commons. Successive governments have sought to inhibit the Lords by pointing to its position of weakness — its lack of a satisfactory electoral mandate. Yet, in order to secure a more inde-

[27] *The House of Lords — Completing the Reform* Cm 5291, November 2000.

pendent House of Lords, it is necessary to advance appointments through an independent and transparent system. Expertise thus appointed will allow the Lords to fulfil its role of scrutiny and advice separate from the pressure of party politics. This is an argument for preserving the appointed elements to the Lords. A compromise faces the difficulty of having an unsatisfactory outcome.[28] Members who are elected may appear to have a greater mandate than those members appointed because of their expertise. A two-tier Lords may gain neither authority nor self-confidence and certainly may never *represent* British society as a whole. Lords reform appears to have become more difficult than the government first realized.

## Conclusions: Reforming the Office of Lord Chancellor

As noted above a certain cultural reluctance and intransigence have characterised the traditional British approach to constitutional reform. The cultural resistance of the past appears to be in direct confrontation to the current modernization programme of the government. In the midst of the major constitutional reforms outlined above, the Supreme Court of the United Kingdom remains as a committee of the legislature of the House of Lords. The Appellate Committee as it has been technically known since 1947, works in a Committee room off one of the corridors of the Palace of Westminster. The Law Lords comprising 15 Judges of the House of Lords work within a Corridor of the House of Lords. It is easy to become confused as to the status and work of the Law Lords when their role appears identical to the casual observer as part of the legislative function of the House of Lords. However, this is deceptive. Despite the absence of any formal doctrine of the separation of powers there is in practice constitutional principles of judicial independence, the operation of the rule of law and the working practice that judges must distance themselves from the party politics of the day or the government. However, it would appear anomalous that the Lord Chancellor[29] may participate in judicial business and that serving Law Lords are able to vote and speak on legislation as it passes through the House of Lords. The question arises as to whether the long traditions and history of the office of Lord Chancellor are today compatible with the need for a modern Supreme Court and the Human Rights Act 1998? It is argued that despite reluctance to the contrary it is time for change and the separation of the judges from the physical facility of the House of Lords will raise the opportunity to create a modern Supreme Court.

---

28 *House of Lords Reform- the 2001 White Paper* House of Commons Research Papers 02/002 8th January 2002 http://www.parliament.uk.

29 Diana Woodhouse, *The Office of Lord Chancellor* Oxford: Hart Publishing, 2001.

In the *Pinochet* case,[30] the panel in the House of Lords consisted of Lord Hoffman, in a case involving the claim for sovereign immunity against extradition made by Senator Pinochet, a former Head of State. In reaching its decision, the House of Lords allowed a variety of human rights interest groups to give evidence, including Amnesty International. Lord Hoffman was chair of a Trust set up to administer funds in connection with Amnesty International. This link was sufficient to establish that Lord Hoffman fell within the category of having an interest in the case. As a result it was considered that Lord Hoffman should have been automatically disqualified from membership of the panel. The earlier decision of the House of Lords had to be set aside and a second hearing had to take place.[31]

The case is illustrative of the potential for judges to become automatically disqualified from hearing cases in which they may have an interest. The need for protecting the independence of the judicial power is paramount in the light of the Human Rights Act 1998 and the right to a fair trial. It is likely that article 6 of the European Convention on Human Rights will deprive the Lord Chancellor of any judicial role.

There remains the anachronism of the Lord Chancellor, a member of the Government of the day and senior minister sitting as a member of the Appellate Committee of the House. The signs are that in practice the Lord Chancellor is virtually unable to make a major contribution to his judicial functions in the Lords. Annually there are about 300 petitions to the House. A committee of three determine which petitions to hear. Annually, the Lords hear about 70 cases. Since May 1997, the Lord Chancellor has sat in only 8 cases. In the Judicial Committee of the Privy Council there are about 60 petitions heard annually. The Lord Chancellor has heard none.

It is highly unlikely that the Lord Chancellor, by virtue of his position can sit in any major case involving substantial rights or constitutional issues covering the range of issues dealing with devolution, public bodies, and public law. This makes any expansion of a judicial role for the Lord Chancellor virtually impossible.

Unhappily the role of the House of Lords and its judicial composition fell outside the terms of reference of the recent Royal Commission, discussed above. This oversight is deliberate and is an example of a missed opportunity to settle an important constitutional issue. It is symptomatic of the ad hoc approach to constitutional reform and the absence of a systematic analysis of the constitution. It is indicative of political considerations outweighing the constitutional ones.

---

30 R v Bow Street Metropolitan Stipendiary Magistrate ex parte Pinochet Ugarte (No. 2) [2000] AC 119.

31 See the first decision (No. 1) [2000] AC 61.

The Lord Chancellor is also a member of the cabinet. The anomaly of the judiciary having a voice in the cabinet is clear when in another context the independence of the judiciary is regarded as a paramount element in the rule of law. Policies settled by the cabinet impact on the administration of justice and the relationship between the Home Office and the Lord Chancellor's department is at sharp end of policy implementation and resolution. This role calls into question the current constitutional position and status of the Lord Chancellor. This is underlined when consideration is given to that role in the appointment of judges and in the management of the judiciary.

The conclusion is clear that the office of Lord Chancellor is an anachronism of the past that is incompatible with the constitutional arrangements that today seek to give pre-eminence to the separation of the judicial power from the legislature and the executive.

What is the way forward? There is an opportunity today to consider the creation of a modern Supreme Court that separates the judicial power from the other elements in which it is confused and embedded. At the present stage in the development of the Constitution this is an appropriate moment to take stock. A Supreme Court would provide an opportunity to break with the past. The Lord Chancellor might severe his judicial role from the court, thus creating in the Lord Chancellor's office a Department of Justice. The new Supreme Court might be separately located in a purpose built building. This would be symbolic of a new beginning, a recognition of a reality that much power is in judicial hands and as guardians of the judicial power the judges might seek to balance their stewardship against incursion from political power. The new Supreme Court might incorporate the benefits of including constitutional powers of review over devolution matters and human rights. This might provide an opportunity for the jurisprudence of the commonwealth to become more fully integrated into the ideas of the common law. In defining such a role Britain might find that a written constitution may best settle the reality of where power is distributed between the political, legal and economic. The historic culture of resistance against change may find that thinking about the future leads to a better understanding about the past and underlines the need for a different kind of constitutional future than the existing one allows. As Colls has acknowledged, Englishness is no longer the defining element in our constitutional arrangements. The state is too centralized, despite devolution and regionalism. Government is too secretive and unaccountable. Society and culture are too heterogeneous to conform to one idea of a Union state or a homogeneous nation. The Englishness of the constitution is no longer uniquely important or characteristic of the whole. Parliament is too weak and confused about its role to be effective. Party politics too strong and fragmented to be trusted. Law is too complex and technical to be understood in a universal way and lawyers are too expensive to be readily available to many. The European Union and globalisation provide a more multicultural and multilingual society than ever in our history. An ancient history and peoples need to understand their past in order to contemplate the manner of their future survival through change.

# Remarks Concerning the Normative Structure of a Modern World Order in a Historical Perspective*

*Prof. Dr. Heinhard Steiger, Universität Gießen*

## I. Introduction

Compared with the classic, traditional legal world order as it developed essentially in the 19$^{th}$ century, the contemporary normative structure of a world order has become more and more pluralistic, fragmentated, obscure and contingent. It seems to be imprinted essentially by a differentiation into two spheres of activities: the political sphere and the social sphere, whereas the classic world order was predominantely an order of the political sphere. Both spheres differentiate in themselves into several subspheres, the political sphere in the spheres of classic interstate relations, the cooperative supranational sphere of the intergovernmental organizations (IGOs) and the integrative supranational sphere, represented paradigmatically in Europe by the European Community (EC) as main pillar of the European Union (EU); the social sphere in the multiple spheres of economics, finance, sports, communication inclusive cyberspace, culture etc. These processes of differentiation are tottering and fundamentally transforming the traditional normative structures of the world order.

The different spheres of activities are all developing their own normative structures more or less autonomously and contingently. Some of them are strongly institutionalized, in the political sphere by the states and the IGOs, in the social sphere by national and international non governmental organizations (NGOs and INGOs). Others are more loosely organized. But they all may, in the notions of general systems theory, be regarded as systems or subsystems. The discussion on the consequences of the modern developments in the legal structure of the world order is vivid.[1] It is not my intention to discuss them all. My

* Revised and enlarged version of my presentation. The form of the presentation has been kept. I thank the participants for their comments during the discussion. I have tried to take up at least some of them.

1 The discussion started already several decades ago. Philip C. Jessup, Transnational Law, New Haven 1956; C. Wilfred Jenks, The Common Law of Mankind, New York 1958; Wolfgang Friedmann, The changing structure of International Law, New York 1964; for recent literature see: Richard Falk, Law in an emerging Global Village, A Post-Westphalian Perspective, New York 1998; Gunther Teubner (ed.), Global Law without a State, Aldershot etc. 1997; Klaus Dicke, Waldemar Hummer, Daniel Girsberger, Katharina Boel-Woelki, Christoph Engel, Jochen A. Frowein, Völkerrecht und Internationales Privatrecht in einem sich globalisierenden Internationalen System – Auswirkungen der Entstaatlichung transnationaler Rechtsbeziehungen, Heidelberg 2000; German Yearbook of International Law, vol. 44 (2001), with articles by Anne Peters, Martin Borowski, Stefan Oeter, Siegfried Wiesner/Andrew R. Willard, Berta E. Hernández-

question today is mainly whether we can still speak of a unity of a legal world order.

The differentiation of a world order into systems and subsystems is a contingent process, not steered by a general institution and not even following a general programme. The activities in both spheres often concern the same fields of problems and tasks. There is no clear-cut separation of functions. In the traditional classic world order the questions of war and peace, delimitation of spheres of sovereignty, the formal regulation of diplomatic relations were dominant, even though economic questions already played an important role in the $19^{th}$ century, the first phase of globalization. It was an order of coexistence with merely formal rules. Today all fields of tasks and problems of a modern national and global society such as: economics in all their dimensions, social welfare, protection of human rights, development, environment, scientific research, formation, health, communication, various necessities of aid and support in all its forms and outer space have become of equal importance for the functioning of the world order. They are deeply interrelated with the questions of war and peace and security. Therefore they are not only to be dealt with by the social sphere and its systems, but also by the political sphere, the states and the IGOs. The World Order becomes more and more an order of cooperation, even integration with material rules.

A first consequence of the differentiation process of the World Order is the emergence of new actors on the international scene in addition to the states. Whereas in the classic World Order they were the sole, in any case the dominant actors on the international scene; now new actors of very different structure are increasingly playing very influential and decisive roles: IGOs, NGOs, INGOs of a great variety, multinational companies (production, trade, finance, designers), and even individuals solely for themselves.

Another consequence is the transformation of the traditional, relatively strict separation of the legal orders of the „internal" sphere of the states and the „external" sphere of the international scene. The distinction as such is the consequence of the development of the modern sovereign state in Europe since the $16^{th}$ century, *Francisco di Vitoria* for the first time definded the term *ius gentium* as *ius inter omnes gentes.*[2] It was familiar to the classic authors of the Law of

---

Truyol, Christian Walter; American Journal of International Law, vol. 93 (1999), p. 291 sq. with articles by Steven R. Ratner and Anne-Marie Slaughter, Bruno Simma and Andreas L. Paulus, Siegfried Wiesner and Andrew R. Willard, Mary Ellen O'Connel, Martti Koskeniemi, Kenneth W. Abbott, Hilary Charklesworth, Jeffrey L. Dunoff and Joel P. Trachtman, Anne-Marie Slaughter and Steven R. Ratner.

2 Francisco de Vitoria, Relectio De Indis, 1538/39, New edition in: Francisco de Vitoria, Vorlesungen II, Latin/German, ed. by Ulrich Horst and others, Stuttgart 1997, p. 370 sq., sect. tertia, § 1, p. 460.

Nations as *Emer de Vattel.*[3] But it was *Jeremy Bentham* who created the conceptual distinction of the two „branches of jurisprudence" by the introduction of the terminology of „internal" and „international".[4] He wanted to replace the old notion „law of nations" which he found had „an appellation so uncharacteristic, that, were it not for the force of custom, it would seem rather to refer to internal jurisprudence".[5] But looking closer to his argumentation, we see that his distinction between „internal" and „international" jurisprudence is as ambiguous or equivocal.[6] On a first level he distinguishes the two branches of jurisprudence „with regard to the *political quality* of the persons whose conduct is the object of the law", which means law in its concrete sense. „*Internal*" jurisprudence is that branch concerning the conduct between the „members of the same state" and „*international*" jurisprudence is that branch regarding the conduct of „members of different states". But he than introduces a second criteria. He noticed that the transactions between individuals of different states are regulated by internal law and decided by internal courts or tribunals of the one or the other state, and similarly the transactions between a state and a private member of another state. He concludes that „there remain then the mutual transactions between sovereigns, as such, for the subject of that branch of jurisprudence which may be properly and exclusively termed *international*".[7] *Bentham* uses a wider and a narrower term of „international". The first applies, as he says, to the persons concerned, the second has regard, what he does not say expressively, to the law-creator. The consequences of this ambiguity of the term „international" are still felt today, as you know very well. The „international private law"[8], „international penal law", as distinguished from „international criminal law", „international administrative law" are international in the wider sense, and internal in the narrower sense, poses a major problem to explain to our students. On the other side only the narrower sense of „international" applies to the common, consensual, reciprocal law of the sovereign states between them, the former „law of nations", „droit des

---

3 Emer de Vattel, Le Droit des Gens ou Principes de la Loi Naturelle, London 1758, reprint (with English translation) 3 vol. Geneva 1983 (Classics of International Law), „Livre I De la Nation considérée en elle même" and „Livre II De la Nation considérée dans les rélations avec les autres".

4 Jeremy Bentham, An Introduction to The Principles of Morals and Legislation, 1789, Cap. XVII, § XXV.

5 Ibd., footnote 1.

6 It seems that he uses the term „jurisprudence" as equivalent for „ius", „Recht", „droit", „diritto", and „law" as equivalent for „Lex", „Gesetz", „loi", „lege", see § XXIII, footnote 2, because at the difference to the other languages the english language knows only one term „law" for „the abstract and the concrete senses of the law".

7 All emphases are original.

8 In English terminology it is replaced mostly by the term „conflicts of law", but in German, French and other languages „Internationales Privatrecht", „droit international privé" etc. are still used regularly.

gens", or „Völkerrecht", which term is still generally used in the german terminology. „International Law" is in this strict sense only interstate law.[9] To reduce the ambiguity, the term „International Public Law" is now commonly used for this branch of jurisprudence.[10] But nevertheless it may be true what *Richard Falk* wrote recently: „International law, in a real sense, has never been international law!"[11]

Since *Bentham* the distinction of „internal" and „international jurisprudence", or in the terminology of today of „internal" and „international law", is unquestioned for the 19th and the 20th century. No third category existed above or in between those two branches, spheres or „Rechtskreise". Only the relation between internal, national or domestic law and international law was discussed by the theories of monism and dualism or pluralism. Especially the latter made of the distinction a clear cut division in two separated spheres of law.[12] The decay or decline of the natural law theory on the one side deprived the conception of one law of its material foundations.[13] On the other, the rise of the principle of state sovereignty to its absolute, unconditioned, unbound, rigorous quality after 1800 excluded any direct influence from the international into the national law. Only the state had the power to decide what should become valid inside the state legal order.

---

9 Immanuel Kant spoke of „Staatenrecht (*ius publicum civitatum)*", Metaphysik der Sitten, Rechtslehre, II. Teil, Das öffentliche Recht, 2. Abschnitt, Das Völkerrecht, § 53.

10 As such the notion „International law" is generally used by English writing authors in the title of their treatises on the „law of nations" see Hans Kelsen, Oppenheim-Lauterpacht-ed. by Robert Jennings, Arthur Watts, Georg Schwarzenberger, Malcom N. Shaw, J. G. Starke, Akehurst ed. by Peter Malanczuk; exceptions are Max Brownlie, Max Sorensen, who use the term „Public International Law". French authors use generally „Droit International Public", Charles Rousseau, Paul Reuter etc. Despite the terminology used for the „Encyclopedia of International Public Law" (ed. by Rudolph Bernhardt) the article treating this law is named „International Law" by Robert Y. Jennings, vol. 2, Amsterdam 1995, p. 1159.

11 Falk, Law (Fn. 1), p. XXVI.

12 For the monistic theory see Hans Kelsen, Principles of International Law, New York 1959, p. 401 sq., esp. p. 424 sq.; for the dualist or pluralistic theory see Heinrich Triepel, Völkerrecht und Landesrecht, Leipzig 1899; Dionisio Anzilotti, Lehrbuch des Völkerrechts, Berlin 1929, p. 36 sq.

13 The natural law theory did not disappear completely in the 19th century, neither in general nor concerning the theory of the law of nations, with whom it was strongly interrelated, Heinhard Steiger, Völkerrecht und Naturrecht zwischen Christian Wolff und Adolf Lasson, in: Naturrecht im 19. Jahrhundert (ed. by Diethelm Klippel), Goldbach 1997, p. 45 sq. But the theory of natural law changed into legal philosophy, in the terminology of Jeremy Bentham it was transformed from *„expository"* jurisprudence to *„censorial"* jurisprudence, Introduction (Fn. 4), chap. XVII, § XXI.

The traditional world legal order with its basic distinction of the internal and the external legal orders is often called „Westphalian“[14], referring to the treaties of Münster and Osnabrück of Oct. 24th 1648.[15], This concept takes up the widespread idea, that the modern law of nations or international public law and its European order based on the sovereign state starts with these two treaties.[16] It is at least doubtful whether this is historically correct.[17] The two treaties were peace treaties between the kings of France and Sweden on the one side and the Emperor and the Reich on the other. All the other monarchs and states of Europe were not concerned directly, even if most of them were included in the peace, but not in the treaty.[18] Sovereignty in the full and strict sense of the word was not yet a necessary perquisite of state-subjects of the European order. Neither the Empereror nor the Reich and its members were really sovereign in the full sense of the term as developed by *Jean Bodin, Thomas Hobbes* and their adherents. The members of the Reich were called „mi-sovereign“.[19] But all were subjects of the European public law (droit public européen).[20] The legal structure of the European order in the 17th and 18th century was not only formed by the positive law of nations, customs and treaties, but also by natural law, feudal law, constitutional law of the Reich, laws of succession to the throne, and even in some respect still by canon law.[21] Christendom as a general non-confessional

---

14 For instance Falk, Law (Fn. 1), p. XXVI; Beyond Westphalia? State Sovereignty and International Intervention (ed. by Gene M. Lyons and Michael Mastanduno), Baltimore 1995.

15 Instrumentum Pacis Osnaburgensis (IPO); Instrumentum Pacis Monasteriensis (IPM), Acta Pacis Westphaliae ed. by Max Braubach, Konrad Repgen and others, Sec. 3, Abt. B, Teil 1 Urkunden, Münster 1998.

16 See for instance the classic study in history of the law of nations by Henry Wheaton, Histoire des Progrès du Droit des Gens en Europe et en Amérique depuis la Paix de Westphalie jusqu'à nos jours, Leipzig 1853.

17 See Heinhard Steiger, Der Westfälische Frieden – Grundgesetz für Europa?, in: Der Westfälische Friede (ed. by Heinz Duchhardt), München 1998, p. 32 sq.; critical also Karl Heinz Ziegler, Die Bedeutung des Westfälischen Friedens von 1648 für das europäische Völkerrecht, Archiv des Völkerrechts (AdV), 37 (1999), p. 129 sq., p. 131 and 149.

18 Art. XVII §§ 10, 11 IPO; § 119 IPM.

19 For instance Georg Friedrich Martens, Einleitung in das positive Europäische Völkerrecht auf Verträge und Herkommen gegründet, Göttingen 1796, § 17, and Précis du Droit des Gens moderne de l'Europe, Göttingen 1783 l. I., ch. II, § 20. In the edition of 1831 the term was kept, but it was made clear that after the fall of the Old Reich in 1806 no important mi-sovereign states did anymore exist.

20 Heinhard Steiger, Die Träger des *ius belli ac pacis* 1648 –1806, in: Werner Rösener (ed.), Staat und Krieg – Vom Mittelalter bis zur Moderne, Göttingen 2000, p. 115 sq.

21 Heinhard Steiger, Rechtliche Strukturen der Europäischen Staatenordnung 1648 – 1792, Zeitschrift für ausländisches öffentliches Recht und Völkerrecht/Heidelberg Journal of International Law (ZaöRV/HJIL), vol. 59 (1999), p. 609 sq.

concept still formed an essential material basis of the whole order.[22] All this disappeared only during the French revolution and the Napoleonic era, definitely so with the final act of the long lasting and painful breakdown of the Reich in 1806. It was the Act of the Congress of Vienna of 9th June 1815 which established a new order on the sole and exclusive basis of sovereign states of the civilized nations.[23] Therefore it would be more precise to speak of a Vienna or Austrian order.

Today we have to acknowledge that on the one side the walls between the two spheres are shaken, for instance by the growing international promotion of human rights or of obligations concerning the environment within the states. On the other hand a transnational sphere is emerging, for instance in the fields of economics, communication or sports, development and again global environment. Thus, a multitude of public, private and mixed networks of activities cover the whole globe which expressively and purposely do not respect national boundaries but are constituted as transnational networks. We generally call this development „globalization“ without knowing exactly what this is. Thus, the traditional strict distinction and separation of the two spheres does not disappear, but it is shaken in reality and must therefore be re-examined in theory and doctrine of the legal structures of World Order. Other supranational and transnational law systems have already emerged and are developing. The question is, whether and how they are interrelated.

At first, I shall briefly sketch the changes within the political sphere (II) and some essential aspects of the social sphere (III). I then shall discuss the normative character of the norms applied in the different systems (IV). Afterwards I shall deal with the question of the unity of World Order (V). I shall conclude by turning to a newly raised proposition of a World State or World Republic (VI).

## II. The political sphere and international public law

In a historical perspective the international public law changes not only its structure but also its essential basis: The sovereignty of the states is coming to an end, paradigmatically for the member-states of the European Community. This is not a question of might, power, capacity, but a structural development of the status of states in the World Order. I have described this process elsewhere and will not repeat myself.[24] As one consequence international public law is un-

---

22 Wilhelm G. Grewe, Epochs of International Law, Berlin 2000, p. 287 sq.; Heinhard Steiger, Die Friedenskonzeption der Verträge von Münster und Osnabrück vom 24. Oktober 1648, in: Rechtstheorie, vol. 29 (1998), p. 189 sq., 196 sq.

23 See the text (French, German, English) in Fontes historicae Iuris Gentium, vol. 3/1 1815 – 1945 (ed. by Wilhelm G. Grewe), Berlin 1992, p. 3 sq.

24 Heinhard Steiger, Geht das Zeitalter des souveränen Staates zu Ende?, in: Der Staat 41 (2002), p. 331 sq., with some further literature; see also Peter Malanczuk, Globalisierung

dergoing a process of „institutionalisation“ or even „constitutionalisation“[25] and thereby, as seems to me, of „hierarchisation“ within itself and in its relation to internal law.This process has a material and an institutional dimension.

On a material basis typical elements of state constitution are becoming fundamental elements of the international public law, as human rights, solidarity of the peoples, and especially the development of ius cogens, which is no more at the disposal of the single states, objective obligations erga omnes, which are directly binding on all states in their law creating activities and in their political behaviour. Without entering into the theoretical and doctrinal problems of a ius cogens without a law giver placed above all states or a conception of a preexisting general law, as the natural law doctrine, it may be said that today ius cogens as such is generally recognized by the states.[26] Its content is disputed. But the prohibition of the use of force in interstate relations is at its core. Human rights or at least the most basic rights also form part of it. Art. 103 UN-Charter gives the obligations of the Charter priority in case of a conflict with obligations arising from other treaties. In many declarations, treaties etc. this priority is expressively repeated.[27]

The institutional dimension is still not very clearly developed. Several methods of law creation exist side by side. The traditional procedure to create international public law solely by the states themselves in a consensual procedure, that is to say by multilateral treaties, is still the main procedure of the creation of international public law. Firstly however, it is directed more and more by the UN and other IGOs, which means it becomes centralized. Secondly it is no longer the only method.

Art. 13 § 1 UN-Charter charges the General Assembly with the duty to „initiate studies and make recommendations for the purpose of a)...... encouraging the progressive development of international law and its codification“. The Gen-

---

und die zukünftige Rolle souveräner Staaten, in: Matthias Lutz-Bachmann/James Bohman (ed.), Weltstaat oder Staatenwelt?, Frankfurt/Main 2002, p. 125 sq.

25 Already in 1926 Alfred Verdroß wrote about Die Verfassung der Völkerrechtsgemeinschaft, Wien/Berlin 1926; see e.g. Jochen A. Frowein, Konstitutionalisierung des Völkerrechts, in: Klaus Dicke, Völkerrecht (Fn. 1), p. 427 sq.; Rainer Wahl, Konstitutionalisierung - Leitbegriff oder Allerweltsbegriff?, in: Festschrift für Winfried Brohm, München 2002, p. 191 sq., esp. 199 sq.

26 Lauri Hannikainen, Peremptory Norms (Jus Cogens) in International Law. Historical Development, Criteria, Present Status, Helsinki 1988; Jochen A. Frowein, Jus Cogens, in: EPIL (Fn. 10), vol. 3, Amsterdam 1997, p. 65 sq. with further literature; Stefan Kadelbach, Zwingendes Völkerrecht, Berlin 1992.

27 E.g. Final Act of the Conference on Security and Cooperation in Europe (CSCE) of Helsinki, 1 August 1975, 13 I.L.M. 1292 (1975), and Charter of Paris, 11 November 1990, 30 I.L.M. 190 (1991).

eral Assembly has developed different strategies to perform this duty.[28] It created the International Law Commission (ILC) to prepare projects of codification and development of the international public law in nearly all fields, in classic fields as well as in new ones. The members of the ILC are chosen not as representatives of the member-states but in their personal capacity of outstanding experts in international public law. Their proposals are discussed by the states, in the Sixth Committee of the GA, which consists of state representatives. But projects of conventions may also be prepared by other bodies of the UN as UNCITRAL.[29] Finally these projects are adopted by the General Assembly by two thirds majority vote or informal consensus. Another strategy consists in the calling of an interstate conference by the GA to prepare an international convention on or without the basis of prepared proposals by the ILC or other bodies. Again the Conference and eventually the GA itself adopts the final text by majority vote, but also eventually by informal consensus. In both cases the convention does not enter into force by the vote of the conference or the GA. It must still be signed and ratified by the states to enter into force. Viewed only from these final acts nothing seems to have changed in the decisive importance of the sovereign will of the states. But on looking closer we shall discover important changes. The initial proposals of the ILC are not politically but legally founded. The final text does not need the positive vote by all states. The influence of the individual state is very restricted. Only with allies a state may have the chance to get its point of view accepted by the majority. This is true even for the big states. The acceptance of the convention and its ratification is often devoid of choice for a single state, if it does not want to become isolated. Other IGOs have even stricter procedures, as the ILO with its reporting system concerning the labor conventions adopted by its general assembly[30] or the WHO with its opting out procedure.[31]

But not only the IGOs as state-representing actors play an initiating and concentrating role in the treaty law making process of international public law for themselves. By their very functions they have opened the possibility to various kinds of private actors, INGOs, multinational enterprises of all kinds, (production enterprises banks, stock exchanges, other financial institutions, trade com-

28 See Oscar Schachter, Christopher C. Joyner (ed.), United Nations Legal Order, vol. 1, Cambridge 1995, Part One: The UN System as a Source of Law, §§ 1 and 2, p. 33 sq.; Carl-August Fleischhauer Art. 13 note 12 sq., in: Bruno Simma (ed.), Charter of the United Nations, Commentary, 2nd ed. Oxford 2002. For the work of the ILC see the Yearbooks of the ILC. Important aspects of the law creating role of the UN and other IGOs have been treated in the Max Planck Yearbook of United Nations Law, vol. 2, 1998, ed. by Jochen A. Frowein and Rüdiger Wolfrum, London etc. 1998.

29 For its work see The Yearbook of UNCITRAL.

30 Art. 19 of the Constitution of the International Labor Organization, 9 October 1946.

31 Art. 20 Constitution of the World Health Organization, 22 July 1946 as amended 12 May 1986.

panies) etc. take a very active part in the development of international public law and the law creating process. Especially the second method of creating international law by international conferences opens a large gateway for the participation of NGOs and INGOs and also transnationally active enterprises to influence the law creating process formally or informally. NGOs and INGOs are registered as observers. They deliver their opinions; they are heard and often consulted.[32] They prepare their own proposals and introduce them into the procedure.[33] Even if they do not take part in the formal act of voting the final text, their material influence is often very important. Some may appreciate this participation of INGOs as a global or transnational democratic element entering into the law-creating process of international public law.[34] But this can be admitted only under various reservations. The democratic legitimation and structure of many INGOs is doubtful. Often they are bound to more or less special group-interests. But even if they represent common interests, as Amnesty International or Greenpeace, their democratic legitimacy is not always clear. Nevertheless representatives of the civil society and not only state officials are now shaping the creation of the new international public law to a greater extent, mainly in new fields such as protection of human rights, sustainable development, protection of the natural environment, the development of international criminal law, the banning of anti-personal mines etc. and others.[35]

All IGOs have the power/competence to set binding norms for their own internal order. But what is more important, some IGOs are directly creating binding law for their member-states. Besides the traditional consensual interstate public law, authoritative regulations and decisions of IGOs appear, creating elements of a new supranational legal order. This order does not replace interna-

---

32 An intensive and very detailed study of the overall role of the INGOs has recently been presented by Waldemar Hummer, Internationale nichtstaatliche Organisationen im Zeitalter der Globalisierung, in: Dicke, Völkerrecht (Fn. 1), p. 45 sq. with English summary p. 264 sq.; especially for their role in international law-making see: Anne-Marie Slaughter, International Law and International Relations, Académie de Droit International, Recueil des Cours 2000, vol. 285, p. 9 sq., 96 sq. with further literature.

33 For instance the Convention on Biodiversity, adopted at the Conference of Rio de Janeiro, was largely prepared by the International Union of the Conservation of Nature (IUCN) and its legal service and experts. An important role for the development of the humanitarian law is played by the International Comittee of the Red Cross (ICRC), which is, despite its name, corporated under national Suisse law. The first drafts of the Geneva Conventions of 1949 and of the Protocolls of 1975 were prepared by its services.

34 Concerning the question of the democratisation of the World Order see James Bohman, Internationale Regime und demokratische Governance: Gleicher Einfluß auf globale Institutionen, in: Lutz-Bachmann, Weltstaat (Fn. 24), p. 75 sq.; Boutros Boutros-Ghali, Pour un droit international de la démocratie, in: Theory of International Law at the Threshold of the 21st Century, Essays in honour of Krzysztof Skubiszewski, ed. by Jerzy Makarczyk, The Hague 1996, p. 99 sq.

35 See also Falk, Law (Fn. 1), p. 57, 81.

tional public law in all respects, all fields and not in a universal sense. But in the European Community, which is at the top of this development, such essential fields as internal and external trade and customs, competition, agriculture, currency, and soon immigration and questions of internal security and others are regulated by authoritative quasi laws of the Community organs and no more by the member-states. On the global level the Security Council has tried at least twice to substitute regulations by convention by its obligatory regulatory decisions under Chapter VII of the Charter, the establishment of the Criminal Tribunals for former Yugoslavia and Ruanda before the entry of the Statute of the International Criminal Tribunal[36] came into force and the creation of the obligation of the member states to freeze and eventually confiscate the financial sources of terrorist groups.[37] Other IGOs have similar partial competences to take binding decisions.[38]

More and more institutionalized procedures of third party decisions of conflicts between states are established, from the International Court of Justice (ICJ) to the panels of the World Trade Organization (WTO). Even if the jurisdiction of the ICJ is not yet obligatory, other institutions such as the panels of the WTO[39] and the European Court of Human Rights [40] have already obligatory jurisdiction over states. As is the case with all courts and tribunals, all these institutions decide individual cases only, but their decisions form a whole body of formal or informal precedents and thus create general norms. Montesquieu was wrong, judges are not „en quelque façon nul".

Besides the traditional and new international and the new supranational sources of formal, strict, „hard" law, new international norms are appearing to regulate the behaviour of the states: different forms of formally not legally binding recommendations, declarations, charters adopted by the states on international conferences or by the IGOs by their organs. These norms are summarized today under the notion of „soft-law". This is without doubt a very imprecise and ambigious notion. But it expresses the conviction that these norms have after all

36 For Yugoslavia: Res. SC 827 (1993), 25 May 1993, amended several times, see http://www.un.org//icty/legaLDOC/index.htm; for Rwanda Res. 955 (1994) amended several times, see http://www.ictr.org.

37 The GA had adopted a Convention in December 1999, but it has not yet entered into force, GA-MS 54/109, 12 December 1999, A/RES./54/109; the SC adopted several resolutions, the last after the terrorist acts of september 11th 2001, S/RES/1373 (2001).

38 E.g. Art. 6 OECD.

39 See Dispute Settlement Understanding (DSU) with its different Annexes, 15 April 1994, as a core part of the whole WTO treaty-complex. More than 275 cases have been brought, see http://www.wto.org. Again the literature is abundant. See for general information David Palmezer/Petros C. Mavroidis, Dispute settlement in the World Trade Organization: Practice and Procedure, The Hague etc. 1999.

40 For the European Court of Human Rights Art. 32 – 34 European Convention on Human Rights of 4-11-1950 as amended by the 11th Protocol 11 May 1994.

a certain binding force. I ask myself whether we should not regard as an important category of law-creating activities of the IGOs the contracts and agreements of IGOs not only with states but also with NGOs, multinational enterprises and even private actors to realize and assure international projects of various kinds, especially in the fields of development, environment, human rights, formation, aid etc. As contracts or agreements they may have first a more subjective character. But it seems to me that the steady practice, repetition and perhaps standardisation may leed to a set of objective norms. A whole body of law of international administration is thus developing.[41] Again the role of the INGOs in this field of norm creating activities is great and important. The norm-creating character of the scientific discourse-practices, especially developed by private institutions as the International Law Association and the Institut du Droit International has already been recognized by Art. 38 § 1 d) of the Statute of the ICJ.

Whereas the institutionalization concerns essentially the creation and assurance of the performance of the international public legal order, the hierarchisation touches the relaton of international law and internal law. More and more, norms from the international or supranational sphere are steering more or less directly or at least strongly influencing the internal or domestic sphere. This has been called „internationalization of domestic law“.[42] The new supranational legal norms of the EU and other IGOs have already been mentioned. Art. 6, 7 and 49 TEU make the democratic principle and the fundamental rights obligatory for the member-states and for the aspirants.[43] They are directly binding and applicable within the states. But often more indirect strategies by universal or quasi universal legal and other norms are used. The Declaration on Human Rights of 1948 and the mass of general and specific Conventions of Human Rights concluded on the universal and on regional levels oblige the states to respect human rights within their territories vis a vis all persons under their rule.[44] The interna-

41 It would be necessary to analyse the activities of the different IGOs to get a comprehensive insight; two examples may be cited: the financing activities of the World Bank together with the International Finance Corporation, The International Development Association and the Multilateral Investment Guarantee Agency, which give credits and other financing not only to states, but also to subdivisions of states and even private investors or project developers; the WHO which has established formal relations with INGOs and NGOs as well as with collaboration centres in the member states to perform essential parts of its functions under Art. 2 of its Constitution inside the states, see http://www.who.org. Research concerning this new field of international law seems at least to be rare. Rüdiger Wolfrum, International Administrative Unions, EPIL vol. II p. 1041, gives only a short overview.

42 See Brun-Otto Bryde in this volume.

43 Heinhard Steiger, Der Vertrag von Amsterdam: Auf dem Weg zu einer Europäischen Republik?, in: Günter Weick (ed.), Competition and Convergence – The Future of European Legal Culture, Frankfurt a. M. 1999, p. 31 sq.

44 What this can mean for the interior legal order has been shown recently by Anja Seibert-Fohr, Domestic Implementation of the International Covenant on Civil and Political

tional community is watching over the compliance by the states by different means, from commissions to international courts and in extreme cases the Security Council or the GA of the UN will intervene with measures of their choice.[45] Human rights are no more „matters essentially in the domestic jurisdiction" in the sense of Art. 2 para. 7 UN-Charter. The recognition of new emerging states in Europe by the EU and its member states was bound to the acceptance and introduction of the basic principles of democracy and fundamental rights.[46]

But equally important are the intruding processes in internal commercial and financial matters. States who are by their internal and international financial needs and situations forced to ask for financial assistance from the International Monetary Fund (IMF) or the World Bank are generally obliged to accept the conditions concerning their internal economic and financial behaviour which the two IGOs connect with their financial assistance. Often these conditions are very severe, especially for the social policy of the state concerned.[47]

All these are well known developments, which have been often described, analyzed and evaluated. I have not discovered anything new. But in a historical perspective these well known developments of international public law are very recent and very new. They began very slowly and hesitantly after the Second World War and developed more intensively only in the last quarter of the 20[th] century when the Cold War began to come to its end with the adoption of the Helsinki Charter in 1975. These developments are very complex, in many respect contingent, fragmented, not following a single plan but appear as a sum of quite different lines of conduct of the different actors.[48] But it is necessary to take these developments together, see them as a whole, and not each development alone for itself. On the whole, it seems that a common direction may be ascertained. I will come back to that question later.

---

Rights pursuant to its article 2 para. 2, in: Max Planck Yearbook of United Nations Law, vol. 5 (2001), ed. by Jochen A. Frowein/Rüdiger Wolfrum, The Hague 2001, p. 399 sq. and Neue internationale Anforderungen an die Überführung von Menschenrechtsabkommen in nationales Recht – Das Verhältnis des Internationalen Pakts über bürgerliche und polische Rechte zu nationalem Recht, ZaöRV/HJIL 62 (2002), p. 391 sq., where she critises with good reasons the German practice, p. 413 sq.

45 See S/RES/418 (1978), 4 November 1977, concerning the apartheid system in South-Africa.

46 Declaration on the „Guidelines on the Recognition of New States in Eastern Europe and the Soviet Union", 16 December 1991, 31 I.L.M. 1486 (1992); Richtlinien für die Anerkennung neuer Staaten in Osteuropa und in der Sowjetunion, Europaarchiv 1992 D. 120 sq.

47 The practices of the IMF vis à vis the states seeking its assistance are very much disputed, see Joseph E. Stiglitz, Globalization and its Discontents, W.W. Norton 2002.

48 „The risks of fragmentation of International Law" have already become a topic of the ILC, which established a special Study Group in 2002 after a feasibility study, see G. Hafner, „Risks Ensuing from Fragmentation of International Law", Official Records of the General Assembly, Fifty-fifth session, Supplement No. 10 (A/55/10), annex; ILC Report of its fifty-fourth session, 2002 , Chap. IX, §§ 489 sq., p. 237 sq.

## III. The social sphere and global non-state law

Civil society is traditionally a national civil society, which is more or less identical with one state, the modern sovereign nation-state. This became the leading concept of political-legal organization during the 19th and 20th centuries after its birth during the French Revolution. Its realisation often meant and means freedom and self-determination of peoples of multinational states, but it meant and means not seldom also, repression, ethnic cleansing and even genocide of minorities, civil war and even international war right up to our own present time. Still today the national civil society is the primary basis and frame of social life in all its dimensions, economy, culture, welfare, security, legal protection etc.[49] But on the one side national civil societies are no more closed societies but open to and for other national civil societies and their culture, religion, immigration from them etc. On the other side a transnational civil society on regional and global levels, a world civil (Weltbürgergesellschaft) society is emerging. From a legal perspective both developments were made possible by the fundamental rights of freedom of human activities of very different kinds: freedom of communication, freedom of religion, freedom of economic activities, freedom of migration, free flow of capital etc. guaranteed in the national constitutions of modern liberal-democratic states, and also by the international established body of human rights mentioned above. Only those nation-states which recognize at least the economic freedoms participate in this development of an emerging world civil society. Former Albania of Enver Hodja, the european socialist bloc before the „Wende“ and China before its economic reforms and opening did not and could not participate in this movement. This was perhaps one reason for the breakdown of the socialist system in Europe.[50] From an empirical perspective the developments of the second industrial revolution after World War II and of the new technologies initiated are described today by the very unclear, sweeping and multifunctional notion of „globalization“.

„Globalization“ in a very general sense means, as used here, developments or processes versus the constitution of a world civil society in all fields of social intercourses: economy, finances, culture, architecture, religion[51], communication, sports, cyberspace, civil protest, assistance movements etc. It would be wrong to confine the term and the concept of globalization only to economic and financial movements or structures. It seems that the idea of „mankind“, already developed by *Francisco di Vitoria* in the 16th century after the discoveries of the

---

49 Steiger, Zeitalter (Fn. 24), p. 347 sq.

50 North-Corea and Cuba, but also most of the African states are still outside the general development, also because they do not realize these freedoms.

51 Christendom and Islam are perhaps the oldest globalizing movements in this sense and both have constituted transnational religious societies. The appearance of Buddhism and Hinduism in Europe and America with own organizations and temples constitutes a new phenomenon, but it is in the same line.

pagan non european peoples in America, Africa and Asia [52] and the basis of the natural law theory of the law of nations in the following centuries becomes more and more reality as a leading concept of civil society activities and transactions.

This emerging world civil society and its actors are creating rules in all these fields of activities, what we may call a global or regional non-state or a-national normativity.[53] It is not completly independent from nation-state or interstate created law, but is largely autonomous in its institutional creation, its material content as well as in its procedural assurance of compliance. Rule creating actors differ for the different fields but their general characteristic is their international or better transnational foundation and status largely independent from national or interstate law. This does not exclude that interstate or state actors are participating in the rule creating and especially in the rule enforcing processes by international conventions and by national court decisions. But they are not the primary rule makers.

The most important and most discussed branch of autonomous global non-state normativity is the modern lex mercatoria.[54] It is the autonomous normativity for the world commercial system, the transactions of transnational commerce, trade and services. The concept of lex mercatoria comprises in a narrow sense only non-state rules. In a wider sense also state and interstate rules are included.[55] For the purpose of this paper I intend to follow the narrower understanding because the wider notion conceals the key problem of the relationship between non-state and interstate/state commercial rules as different but nevertheless interrelated parts of the general system of international commercial or economic law. Lex mercatoria is created by the actors of the commercial system, multinational enterprises, financing institutions, media, etc. and their common institutions, such as UNIDROIT, the International Chamber of Commerce (ICC) in Paris, the International Law Association (ILA), the Institut de Droit International etc, and the different courts of arbitration. If lex mercatoria is used in the wider sense also IGOs as the UN by UNCITRAL, the UN Economic Commission of Europe (ECE), the EC, and others as well as the states are involved in or associated to its creation.

It is still very much disputed whether lex mercatoria is an autonomous non-state legal order. But the empirical analysis and the theoretical evaluation by its protagonists seem to be very strong and convincing.[56] The creation and devel-

---

52 De Indis (Fn. 2).

53 See Teubner, Global Law (Fn. 1) p. XIII sq.

54 The term has been chosen by association with the lex mercatoria of the late middle ages and the early modern times, Ursula Stein, Lex mercatoria – Realität und Theorie, Frankfurt/Main 1995, p. 4.

55 See Stein, ibid., p. 184 sq.

56 I refer myself mainly to Ursula Steins research (Fn. 54), who, in the first part, has undertaken a very thorough analysis of the reality of the normative elements constituting lex mercatoria, p. 13 sq., and, in the second part, has developed by an intensive discussion of

opment of Lex mercatoria is based upon two grounds, the establishment of material rules, and the organising of private arbitration to assure its application and compliance in cases of conflict.[57] Both have the function to exclude state or interstate interference as far as possible, in general rule making as well as in its application and assurance of compliance. The material rules are created in complex procedures. These are very elaborate and detailed contracts, which may be used as models, especially by the same actors, by standardized contracts often developed and proposed to the actors by the institutions mentioned above, by multinational companies, international affiliated groups etc for their internal worldwide transactions between their different entities.[58] Furthermore, by rules of international federations of commercial actors and other associations for their members, but also by the development of commercial practices and customs in the daily behaviour of the merchants their companies etc. Reading the literature I got the impression that the rule-making processes are not unified or coherent, but contingent, diversified, fragmented and in some respect even chaotic. There is no single law maker, not even a coordinator, even if some institutions such as UNIDROIT, ICC; UNCITRAL are trying to steer the development of this law. But they seem to be only partially successful in creating general and unified rules for all kinds of transactions. This may be one of the reasons why states and IGOs try to set general frames and regulations by interstate conventions.[59] However, nevertheless the elements of the Lex mercatoria and of the regulations in other fields are of course thoroughly prepared and refined by highly skilled lawyers and perhaps even by professors and most of them are in written form.

The international private arbitration forms the necessary and cohesive keystone of the whole system of lex mercatoria. The arbitrators are moreover people with an intensive formation in law and other fields. The system of international arbitration assures the application of and the compliance with the lex mercatoria again by an autonomous, and a-national jurisdictional procedure in concrete conflicts and develops further by its awards the material content of the lex mer-

---

the arguments of the critics of lex mercatoria a well founded theoretical framework, p. 203 sq. But the strictest concept has already been developed by Berthold Goldman in several writings since the 60th of the 20th century. See also Teubner, Global Bukowina' in Global Law (Fn. 1); Hans-Joachim Mertens, *Lex Mercatoria*: A Self-applying System Beyond National Law?, in: Teubner, Global Law (Fn. 1), p. 31 sq.

57 The modern Lex mercatoria is not a new or recent phenomenon. It has its roots in the first phase of „globalization" of the market in the 19th century. But the second phase in the second half of the 20th century had new demands for the development of an autonomous normativity and gave an enormous push to it.

58 See Peter T. Muchlinski, Global Bukowina' Examined: Viewing the Multinational Enterprise as a Transnational Law-Making Community, in: Teubner, Global Law (Fn. 1), p. 79 sq.

59 One of the last examples is the Model Law on Electronic Signatures, developed by UNCITRAL and adopted by the GA of the UN on Dec. 12, 2001, 41 I.L.M. 303 (2002).

catoria. It is partly based on state or interstate law, but largely instituted by autonomous organisational acts and rules.[60] But in both cases the arbitration itself is private arbitration and applies largely to autonomous material and procedural rules. Most important is the general function of arbitration for the development of the material content of lex mercatoria. Despite the still existing pluralism of arbitral courts or tribunals and the lacking of an overall well organized, coherent, perhaps hierarchal system of arbitral courts or tribunals, arbitration forms a jurisdictional system in which the institutional stabilty of certain arbitral courts and tribunals, the continuity of the jurisprudence, the growing procedural harmonization, the increasing publication of arbitral awards which allows for exchange and reciprocal influence between the arbitrators. It also assures an improving general coherence and common development of the lex mercatoria and its elements.[61]

Closely related to the general economic system or even part of it but presumably forming a subsystem of its own is the financial global network. National, transnational and multinational banks, stock exchanges and other institutions form its actors. State and interstate global and regional institutions are also participating. Nevertheless it seems that many rulings concerning the financial subsystem in its transnational as well as in its internal sphere are non-state rules and norms. As an example I cite the „ICC Uniform Customs and Practice for Documentary Credits UCP 500“. This is clearly an autonomous regulation since the ICC is a private institution.[62] Viewing the matter from the outside it seems that the rules and norms in the field are very complex and difficult to analyse. Without entering into the literature, I may, as in other fields, only give some hints, since I am not an expert. Of course the states, in Europe the EC, are not excluded from this field, to the contrary. But autonomous regulations and state or interstate regulations are combined.

In the economic and social field international labour regulations are playing a growing role, following the internationalization of labour relations as consequence of the internationalization of production and services.[63] On the one side multinational enterprises try to introduce their own private internal regulation for the labour relations in the different parts of their world-wide activities, on the other side in some parts of the world, especially in third world countries transnational NGOs and not local or national trade-unions are their counterparts.

---

60 Peter Schlosser, Das Recht der internationalen privaten Schiedsgerichtsbarkeit, 2nd ed., Tübingen 1989.

61 Stein, Lex mercatoria (Fn. 54), p. 96 sq.

62 Jens Nielsen in: Bankrechts-Handbuch, ed. by Herbert Schimansky and others, vol. III, München 2002, § 120 p. 4090 sq.

63 Brian Bercusson, Globalizing Labour Law: Transnational Private Regulation and Countervailing Actors in European Labour Law, in: Teubner, Global Law (Fn. 1), p. 133 sq.

Looking at other fields of transnational relations and activities constituting a globalizing civil society the global religious entities must also be taken into consideration. We discover the classic and oldest transnational society, the Roman Catholic Church, and its not only autonomous, but even independent non-state law, the canon law. It was developed since the late roman antiquity and today regulates the organization of the church and the status, rights and obligations of over a billion church members in nearly all states of the world, with a transnational head, the Pope in Rome.[64] But also other transnational religious corporations, federations and entities have created legal rules for their world-wide organization and membership.[65] And for all muslims in the world the Koran is likewise a legal basis, also for their transnational or international behaviour.

Between other globalizing fields of social intercourse sports is not only of a growing economic relevance and cultural influence but has developed an effective world-wide network of organisational structures in creating global and regional federations such as the International Olympic Comittee, FIFA, UEFA, to conduct the very different global and regional activities such as the olympic games, the regional as well as the world championships in nearly all disciplines, etc. Again we find a well developed autonomous system of organisational and material rules and procedural provisions and institutions of the national and international federations, courts, tribunals, commissions, arbitration institutions, to deal with disputes and conflicts between athletes and their organisations, for instance in doping cases, disputes between the organisations etc., etc.[66] The notion of *lex sportiva internationalis* has been proposed.[67] But again state or interstate norms are supplementing the autonomous rules and norms and perhaps enforcing certain rules, for example doping has been penalized in France.

A fundamental structural change of transnational communication has been initiated by the development of Internet and the creation of cyberspace. It is per-

---

64 The current codification, the Codex Juris Canonici (CIC) has been promulgated by Pope John Paul II in 1983. It is not a „new“ law, but in the understanding of the Church only a renovation and modernisation of the Codex 1917 after the Council of 1962 – 1965 and it is based on the unshakable foundations of the Old and New Testaments, see the Introduction to the Promulgation by Pope John Paul II.

65 See e.g. the Constitution and the Rules of the World Council of Churches, http://www.wcc-coe.org.

66 James A. R. Nafziger, International Sports Law as a Process for Resolving Disputes, in: International and Comparative Law Quarterly, vol. 45 (1996), p. 130 sq.; a comprehensive study of international or better transnational sport regulations of the different international federations etc. seems not to exist, at least not in German, not even a list of these regulations. Some may be found on http://www.sportgericht.de, other on the homepages of the federations themselves. Under „sportgericht.de“ and in the Review „Sport und Recht“ decisions of sport tribunals and state courts as well as arbitral awards are published.

67 Reference see Teubner, Global Bukowina, Global Law (Fn.1 ), p. 4.

haps the most advanced transnational technical structure of world civil society, the technical incarnation of transnationality since its technical structure inherently completely disregards state boundaries. What is meant here is not e-commerce or e-banking etc itself, but the regulation of the access to the Internet and its use for communication and for other activities, in different instances, forms and dimensions, e.g. the web side address and the using of it for transmitting informations, texts etc., the e-mail adress, the surfing in the net etc. etc. The regulation of cyberspace is largely and predominantly private non-state regulation. The crucial question who with what address will be admitted, is decided by a private-sector corporation under californian law, the Internet Corporation for Assigned Names and Numbers (ICANN).[68] The individual access and use is based on private law contracts. Individual states have extreme difficulties to exert any control over the use inside their own territory, especially concerning criminal activities, data-protection, consumer protection etc. But also the regulation by and applicability of the national state law in commercial, financial and other activities is uncertain and difficult[69]. This is especially the case for transboundary legal as well as illegal activities. Here elements of lex mercatoria may play an essential role, e. g. the ICC Guidelines on Advertising and Marketing on the Internet.[70]

In conclusion we may state that in many important fields of world wide activities and transaction in the social sphere of civil-society transnational networks have developed and are developing at an accelerating pace. They create their own autonomous regulatory structures. They are not completely independent from state or interstate law, but they try to become as selfdependent as possible. In some fields the influence of state and interstate law is stronger in others weaker. Indeed, in the last ressort the enforcement of the the self-regulatory and self-applying non-state rules depends on the states, which still are the sole holders of legal enforcement power. Therefore the recognition and acceptance of these rules by the states is neccessary. But the question is, whether the states may refuse this recognition ad libitum or whether, at least in their own interests, they have principally to accept it and may refuse enforcement only in special cases of contravention against the public order. It may be easier in some fields and safer to have universal interstate conventions as a basis of the transactions.

---

68 See ist own home page http://www.icann.org.

69 Legal research, at least in Germany, seems to concentrate on the questions of the legal frames set by state law for the regulation of contracts etc. for the use of internet, and to neglect the analysis of its internal normative structures, e.g. Thomas Hoeren, Grundzüge des Internetrechts, 2nd ed., München 2001; Frank A. Koch, Internet Recht, München 1998; Armin Schwerdtfeger and others, Cyberlaw – Grundlagen. In my opinion, this state law oriented approach to the legal problems of internet is too one-sided and too narrow.

70 http://www.iccwbo.org/home/statements_rule/rules/1998/internet_guidelines.asp.

But again the question is how far they are ius cogens for the parties and how far they are followed if this is not the case.

## IV. Legal or non-legal norms?

If we follow a traditional positivist legal theory that all law must be state law, enacted in a formal process by a formal legal act by competent state organs or institutions to whom the states have delegated the power to enact law, than, in the international field, only treaty-law and acts of IGOs endowed with those competences, as for instance the European Community, are law. Neither the so-called „soft law "of the political sphere nor the „global autonomous law" of the social sphere then are „law". This theory comes up with clear-cut answers, but unfortunately it does not reflect the normative reality of our days.

But in a historical perspective not only the social, political and legal reality is changing and historically different in the lapse of time, but also the methods and theories of its understanding are historically conditioned theories, bound to special historical situations of society, its political, economic, cultural and legal organization and institutionalization and also to historically given scientific pre-suppositions. And this also means that legal theories are not strictly right theories in an absolute sense, but reflect the special historical situation in which and for which they have been or are developed. If the natural law theory is no more accepted today, this does not mean that it was wrong in former times, but only that it is not appropriate to explain our legal situation in the 21$^{st}$ century (which may be even wrong in some respects). On the other side, this means, that legal theorists have to look for new approaches if the old theories, in this case the positivist law theory is no longer in a position to deal with the existing normative order. Therefore it is necessary and legitimate that several modern legal theories try to ascertain the legal or non-legal character of these norms by other criteria. I cannot go through all of them.[71] In my opinion the legal theory based on the general systems theory of *Niklas Luhmann*[72] and *Gunther Teubner*[73] seems to be the most apt to explain why a norm is a legal and not only a „soft legal", political, social or moral norm.[74]

The positivist theory was born with the sovereign state, which has since the 16$^{th}$ century more and more monopolized law making as one of its chief instruments of creating itself as an independent political, social and legal entity. But, as we have seen, the state is no more the sole actor in creating norms. It was, by

---

71 See the literature cited in footnote 1.

72 Niklas Luhmann, Das Recht der Gesellschaft, 2. Aufl. Frankfurt/Main 1997, and Rechtssoziologie, 2 vol., Hamburg 1972.

73 Gunther Teubner, Law as an autopoietic system, Oxford 1993, Recht als autopoietisches System, Frankfurt/M. 1989; Global Bukowina, Global Law (Fn. 1), p. 3 sq.

74 For a thorough but more critical discussion see Stefan Oeter, International Law and General Systems Theory, in: German Yearbook (Fn. 1), p. 72.

the way, never fully the case. Canon law constituted always a second, non-state law system, which until the 19th century competed in many fields with state law. The modern lex mercatoria began its development in the 19th century, the first phase of globalization. And also already in the 19th century international organizations decreed binding regulations at least of an administrative character, such as the stream Commissions and others.[75]

It does not lead us much further to construct a system of a hierarchy of norms by successive delegation finding somewhere in this hierarchy of norms a state norm which like a fundamental norm of Hans Kelsen[76] authorizes the private actors to create their own law, and thus put on the state seal on those global autonomous norms.[77] Also the other way round does not make non-state global law state law, I mean the approval of an arbitral award by a national court for its enforcement, which is necessary from time to time.[78] The national court does not transform the award into a legal act or the law applied by the arbitrators into national law. It accepts it because it considers the award as a legal act, and the norms as law, in the same way as the german court accepts a judgment of an english or a polish court because it is - english or polish - law. § 1051 of the german Zivilprozeßordnung states clearly that the arbitral tribunal has to decide „in Übereinstimmung mit den Rechtsvorschriften, die von den Parteien als auf den Inhalt des Rechtsstreits anwendbar bezeichnet worden sind". The french regulation of Art. 1496 NCPC is similar. Both are following Art. 28 § 1 of the UNCITRAL Model-Law. It is generally accepted that the norms of the lex mercatoria as non state law fall under this wording.[79] This seems to be a convincing example of a complementary regulation of a global legal problem by autonomous, international public and national/state procedural law.

Non-formal norms set by state actors or IGOs in the political international field as general declarations, charters, resolutions etc. and global or regional autonomous norms set by international or transnational non-state actors as

---

75 Perhaps the most powerful was the Commission for the Danube, established by Art. 30 of the Peace Treaty of Paris, 30 March 1856, and further developped by the Act relating to the Navigation on the Danube, 11 November 1865, Grewe (ed.) Fontes (Fn. 23), vol. III/1 p. 19 and 464.

76 Hans Kelsen, Reine Rechtslehre, 2. Aufl. Wien 1960, Neudruck 1967, p. 228.

77 But so some critics of the autonomous legal character of the lex mercatoria, cited by Stein, Lex (Fn. 54), p. 205.

78 H. P. Schroeder und B. Oppermann, Anerkennung und Vollstreckung von Schiedssprüchen nach lex mercatoria in Deutschland, England und Frankreich, ZvglRWiss 99 (2000), p. 410 sq.

79 Schroeder/Oppermann, ibid. p. 425; Wolfgang Voit, in: Hans-Joachim Musielak (ed.), Kommentar zur Zivilprozeßordnung, 2. Aufl., München 2000, § 1051 note 2; Joachim Münch, in: Gerhard Lücke/Peter Wax (ed.) Münchner Kommentar zur Zivilprozeßordnung, 2. Aufl., vol. 3, München 2001, § 1051, note 8.

model-contracts, codes of conduct, rules of good practice, etc. can be considered as legal norms if the following conditions are given cumulatively.

1. General and continued observation and application of the norms by the actors in the system, also by refererence to them in speeches (speech acts, coding, grammar);
2. Increasing and continuing strenthening of the norms by practice, for instance steady repetition in resolutions of the General Assembly of the UN;
3. Steady systematization, differentiation, and downbreaking of the more general norms to more and more specific formulations;
4. Institutionalization of the formative and norm-creating processes, of the surveillance of their application and perhaps but not necessarily of the sanctioning of default by all kinds of institutions: e. g. IGOs, INGOs, commissions, courts, tribunals, associations etc.

If these conditions are given the norm or rule performs exactly the same function as a formal state created norm or rule, a statute, a treaty, a binding regulation of the EC etc. Their legal character is not dependant on certain formalities but on the function it has to perform.

At first sight that seems to mean customary law. But the legal character of a norm is not as in customary law determined by the generally very uncertain and circular relation of „custom“ and „opinio iuris“.[80] The category of customary law is not apt to cover all kinds of law originating in both systems. The systems theory by *Luhmann* and *Teubner* applies what they call „second level observation“. This means as *Teubner* puts it „It observes the observations of legal practice“.[81] This is certainly an empirical and not a dogmatic or doctrinal approach. The four conditions must be empirically ascertained conditions, but their application is normative in the sense that they ought to be given to consider a norm as a legal norm.

If we negate the legal character of those norms, as certainly may be possible, we must admit, that besides legal norms or rules norms and rules of another but also obligatory and enforced character exist besides legal norms. They may not be classified between the traditional norms, as moral or ethical norms, political norms or mere social norms. Despite the fact that the latter are often generally recognized and applied norms by the social sector to which they belong, the functions and their structures are fundamentally different. Their content is uncertain and depends very much on practice. They are not part of written acts. They are not really obligatory. Their creation as well as the assurance of compliance with them is not institutionalized. There may be a certain resemblance to the „conventions“ in english constitutional law. But this would only be acceptable for „soft law“ in the political international field. In reality these norms

80 See for the discussion of these difficulties in this field Teubner, Global Bukowina, in Global Law (Fn.1), p. 9 with further references.
81 Teubner, ibid. p. 11.

would form a new category of norms with the same functions and structures as legal norms, lacking state creation, but not state application. It would be difficult to find differences of practical importance. It seems therefore more rational for the construction of a functioning global legal order to admit and recognize the legal character of those norms if the said conditions are given.

Is this a „retour au moyen-age"? I do not think so. After all, the states still exist and they are still the primary law creating agencies, but no more the only ones. Already custom or customary law was not in general state-made law. It comes out of the society, the behavior of the people participating in the law creating processes. Again custom is not law because the state recognizes it, but the state recognizes it because it is law. We are turning to new forms of diversification of the law creating processes by different or diverse actors, the states, the IGOs and private actors of very different kind and status. The sovereign state loses its exclusive absolute competence to create law. The earthly god has to accept other gods beside him. A pluralism of legal systems is the consequence. The next question therefore is whether we can still speak of „The " international legal order, or the unity of the international legal system.

## V. Unity of the International Legal Order?

We have seen in the analysis of the two legal systems, the international public law system and the non-state autonomous law system, that no single coherent international legal order or international legal system exists. The sources of law are different, the law-makers are different, the institutions are different and a common basis does not seem to exist, neither formally nor materially. The systems theory therefore negates the unity of the international legal order. It speaks of pluralism, fragmentation etc. [82]

But we should try again. I am looking only to the relations between the two systems of international public and global non-state autonomous law.

1. The sources are not the same but they are interrelated.
In many fields international public law, nation-state law and global non-state autonomous law have to cooperate to create adequate legal regulations and solutions. e. g. in the field of purchasing [83] or, as shown, in the field of arbitration. Again that does not mean that only by the international public law or by the nation-state law the global non-state autonomous norms become law, in reality in many fields outside war and peace and international security on the international as on the national levels the state- created law follows the global non-state autonomous legal developments.

---

[82] Teubner, Foreword and Global Bukowina, Global Law (Fn. 1), p. XIII and 8.

[83] On the one side UN-Convention on Contracts for the International Sale of Goods, April 11, 1980, (CISG), BGBl. 1989 II, p. 586, on the other UNIDROIT Principles of international commercial contracts, 1994.

2. As already shown the law makers are not the same but they cooperate. On the state level as well as on the international public level private organizations of various kinds take influence on the state legal process by formalized as well as by informal procedures. [84]
3. A common institutionalized system does not exist, but institutions of the different orders are interrelated, e. g. in arbitration.
4. There does not exist a common legal meta-order or meta-system as for instance natural law was. But we have alsready ascertained certain common freedom in its different elements as necessary basis of both spheres and their respective legal orders. There is the strong and legitimate social demand that also other human rights, including social rights are taken up by both legal systems. At this point the states and their IGOs have their primary role to play, but again not alone but together with autonomous actors such as the INGOs active in these fields.

I think that we may not speak of the unity of the international legal order in the traditional sense. But common structures exist, even if we must admit that legal World Order has a very pluralistic and even fragmented structure, that it is not coherent and that its different elements even partly conflict. The other question is, whether we need or only want a unity of World Order. The systems theory not only denies it, but sees on the contrary, the pluralistic structure as a nescessity of its further development.[85]

If we would negate the legal character of the non-state created norms in the political as well as in the social field, the unity of the normative world order is excluded structurally. It must be conceived as a pluralistic order not only from the point of view of different legal systems and subsystems but also from the point of view of norms. This is not new. It was always recognized that besides legal norms ethical or moral norms, values or similar concepts must be recognized in the relationships on all levels between individuals, peoples and states. Already *Vattel* claimed that states had moral obligations versus each other.[86] But whereas the legal norms and the ethical norms lay on different levels, the interior conscience and the exterior behaviour, the two categories of norms, we are speaking of, would lie on the same level, the exterior behaviour. This kind of normative pluralism would therefore not only create enormous theoretical and doctrinal but, what seems more important, enormous practical problems, which finally may not be solved because a common denominator is lacking. This again

---

84 UNIDROIT has prepared and drafted several conventions which than have been adopted by the member states of UNIDROIT, see the list http://www.unidroit.org/english/conventions/c-main.hm.

85 See e. g. Teubner (Fn. 1).

86 Emer de Vattel, Le Droit des Gens ou Principes de la Loi Naturelle, London 1758, new edition French/English Geneva 1983 (The Classics of International Law), L.II, Chap.1 p. 255; see Emmanuelle Jouannet, Emer de Vattel et l'émergence du droit international classique, Paris 1998, and my review in: Archiv des Völkerrechts (in print).

is a reason to recognize our non-state norms as legal norms, if the four conditions are given or ascertained by the observer of their observations.

## VI. World-State as an answer?

Since the beginning of the decline of the one hierachical medieval order and the rise of the multitude of modern sovereign states since the 13th century plans for a federation of the states have been developed by politicians, jurists, theologians and philosophers from the plan of *Pierre Dubois*, passing by the bohemian King *Podiebrad,* the chancellor of Henri IV of France *Duc de Sully*, *William Penn*, *Jean Jacques Rousseau, Jeremy Bentham* to *Immanuel Kant*.[87] They all wanted to outlaw war and to assure peace by a centralized political-legal power. *Kant* pleaded for a „World Republic“, even if he himself did not believe that its establishment would be wise and possible.[88] But he wanted at least a „League of Nations“. After the First World War and much more intensively and comprehensively after the Second World War global and regional supranational institutions have been established to deal with all fields and matters concerning the peace of mankind and between the states in all its aspects and elements; the centre is surely formed by the UN, but around it the very differential UN-System and the equally differentiated mass of regional organizations have been established. But they do not form a World-Republic, not even a coherent system.

Recently *Otfried Höffe* has taken up the idea of a World State or World-Republic.[89] I will not discuss his proposal here. I have done it elsewhere.[90] But let me make some final remarks.

The traditional concept of sovereign statehood as scientifically developed by *Jean Bodin, Thomas Hobbes* and their followers and realized since the 17th century is without doubt no more realistic. As already mentioned above, individual states are no more able to assure the performance of all the necessary functions of the traditional sovereign state. This loss of the capacity of the traditional individual state of the 21st century to perform its functions for the people is not only a loss of factual power, might, strength and means. It is a structural loss and therefore it concerns all states, not only the „failing states“, the states of the third world, but also the developed states and even the United States.[91] The establish-

87 See Kurt v. Raumer, Ewiger Friede, Freiburg/München 1953; Hans-Jürgen Schlochauer, Die Idee des ewigen Friedens, Bonn 1953.

88 Immanuel Kant, Zum ewigen Frieden, Königsberg 1795, often reprinted since, 2nd Definitivartikel.

89 Ottfried Höffe, Demokratie im Zeitalter der Globalisierung, München 1999, 2. Aufl.

90 Heinhard Steiger, Brauchen wir eine Weltrepublik? (Review of the book of O. Höffe) in: Der Staat (in print).

91 The struggle for the mandate by the UN-Security Council in October/November 2002 concerning the Iraq case is sureley an ambivalent case. But it seems, that the US wants the support of the UN for its actions and needs at least a wide support of other countries if

ment of global and regional IGOs is a reaction to this development. Cooperation and even integration of the states into bigger supranational entities has since long become unavoidable and necessary. This seems to be an argument for a world-state or world-republic.

The principles of general freedom of action, especially economic and communication freedom, and freedom of private property, democracy, which are the constituent principles of the modern state, have set free society and individuals not only to act inside the legal frame set by states, but to create the transnational autonomous systems of communication, economy, finance, sports, etc etc described. The differentiation/diversification of social systems leads to their emancipation from the state inside the states and on the transnational level.

Therefore the concept of a World-State or World-Republic will not solve the problem of a pluralistic legal world order. Already *Kant* feared the suspension or even the suppression of freedom by a World-State[92] and *Höffe* in his proposal insists on the guarantee of human rights, freedom and property as the fundament of a World Republic.[93] But than the autonomy of the cultural, economic, comunicative, sportive and other social systems will be upheld and even develop further and with them their autonomous global law as one element or structure besides the public world law.

In the political sphere a coherent complementary system of global and regional, cooperative and integrated supranational IGOs must be further developed, not only to help states to assure the performance of their specific duties, but mainly to assure the general, global, transnational tasks, especially and mainly the assurance of international peace and international and national security, the protection of the global environment, the general assistance to sustainable development, etc. This can not only be done by one single general world institution on a global basis but also needs interrelated specialized global and regional institutions or organizations.[94]

In the social sphere it seems to me, as someone who is not an expert but only an exterior observer, that the institutional framework within the different subsystem should be better developed. The fragmentated and partly even chaotic development of the different parts of the non-state autonomous law in some of

---

they will not be isolated, but that, on the other hand, the UN needs some „pressure" to act and to overcome its internal differences.

92 Immanuel Kant, Über den Gemeinspruch: Das mag in der Theorie richtig sein, taugt aber nicht für die Praxis, 1793, III. Im Völkerrecht.

93 Höffe, Demokratie (Fn. 89), p. 58 sq. and 316 sq.

94 It is very questionable whether in a regional conflict, for instance in Europe as in former Yugoslavia the UN and its Security Council must take the necessary decisions, or whether it would not be more adequate to give this competence to a regional IGO. Art. 51 UN-Charter only provides for a regional competence in the case of an armed attack, and only as long as the SC does not take measures. It would be perhaps more effective to give to the SC not the primordial, but only a subsidiary competence.

them, even concerning lex mercatoria, may finally deprive them of their full effectivity. But also their fundamental conditions or presuppositions must be better realized to assure their legitimacy. The heavy protests against globalization as such by large parts of a transnational politically active global public are very significant. They formulate a general suspicion and even conviction that the selfreferential systems of world economy are not legitimate in respect of certain basic conditions of human life. States have therefore the tendency to restrict the autonomy more and more to assure these basic conditions. If the autonomous systems will resist this danger, it seems to the exterior observer that they should firstly take up those demands themselves and secondly organize themselves better. For the autonomy of law creating is necessary for the functional adequacy of this law in the different fields of the social sphere.

But even if both systems, the political-public system supported by the states and their IGOs and the global civil society and its systems need their differentiation and therefore their respective autonomy to perform their functions, to accomplish their specific objectives and to produce the effects and results necessary for the development of the national societies as well as the global society or mankind as a whole for which they are responsible, they also must establish a complementary system which fulfills the demands for a valuable world order of peace, justice, and basic social security. Since both spheres have to contribute to that order they cannot act separately and perhaps against each other, but they have to cooperate.

Therefore, it is thirdly necessary to develop the complementary cooperation between the two spheres, their systems and subsystems and their legal complexes. A complementary system is a necessary, organized, permanent and reciprocal system of systems, a differentiated or diversified whole or meta-system, in which each system for itself but also in coordination, cooperation even integration with the others, fulfills its, as well as the common tasks.[95]

It would be a great error of the states, if they would try single-handedly, on the level of IGOs or individually, to steer and to regulate the different social systems. This is no more possible and would lead to a collapse. Not only the experience of the socialist countries has shown that the steering capacity of the states of modern social development in all fields is not strong enough and that exclusive stateoriented steering concepts are doomed to destruction, not only of the economic but also of the political and eventually of the whole social system.[96]

But it would be an equally great error of the civil society to try to develop its autonomous global non-state law without cooperation with the state actors. As I mentioned already it seems structurally nearly impossible that these systems fulfill adequately and sufficiently by their own the different demands of the so-

[95] In the political sphere the EU constitutes such a complementary system.
[96] This seems to be especially the case of Russia after the breakdown of the USSR.

called „social justice", a very unprecise and vague notion, but which expresses nevertheless one social key element of a global and general conception of the essential basic structure of world order. Others are external peace, general internal security, social welfare and security, environmental protection, human rights, etc. For them the states will stay responsible primarily.[97] The autonomous non-state legal systems must confirm to these so-called „values".[98] They are also more or less intensively interrelated with the economic, communicative, and other systems of the civil society.

My proposition therefore would be, not to create a single, hierarchical legal world order of a world state, but to develop a pluralistic, functionally differentiated and highly complex complementary World Order. In a specific way, such a construction would realize the principle of separation of power, one of the essential and necessary guarantees of freedom. To a certain degree, conflicts and chaos may not be avoided in such a system, but this is the price of freedom. To resolve these, is a question of developing existing and of institutionalizing new methods and instruments of settlement of disputes and conflicts as one necessary and essential element of such a complementary system.

---

97 Teubner seems to fear a „repolitization" of the autonomous global law, even if he takes it for unavoidable, Global Bukowina, Global Law (Fn.1), p. 4. In my opinion, a complementary „politization" of global law is not only unavoidable, but necessary for its legitimacy.

98 This notion is generally used, but has a very ambivalist structure. On the one side it implies a positive content. On the other side „values" have a more or less absolute character, which tends to exclude any rational discussion about it. See for a very heavy critic of the value concept Carl Schmitt and others, Die Tyrannei der Werte, Hamburg 1979.

# Danger – Men at Work: Labour Law in a Comparative Perspective

*Prof. Dr. Alan C. Neal, University of Warwick*

## Labour Law – A Subject in the Eye of Controversy

If there were ever any doubt that the stuff of labour law occupies a particularly controversial and politically-sensitive niche in the rich pattern of Law, one need only consider events in recent years in Italy for confirmation of that reality.

On 19 March 2002, Marco Biagi, Professor of Labour Law in the University of Modena and special adviser to the Italian Ministry of Social Affairs, was gunned down on his doorstep by a team of assassins. The weapon which cut short Biagi's life was the same gun which had been used, three years previously, to strike down Massimo d'Antona, Professor of Labour Law in the University of Rome, and himself a special adviser to the Italian government of the day. Meanwhile, Gino Giugni, formerly Professor of Law in the Universities of Bari and Rome, and a Minister of Labour responsible for reforming the notorious "*scala mobile*" system, continues to carry remnants of the seven bullets fired into him outside his legal studio in Rome.

All three of these figures share the dubious distinction of having been intimately involved in comparative study of labour law and the political debate over how labour law might be modernised with a view to restructuring national labour markets and improving flexibility and competitiveness in the operation of those labour markets.[1]

For this is the world of today's comparative labour law. Whether economic reform and regulatory change are being undertaken within the laboratory of the European Union's "employment policy",[2] or as a part of the broadening of post-

---

1 Most recently, with the *Libro Bianco* on Italian labour market reform, which has met with vitriolic opposition from, in particular, the trade union movement in that country. The backdrop to many of the proposals contained in that document is the framework of employment promoting measures adopted at the level of the European Union through the post-Amsterdam "employment policy" with its associated "Employment Guidelines" and highly intrusive requirements placed upon individual Member States.

2 See, in particular, the framework established by the "employment chapter" of the Amsterdam Treaty. For consideration of some of the implications arising in this context (together with a selection of interesting non-European experiences in the area), see the contributions in M. Biagi (ed.), *Job Creation and Labour Law: From Protection towards Pro-action* (The Hague 2000). This author's comparison of the policy roots for the Community framework with the development of United Kingdom employment policy under successive conservative governments during the 1980s suggests a significant shift towards priority upon the principal "market" issues at the expense of the "social" dimension of this policy field: see *Alan C. Neal*, "From 'Bad Boy' to European Role Model? – The

Amsterdam European "social policy",[3] the role of labour law features large in any initiatives floated or debated. Tampering with the "regulatory balance" at the workplace has become one of the accepted political responses to calls for greater "flexibility", more "deregulation", enhanced "competitiveness", and a host of like-intentioned mantra beloved of corporate directors, employers' organisations, and the politically right-of-centre governments which have steadily regained prominence across the majority of Western Europe at the turn of the Millennium.[4]

Yet, this was arguably never so starkly the case previously. In part, the sharpened prominence is a function of a resort to regulation of working relationships through increasingly normative labour law regimes, something which has been a feature of the last thirty years in most market economies. The rapid ascendancy of the legislative tool as the preferred mechanism for regulating the world of work, to the gradual exclusion of voluntarist "collective bargaining" models, has been a particular feature of this shift.[5] So, too, has the rise of "rights-based" regulatory frameworks, directed towards individual workers, rapidly taken precedence over balancing or "protective" frameworks constructed upon the foundations of collective labour relations and the traditional economic balance of power for so long the hallmark of labour law across continents.[6]

In what follows, there is offered a reminder of what was for long considered to be the subject-matter of labour law, and a brief overview of the contexts within which comparative labour law study and research has commonly been undertaken. This is followed by a number of propositions concerning the make-up of subject-matter now falling within the general description of "social policy" or "social law", which reflects a modern 21st century field of activity for labour law. There is an indication that there has been a shift in recent years from "big names" and "big books" to a different pattern of labour law research, and the

---

Strange Legacy of United Kingdom employment Policies since the Single European Act", in M. Biagi (ed.), *op. cit.*, at p. 269 ff.

3 For the current policy framework within which this is being developed, see the European Commission's *Social Policy Agenda,* COM (2000) 379 final.

4 For recent examples of this "jargon shift", see the European Commission's Communication promoting core labour standards and improving social governance in the context of globalisation, COM (2001) 416 final.

5 See *Alan C. Neal*, "Industrial Relations in Europe: Assessing the Regulatory Challenge for Labour Law", in M. Biagi (ed.), *Towards a European Model of Industrial Relations? – Building on the First Report of the European Commission* (Deventer 2001).

6 For discussion of the traditional "protection of the weaker party" approach which featured so prominently in a variety of "social relationship" contexts, see the contributions to the 5-volume work *Law and the Weaker Party: An Anglo-Swedish Comparative Study* (under the direction of S. Anderman, A. Neal, T. Sigeman & A. Victorin), (London 1981-1992). The study deals not only with employment relationships, but also with housing and consumer relationships.

expression of a concern that the traditional categories by which the subject-matter of this field has been drawn up may no longer be apposite for the task now facing labour law researchers. Finally, a few general observations are offered upon recent trends.

## The Subject-Matter of Labour Law[7]

The term "labour law" has often been used to refer to the system of rules which regulates relationships in a system of industrial relations (the "labour market"). This rule system has grown up gradually, and is comprised of a mixture of custom, agreement, and legislative intervention: what has been said by one writer to constitute "an amorphous mass of unsettled, continuously changing rules of law".[8]

Nor, it may be noted, has it much mattered whether one was approaching the subject from a particular political standpoint, since, even before the dramatic events of 1989 in relation to the former socialist countries of Eastern and Central Europe, labour law in the Soviet system had itself been represented as

> "the branch of socialist law which regulates the labour relations of the workers ... and certain other relations which are inseparable from labour relations".[9]

The emphasis in both of these approaches upon the rule system as opposed to the subject-matter which has given rise to a system of regulation is, it may be suggested, typical of the answer given to the basic question "What is labour law?"

The late Professor Kahn-Freund used a broader sweep. He saw labour law as chiefly concerned with the "elementary phenomenon of social power", with a principal purpose to "regulate, to support, and to restrain the power of management and the power of organised labour".[10] Speaking primarily of the situation in England, he wrote of

---

7 The following comments reflect some of the author's observations published as *Alan C. Neal,* "Comparative Labour law and Industrial Relations: "Major Discipline?" – Who Cares?", in C. Engels & M. Weiss (eds), *Labour Law and Industrial Relations at the Turn of the Century: Liber Amicorum in Honour of Prof. Dr. Roger Blanpain* (The Hague 1998), p. 55 *ff.*

8 I. Szaszy, *International Labour Law: A comparative study of the conflict rules affecting labour legislation and regulations* (Leyden 1968), at p. 5.

9 L. Aleksandrov, *Soviet Labour Law* (3rd ed., 1963), at p. 15, quoted in Szaszy, *op. cit.*, at p. 3, note 3.

10 O. Kahn-Freund, *Labour and the Law* (2nd ed., London 1977), at p. 3 *ff.*

"the triangular relationship between organised labour, organised management and government, which is the framework of all labour law".[11]

Yet, it may be noted that in England, unusually, it is common to speak of "the system of industrial relations", and to distinguish this in some way from "the system of labour law" – thereby giving rise to a "Chinese wall" which continues, even today, to stand in the way of comfortable co-existence between "labour lawyers" and "social scientists concerned with matters touching employment". In this context, the expression "labour law" has tended to be used to denote the formal rules which define and limit the area within which the system of industrial relations may operate.

However, it must be questionable whether any valuable purpose is served for the purpose of this short contribution by attempting a systematic analysis with a view to identifying the boundaries of that part of the legal system which might reasonably be said to qualify for the description "labour law". Even the issue of whether existing rules are to be classified into boxes labelled "individual" or "collective" labour law is of little relevance when assessing the content of those rules and the way in which they operate in a broader socio-legal context. Arguably of rather more help have been attempts to present what is sometimes described as a "functional perspective" on the various materials which go to make up the body of what is often described as "labour law".

On the other hand, it would be misleading and unhelpfully narrow to represent the subject-matter of labour law as being merely a system of rules, with the commentator's role being confined merely to describing this system. The description of a system of rules cannot be separated from an evaluation of the way in which that system operates. Nor can the system be properly understood without some knowledge of the notions and driving forces which impinge upon the relevant field. This is arguably even more the case when it comes to comparative legal study.

Indeed, as Ernst Rabel has observed,[12]

"The inner relationship between the...legal systems is only discernible if in our comparative portrayal of their institutions we take the similarities and differences together".

---

11 O. Kahn-Freund, "Labour law", in M. Ginsberg (ed.), *Law and Opinion in England in the 20th Century* (London 1959), at p. 215 ff., reprinted in O. Kahn-Freund, *Selected Writings* (London 1978), at p. 4.

12 See *E. Rabel*, "Die Fachgebiete des Kaiser-Wilhelm-Instituts für ausländisches und internationales Privatrecht", in *Gesammelte Aufsätze III* (1967), at p. 186. The English language version is drawn from K. Zweigert & H. Kötz, *An Introduction to Comparative Law, Volume I* (2nd ed., Oxford 1987), at p. 41.

To take the view of Konrad Zweigert & Hein Kötz,[13]

> "The objective report which sets out the law of a particular jurisdiction will give a comprehensive portrayal of its legal solution to a practical problem, but it does so 'on its own terms', with its particular statutory rules or decisions, its characteristic conceptual form, and in its systematic context...But when the process of comparison begins, each of the solutions must be freed from the context of its own system and, before evaluation can take place, set in the context of all the solutions from the other jurisdictions under investigation."

Nevertheless, one arguably remains faced with the problem identified by the same writers in relation to "comparative law" in general, that, "so recent a discipline could not be expected to have an established set of methodological principles. Even today the right method must largely be discovered by gradual trial and error".[14] A number of starting premises may therefore be suggested.[15]

"Labour law" tends to have been seen historically as essentially a means of interfering with the normal market forces on the labour market, in order to protect the weaker party in the work relationship. The central question has concerned the extent to which this is to be done, although the issue is one which is characterised by a variety of tensions, not least of which is the difficulty posed by the relationship of "individual" to "collective" rights.

Whatever is eventually regarded as being the essential substance of labour law, however, it seems that in all systems the usual subject-matter consists primarily of three "fundamental" elements:

1. Individual agreements made between workers and their employers (commonly, in the form of "contracts of employment");
2. Agreements made between employers and organisations of workers ("collective agreements", or the product of "social dialogue"); and
3. Such legislative regulation as may be considered necessary to ensure the stable social operation of these first two relationships.

On a broader front, it can be seen that the components identified as forming the "fundamental" elements of labour law, in turn, reflect the meeting of three major processes:

---

13 See K. Zweigert & H. Kötz, *An introduction to Comparative Law, Volume I* (2nd ed., Oxford 1987), at p. 42.

14 K. Zweigert & H. Kötz, *An Introduction to Comparative Law, Volume I* (2nd ed., Oxford 1987), at p. 29.

15 I have drawn freely upon ideas addressed and set forth in an earlier collaborative work in memory of my late friend and mentor, Folke Schmidt. See Ole Hasselbalch, Alan C. Neal & Anders Victorin, *A Perspective on Labour Law* (Stockholm, London & New York 1982), especially in Chapter 1.

1. The development of freedom of contract;
2. The societal goal of regulation for freely bargained contracts within acceptable political and economic limits; and, more recently,
3. The introduction into the mixed economy of systems of social security.

Any approach to comparative labour law must, at the very least, therefore, in its *historical component* recognise the explosive forces which nineteenth century *laissez faire* liberal capitalism unleashed on workers within a developing factory system. It must appreciate, as part of its *political component*, the social pressures to which this gave rise, and the threat which these were perceived to offer to the established order. More specifically, when dealing with its *legalistic component*, it must account for the impetus to adapt the traditional instruments of law as the means for limiting collective power or for preventing mass social reactions to what is widely perceived as the inherent imbalance of bargaining power in the work relationship. Furthermore, in addressing the *economic and social components*, it must trace the transition of the *laissez faire* economic order – through two World Wars, by way of a "Cold War", and on into the "post-Communist" era, with its accompanying rise to prominence of so-called "free market" doctrines – into systems of Labour law built upon detailed regulation of contractual relationships, against a safety-valve created by a social security "floor of rights" introduced and regulated by statute. On top of this, that approach to comparative labour law must also, in relation to its inherent *international component*, take into consideration the impact of newly evolved legal systems (such as the developing legal order of the European Community),[16] as well as crucial aspects of international law embodied in instruments of the kind created through global institutions such as the United Nations,[17] or formulated under the auspices of regional bodies such as the Council of Europe.[18]

## Classifying the Stuff of Labour Law

At a recent symposium dedicated to consideration of the state of "scholarship" in Labour Law,[19] a number of interesting contributions from North American colleagues served to remind those of us whose European introspection has lowered our eyes in the matter that an important distinction continues to be made between "collective" aspects of the employment relationship context and

16 Notably, in relation to the "social provisions" of the Treaties establishing the European Communities, along with legislation in the field of labour law through Directives and other instruments such as the 1989 Community Charter of Fundamental Rights of Workers.

17 Perhaps most notably, the Conventions and Recommendations arising within the field of activity of the International Labour Organisation.

18 As, for example, with the 1961 European Social Charter.

19 10th Annual meeting of the International Journal Editors' Club (Philadelphia, May 2002), under the direction of Matt Finkin.

"individual rights" issues arising in that same context. Indeed, the point was made that, for North American teachers of the subject-matter, the term "Labour Law" is classically restricted to the collective dimension of working life regulation.

This point is particularly interesting when one considers the trend in European studies of the field, where, most notably, the "social policy" agenda of the European Communities has increasingly played a defining role in setting the framework for the work of labour lawyers, labour market analysts, and industrial relations specialists. Indeed, if one is to look at the picture through the eyes of the British commentator, one would also note the Continental enthusiasm for placing labour law in a broader context of "social law", including aspects of social security and related welfare state regulatory areas alongside traditional treatment of workplace relationships (both collective and individual).

As has already been noted, the classification of our subject-matter into (for example) "collective" and "individual" components may not prove particularly helpful if one is taking a functional approach to the comparative study entailed in the venture. Nevertheless, it is worth noting that, in the short period since the signing of the Treaty of Amsterdam in 1997, the nature of EU "social policy" has undergone a substantial shift – with significantly greater emphasis upon issues such as "dignity at work", "social exclusion", and "fundamental social rights", with a consequent diminution in the relative focus upon "labour law", as well as more traditional forms of "worker protection" such as that which dominated the European Commission's social policy action plans between 1974 and 1992.[20]

Undoubtedly, today's "labour law" – in almost any national regulatory system one cares to mention – is much more concerned with "the principle of equality", "fundamental rights", and "social inclusion", rather than in freedom of association, collective bargaining, collective agreements, and the legal treatment of industrial action. Which is not to say that these "classical" subjects for treatment are no longer relevant – far from it, as the continuing work of the ILO and the Council of Europe in relation to such matters testifies only too well.[21]

**Big Names**

No Anglo-German discussion of comparative labour law can take place without mention of the name of the late Sir Otto Kahn-Freund, whose influence

---

20 See the materials presented in Part 3 of Alan C. Neal, European Labour Law and Social Policy: Volume I Social Dialogue, Industrial Relations and Labour Law (2nd ed., Kluwer, The Hague 2002).

21 See, for example, the ILO enforcement activities in relation to Conventions No. 87 (Freedom of Association and Protection of the Rights to Organise, 1948) and No. 98 (Application of the Principles of the Rights to Organise and to Bargain Collectively, 1949), together with the work of the Council of Europe (especially in relation to Article 11 of the Convention for Protection of Human Rights and Fundamental Freedoms, 1950).

continues to resonate more than twenty years after his death. Not only did Kahn-Freund donate to British labour law scholars a remarkably sharp frame of reference within which to undertake their research and study, but he also succeeded in embuing the activity of comparative research in the fields of industrial relations and labour market regulation with clear purpose and salient warnings.[22]

The generation of scholars which launched and nurtured comparative labour law as a widely practised field of study in its own right included, along with Kahn-Freund, Wazlav Szubert (the author of the first draft Polish labour code prepared following the emergence of Solidarnosz), Tadashi Hanami (the font of Japanese scholarship and still the focal point for an academic community which boasts a line of succession the like of Kazuo Sugeno, Yasuo Suwa, and Takashi Araki), and Amerigo Plà Rodriguez (who, with Nestor de Buen, stands – well past his 80th birthday – as a colossus for Latin American labour law scholarship).

It also included the members of the comparative labour law group:[23] Folke Schmidt (the father of Scandinavian labour law), Benjamin Aaron (who, with Clyde Summers, for long stood out as one of the few American scholars seriously to engage in comparative study and publication), Gino Giugni (still the icon of Italian labour law scholarship, and the driving force behind that country's *Statuto dei lavoratori*), Xavier Blanc-Jouvan (along with Gerard Lyon-Caen, a giant of the French intellectual establishment of labour lawyers), and Bill Wedderburn (still active, as is his great rival Bob Hepple, in policy formulation, legislative initiative-taking, and trenchant criticism of "New Labour" reformist policies touching employment and the world of work).

Together with these giants must be mentioned Thilo Ramm, whose abrasive relationship with other members of the comparative labour law group eventually ensured the end of the venture after their work on "discrimination" in 1978.[24] So, too, does the name of Franz Gamillscheg stand forth in the post-war years of

---

22 See, for his general propositions, *O. Kahn-Freund*, "Comparative Law as an Academic Subject", (1966) 82 *Law Quarterly Review* 40, and note the employment-related examples offered in *O. Kahn-Freund*, "On Uses and Misuses of Comparative Law", (1974) 37 *Modern Law Review* 1. A number of the particular points had been made earlier in *O. Kahn-Freund*, "English Law and American Law – Some Comparative Reflections, in *Essays in Honor of Roscoe Pound* (1962), at p. 362 *ff.*

23 For the fruits of this team's collaboration, see B. Aaron (ed.), *Labor Courts and Grievance Settlement in Western Europe* (Los Angeles and London 1971); B. Aaron & K. Wedderburn (eds), *Industrial Conflict. A Comparative Legal Study* (London 1972); and F. Schmidt (ed.), *Discrimination in Employment. A Comparative Legal Study* (Stockholm 1978).

24 See F. Schmidt (ed.), *Discrimination in Employment. A Comparative Legal Study* (Stockholm 1978). This was the last successful collaboration between the group's members, and – following remarkable acrimony between certain of those members, including threats and counter-threats of legal action! – marked the end of an era for established patterns of collaboration in this field of scholarship.

German labour law scholarship – a tradition which has subsequently witnessed a good deal of fragmentation, with sharply contrasting schools of research growing up around luminaries such as Peter Hanau in Cologne, Spiros Simitis and Manfred Weiss in Frankfurt, or Wolfgang Däubler in Bremen.

**Big Books**[25]

Mention of German scholars inevitably, also, brings to mind the phenomenon of the "big book" – classic *oeuvres* which, even now, stand the test of time and serve as a point of departure for scholars seeking the golden thread of development for the field of labour law in the late 19th and the 20th century.

While it may be that a work that can take on such a "basic reference" quality as that of Hueck & Nipperdey in Germany,[26] or Schmidt in Sweden,[27] is no longer the norm in national systems of labour law, there remain, nevertheless, numerous examples of significant works contributing to the stock of knowledge in this specialist field. The emphasis has, however, tended to shift towards largely descriptive tomes setting out the law and practice in a particular country, without very much in the way of analytical or systematic critique and analysis to frame the presentation with an intellectual aura of any note. Long gone are the works in the manner of Sinzheimer's *Der korporative Arbeitsnormenvertrag*.[28] Instead, we have an annual diet of updated detail, set in a non-critical framework (largely reflecting the pattern imposed upon the subject-matter by the normative law-giver) with a view to a practitioner audience rather than an academic critique or a judicial policy-forming function.[29]

Nevertheless, the post-war years have seen the important series of French volumes taking up particular aspects of labour law, while a number of "frame-

---

25 Some broader observations were made in this author's 1986 contribution, "Comparative Labour Law: Projects and Publications", in W. Butler, B. Hepple & A. Neal, *Comparative Labour Law – Anglo-Soviet Perspectives* (Aldershot 1986), at p. 29 *ff.* This work was also published in a Russian language version by the Soviet Academy of Sciences, Moscow.

26 See, for example, *Grundriß des Arbeitsrechts* (various editions, Berlin and Frankfurt), or *Lehrbuch des Arbeitsrechts* (various editions, Berlin and Frankfurt). The particular example serves to illustrate how a "standard work" can emerge in a remarkable number of editions. Other post-war examples could, of course, be offered for Germany, including Franz Gamillscheg's *Arbeitsrecht* (various editions, Munich), or Söllner's *Arbeitsrecht* (various editions, Stuttgart and Berlin).

27 F. Schmidt, *Facklig Arbetsrätt* (various revised editions). This work transformed, in 1977, the author's previous presentation of the Swedish collective labour relations system in his *Arbetsrätt II*.

28 H. Sinzheimer, *Der korporative Arbeitsnormenvertrag* (I & II, Leipzig 1907, 1908).

29 Indeed, this tendency has contributed to the emergence of a variety of encyclopedic works, often in loose-leaf format with regular updates – the possession of which constitutes the advocate's technical "white stick" when presenting labour law cases before Labour Courts and tribunals.

work" works have established the particular flavour of specified national systems – including, in Denmark, Allen Rise and Jens Degerbøl;[30] in Italy, Tiziano Treu or Gino Giugni;[31] in Japan, Kasuo Sugeno;[32] in Luxembourg, Romain Schintgen;[33] in Sweden, Folke Schmidt;[34] or in the United Kingdom, Simon Deakin & Gillian Morris.[35]

At the same time, particular features of the systems have been highlighted, as with Gabriel Aubert's work on the peace obligation in Switzerland,[36] Luigi Mariucci's study of collective bargaining and the collective agreement for Italy,[37] Mark Freedland's analysis of the contract of employment under the English common law,[38] or Hugh Collins' study of "justice in dismissal" in the same legal system.[39]

Where comparisons have been drawn, this has increasingly tended to be in the context of collective works, to which a group of scholars contribute their particular national experiences in respect of a given topic, with an overarching presentation being penned by the coordinator of the project in an endeavour to present common features, trends, or individual peculiarities. Some of the better examples of this kind of work – much of the methodology for which was honed by the comparative labour law group in the 1970s – would include Bob Hepple's team looking at the evolution of labour law in Europe,[40] Lammy Betten's presentation of aspects relating to the contract of employment,[41] the EUI work on juridification in social spheres (including a section on labour law),[42] and the

---

30 See A. Rise & J. Degerbøl, *Grundregler i dansk arbejdsret* (Copenhagen 1977).

31 Both former Ministers of Labour in Italy. See, for example, Gian Primo Cella & T. Treu (eds.), *Relazioni industriali* (various editions, Bologna), or G. Giugni, *Diritto Sindacale* (various editions, Bari).

32 See, for example, K. Sugeno, *Japanese Labor Law* (Seattle, London & Tokyo 1992).

33 Now a Judge of the European Court of Justice.

33 See, for example, K. Sugeno, *Japanese Labor Law* (Seattle, London & Tokyo 1992).

33 Now a Judge of the European Court of Justice; R. Schintgen, *Droit du travail* (Luxembourg 1996).

34 *Facklig arbetsrätt*, *op. cit.*

35 See S. Deakin & G. Morris, *Labour Law* (various editions, Butterworths, London 2001).

36 G. Aubert, *L'Obligation de paix du travail: Étude de droit Suisse et comparé* (Geneva 1981).

37 L. Mariucci, *La contrattazione collettiva* (Bologna 1985).

38. M. Freedland, *The Contract of Employment* (Clarendon Press, Oxford 1976).

39 H. Collins, *Justice in Dismissal* (Clarendon Press, Oxford 1992).

40 B. Hepple (ed.), *The Making of Labour Law in Europe: A Comparative Study of Nine Countries up to 1945* (London 1986). This presented the fruits of the work undertaken by the European Labour Law Group (Bob Hepple, Antoine Jacobs, Thilo Ramm, Bruno Veneziani and Eliane Vogel-Polsky, working in collaboration with Ole Hasselbalch and Jean-Claude Javillier).

41 L. Betten (ed.), *The employment contract in transforming labour relations* (Kluwer, Deventer 1995).

ridification in social spheres (including a section on labour law),[42] and the presentation for the Nordic Council of the Nordic systems of employment regulation.[43]

Some important work has also emerged from studies undertaken at the instance of the European Commission – most illustrious of which might be considered to have been the study by Gerard Lyon-Caen of the respective collective bargaining systems of the founding Member States of the Community.[44]

## The Big Idea – "Social Justice"

What, then, are we to make of the state of labour law from a comparative perspective at the turn of the Millennium?

Perhaps the first observation to make is that "there is an awful lot of it around" – albeit of varying quality, displaying varying ambitions, and undertaken with huge variations in available resources (of which the most notorious is finance).

However, the very volume of material may merely serve to disguise a more disconcerting feature of much of the work produced in recent years – namely, the shocking absence of defensible comparative method, compounded by an overwhelming impression of missing components: absence of historical perspective, superficial contrasting of apparently similar terminology without close concern for the import of the technical language being utilised, and an alarming pretence that study of "harmonisation" at the level of the European Communities somehow constitutes comparative evaluation of regulatory mechanisms across different Member States of the European Union.[45]

---

42 G. Teubner (ed.), *Juridification of Social Spheres: A Comparative Analysis in the Areas of Labor, Corporate, Antitrust and Social Welfare Law* (de Gruyter, Berlin and New York 1987).

43 See the work prepared by A. Backman, S. Evju, O. Hasselbalch, T. Sigeman & A. Suviranta, *Arbeidsretten i Norden* (NU 1984:10, Stockholm 1985), (revised version NU 1990:42, Stockholm 1990). This flavour of the Nordic region adopts parallel structures for presenting experience in each of the countries covered, thereby enabling a limited comparative exercise to be undertaken across the respective descriptions.

44 Report for the European Commission, In search of the European Collective Bargaining Agreement, Study of Mr. Lyon-Caen (Doc. V/855/72-E).

45 Where, one might ask, does one now find the kind of presentation in relation to comparative method which characterized the work of scholars in this field during the first three-quarters of the 20th Century? See, for example, the already cited *O. Kahn-Freund*, "On Uses and Misuses of Comparative Law", (1974) 37 *Modern Law Review* 1, or the late Folke Schmidt's exposition of his "multi-axial method" in labour law, contained in the *Festschrift* published in honour of Konrad Zweigert. See *F. Schmidt*, "The Need for a Multi-Axial Method in Comparative Law", in H. Bernstein, U. Drobnig & H. Kötz (eds.), *Festschrift für Konrad Zweigert* (Tübingen 1981). This latter contribution discusses the methodological approach adopted by Schmidt and the present author when preparing their

Indeed, this latter complaint, at a time when floods of writing are emerging in relation to "fundamental social rights", "social dialogue", "corporate governance and the socially responsible restructuring of corporate enterprises", and "social conciliation in dispute resolution", reflects a significant disappointment in the products of research undertaken of late within the rich laboratory provided by the EU legal structure and the socio-political relationships thrown together by membership of the post-1957 European adventure.[46] For it is in this cauldron of social policy development, sharply contrasting industrial relations structures, and shared values as to the nature of social protection for the citizens of the new Europe, that one might have hoped to discover the sparks to rekindle the traditions of high scholarship pioneered in the field of comparative labour law by some of the great names of the 20th Century.[47]

This author bemoans, in particular, growing evidence that the focus for comparative study in relation to labour law appears to have shifted from neutral endeavours to describe and explain phenomena in their particular national contexts, in the direction of a search for "models" which can be applied transnationally or "borrowed" by developing or reforming economies.[48] Such a tendency, it is suggested, carries with it the danger of superficiality and "fig-leaf" policies which pay lip service to the underlying objective of achieving social

joint work for the *International Encyclopedia of Comparative Law*, under the executive direction of Ulrich Drobnig – see F. Schmidt & A. Neal, *Collective Bargaining and Collective Agreements*, International Encyclopedia of Comparative Law, Volume XV, Chapter 12 (Tübingen 1984).

46 Which is not, of course, to suggest that much of the work produced lacks intrinsic value – the point being made here is simply that "studies of harmonization" are too often passed off as today's works of comparative labour law.

47 If one wished to bemoan the myriad "lost opportunities" for a reassertion of dispassionate intellectual critique and analysis in the field, one would only have to look at the limited impact of designated research centers such as the European University Institute, in Fiesole, or the inability of various "think-tanks" throughout Europe to divest themselves of the ideological baggage which tends too frequently to permeate their presentations in relation to social policy and the future of regulatory mechanisms in the face of rapidly changing labour market conditions throughout the Continent.

48 This, indeed, often constitutes the very *raison d'être* for "comparative studies" undertaken for, and financed by, the European Commission. Examples of the difficulties to which this simplistic approach can give rise may be found, most spectacularly, in the attempts by the European Commission to introduce standardized patterns of company law regulation throughout the European Community – notably, by way of the ill-fated "draft 5th company law directive". For a lively debate on the matter of "models" in this field, see *H. J. Glasbeek*, "The Unility of Model Building – Collins' Capitalist Discipline and Corporatist Law", (1984) 13 *Industrial Law Journal* 133.

justice.[49] In reality, however, these may amount to little more than, in the words of the Prince of Denmark, "Words, words, words".[50]

Perhaps more invidious is the growing suspicion, too, that the research agenda has been hi-jacked by national governmental or supra-national bodies whose price for continuing funding and publication support is a demand for non-controversial research findings and a capitulation to the orthodoxy of a post-protectionist labour law.[51]

What Sinzheimer, Kahn-Freund, Schmidt or Szubert would think of many of today's offerings one can only conjecture – but, in the light of what has already been said here, one must have cause to fear that the judgment might turn out to be less than entirely complimentary. Certainly, if labour law in a comparative perspective is to serve the interests of "social justice", as is sometimes claimed by those active in this field, rather more is needed of today's scholars than is currently being delivered. Only with a clear commitment to dispassionate research and analysis of the complex world of work will it be possible to carry the torch in pursuit of the aspiration so succinctly encapsulated by the great English codifier Bracton, over seven hundred and fifty years ago:[52]

> "Justice is the constant and unfailing will to give to each his right."

---

49 See the author's comments in his introduction to Alan C. Neal & Steyn Foyn, *Developing the Social Dimension in an Enlarged European Union* (Oslo 1995).

50 William Shakespeare, *Hamlet,* Act II, ii, 195.

51 A number of issues related to such concerns have been discussed in *Alan C. Neal*, "Labour Law in the 1990s: An Unweeded Garden that Grows to Seed?", (1997) 13 *The International Journal of Comparative Labour Law and Industrial Relations* 11.

52 Bracton, *De Legibus Et Consuetudinibus Angliæ* (1220-1230).

# Aufrechnung in rechtsvergleichender Sicht

*Prof. Dr. habil. Malgorzata Pyziak-Szafnicka, Uniwersytet Łódzki*

## I. Einführung

*„Il vaut mieux tenir que demander"*- laut dieser Volksweisheit ist das, was man hat mehr wert als das, was man fordert. Auf diese Volksweisheit berief sich der ausgezeichnete französische Spezialist für Zivilrecht, Roger Pothier, bei der Erklärung von Wesen und Nützlichkeit der Aufrechnung.[1]

Der lateinische Terminus *compensatio* kommt von *cum pendere,* was den Prozess des Wägens darstellt. Man kann also bildhaft sagen, dass die Aufrechnung wie das Legen von zwei Forderungen auf beide Waageschalen ist; in dem Bereich, wo sie im Gleichgewicht stehen, gehen die Forderungen auf, bedürfen keiner Zahlung; zu bezahlen bleibt die eventuelle Differenz, das was überwiegt. Heute ist die Anwendung des soeben beschriebenen Mechanismus so offensichtlich, dass es keiner weiteren Erklärungen bedarf. Die klaren Vorteile der Aufrechnung im Rechtssystem sind Schnelligkeit, Sicherheit, Entfallen der Handlungen und Kosten der Zahlung, ob bar oder per Bankgeschäft. Die unbestrittene Nützlichkeit und universelle Anwendung bestimmen jedoch nicht näher die Form des Rechtsinstituts in verschiedenen Rechtsordnungen und insbesondere entscheiden sie nicht über Identität des Mechanismus und die Voraussetzungen der Aufrechnung. Die Kenntnis der Unterschiede hilft, die Aufrechnung im internationalen Verkehr zu nutzen. Besondere Bedeutung hat sie für polnische Juristen in einer Zeit, in der sie immer öfter eine rechtliche Bewertung der Handelsbeziehungen im Auslandsgeschäft vornehmen sollen.

Mein Referat über Aufrechnung in rechtsvergleichende Sicht habe ich Herrn Professor Günter Weick gewidmet, und das hat einen besonderen Grund. Es ist nicht nur Anerkennung für seinen enormen wissenschaftlichen Beitrag zur Entwicklung des Komparativrechts und internationalen Privatrechts, sondern auch Ausdruck meiner persönlichen Dankbarkeit für Unterstützung, die ich immer von Ihm bekommen habe, bei meiner Arbeit an Fragen der fremden Rechtssysteme.

Dieser Aufsatz, notwendigerweise kurzgefasst, stellt den Aufrechnungsmechanismus, seine Voraussetzungen und die Verwirklichung im Prozess dar. Bei allen Erwägungen wurden polnische Rechtsregelungen betont, die sicherlich nicht so gut bekannt sind wie die rechtlichen Lösungen in anderen Ländern.

---

1 R. Pothier, Traité des obligations, Kap. IV, De la compensation, S. 623.

## II. Gesetzliche Aufrechnung

Unser Ausgangspunkt ist die Unterscheidung der Aufrechnung in zwei Grundarten, die gegenwärtig in der Gesetzgebung gelten: vertragliche Aufrechnung und Aufrechnung, die man als gesetzlich definieren kann. Ich setze dabei voraus, dass für alle Fälle der gesetzlichen Aufrechnung, im Gegensatz zu den vertraglichen Aufrechnungen, eines gemeinsam ist, und zwar, dass diese unvereinbart, unabhängig von Willen einer Partei und sogar gegen ihren Willen zustande kommt. Unser Interesse in dieser Untersuchung gilt lediglich der so zu verstehenden gesetzlichen Aufrechnung. Es ist nun zu erwähnen, dass das polnische Recht die vertragliche Aufrechnung in vollem Umfang zulässt, sie als Ausdruck des Prinzips der Vertragsfreiheit betrachtet. Mehr noch, die vertraglichen Aufrechnungen waren auch zu Zeiten der zentralen Planwirtschaft voll akzeptiert.

Obwohl fast allen Rechtsordnungen das Rechtsinstitut, das die Merkmale der gesetzlichen Aufrechnung aufweist, bekannt ist, bedeutet das nicht, dass sie mit gleichen Rechtsmitteln zustande kommt. Man kann nämlich von zwei, ja sogar drei Systemen der gesetzlichen Aufrechnung sprechen: (1) Aufrechnung kraft des Rechts, infolge Erfüllung ihrer gesetzlichen Voraussetzungen (auch als automatisch bezeichnet), (2) Aufrechnung kraft der einseitigen Rechtshandlung, der konstitutiven rechtsbildenden Willenserklärung eines der gegenseitigen Gläubiger gegenüber der anderen Seite, unter Einhaltung der gesetzlichen Bedingungen und schließlich (3) die Aufrechnung aufgrund der Gerichtsentscheidung.

Im römischen Recht blieb die Aufrechnung, bis auf die gesetzliche Aufrechnung, immer ein gerichtliches Rechtsinstitut. Ohne auf die Entwicklung der Aufrechnung einzugehen, wollen wir unsere Aufmerksamkeit denjenigen ihrer Aspekte schenken, die das gegenwärtige Recht beeinflusst haben. Zu Beginn, in den Prozessen *iuris stricti iudicium* war die Aufrechnung nur dann zulässig, wenn man *exceptio doli* angewandt hat; der Beklagte konnte den Aufrechnungseinwand erheben, sofern er im Stande war, die Arglist seitens des Klägers zu beweisen, der den Anspruch erhebt statt selbst die Zahlung zu leisten. Erst Justinian hat die Aufrechnung bei allen Arten der Klagen und ohne dass die Arglist der anderen Partei bewiesen werden muss, zugelassen; bei einer Forderung seitens des Beklagten war diese vom Gericht pflichtgemäß zu berücksichtigen. Dieses Prinzip kam in der Formulierung zum Ausdruck, dass die Aufrechnung *ipso iure* erfolgt.[2] Im Mittelalter galten drei konkurrierende Deutungen des betreffenden Fragments von Digesten: die von Azon und Accursius, die die Gerichtsentscheidung über Aufrechnung für notwendig hielten; die von Bartolus, für den *ipso iure* als *sine facto iudicis* zu verstehen war, also ohne Eingriff des

---

[2] Die Entwicklung der Aufrechnung im römischen Recht wurde von W. Osuchowski in Historyczny rozwój kompensacji w prawie rzymskim, PWN 1970, dargestellt.

Gerichts, jedoch auf Grund des Willensaktes des Aufrechnenden und schließlich die von Cujas, für den *ipso iure* gleichbedeutend mit dem Automatismus der Aufrechnung war. Die Juristen, denen der wesentliche Einfluss auf die Konstruktionen im Napoleonischem Kodex von 1804 zugeschrieben wird, Dumoulin, Domat und Pothier, haben die Auslegung von Cujas gewählt, sie setzten also voraus, dass die Aufrechnung ohne Willenserklärung und ohne Eingriff des Richters erfolgt.[3] Heute geben die französischen Juristen zu, dass über die Gestaltung der Aufrechnung im Art. 1290 Code Civil die fehlerhafte Deutung der Texte von Justinian entschied. Um den „Automatismus" der Aufrechnung zu betonen, hat der französische Gesetzgeber im Art. 1290 sogar drei Formulierungen verwendet. Somit erfolgt die Aufrechnung kraft des Rechts selbst - *de plein droit*, kraft des Gesetzes - *par la seule force de la loi*, sogar ohne Wissen der Schuldner - *même à l'insu des débiteurs*. Gemäß dem Napoleonischen Kodex, erfolgt die Aufrechnung zum Zeitpunkt, zu dem sie möglich wurde, also sobald ihre Voraussetzungen erfüllt sind (Art. 1289, Art. 1291 franz. CC). Das Idealbild der Aufrechnung, die automatisch bei Erfüllung der gesetzlichen Voraussetzungen erfolgt, auf die Zeitprobe gestellt, unterscheidet sich heute weitgehend von dem Modell. Bevor wir zur Präsentation des heutigen Standes des französischen Rechts kommen, ist es zu betonen, dass der Aufrechnungsmechanismus in diesem System unter anderem in Belgien (Art. 1289 ff. belg. CC), Spanien (Art. 1195 ff. span. CC) und in Italien (Art. 1241 ff. it. CC) gilt, was seine guten historischen Gründe hat. Er wurde aber auch im österreichischem ABGB aufgenommen, was im § 1438 zum Ausdruck kommt.[4]

Die gesetzliche Aufrechnung, die aufgrund der einseitigen Rechtshandlung des Gläubigers geltend gemacht wird, ist zum ersten Mal im deutschen BGB erwähnt, obwohl noch im 19. Jh. die Überzeugung herrschte, dass die Aufrechnung kraft des Rechts erfolgt.[5] § 388 BGB besagt, dass die Aufrechnung durch die Willenserklärung gegenüber der anderen Partei erfolgt. In der Folge wurde dieses Modell von der schweizerischen Gesetzgebung gewählt, was Art. 124 des Obligationsrechts (OR) beweist, nach dem die Aufrechnung erst dann erfolgt, wenn der Schuldner seinen Gläubiger über den Willen der Aufrechnung in Kenntnis setzt. Diesen Weg hat auch der polnische Gesetzgeber gewählt. Das Obligationsgesetzbuch von 1933 hat im Art. 254 die Aufrechnungswirkung aus-

---

3 Die Informationen wiederholen sich in fast allen Monographien. Vgl. H. L. J. Mazeaud, F. Chabas, Obligations. Théorie générale, Paris 1998, S. 1192; B. Starck, Obligations. Régime général, Paris 1997, S. 137.

4 Grundsätzlich haben die Rechtslehre und die Rechtsprechung von Anfang an angenommen, dass das „Zusammenkommen" der Forderungen allein nicht ausreicht; eine Willenserklärung ist unerlässlich. Rechtsgrundlage der These ist der § 1442 ABGB, der eine Aufrechnungsmöglichkeit durch den Gläubiger besagt.

5 K. Larenz, Lehrbuch des Schuldrechts, t. I, 14. Auflage., München 1987, S. 255. Aufrechnung kraft Rechts ist im § 301 des preußischen Landrechts von 1794 angenommen.

drücklich von der Willenserklärung des Schuldners gegenüber der anderen Seite abhängig gemacht. Diese Erklärung hat konstitutiven Charakter, sie ist unerlässlich – neben den gesetzlichen Voraussetzungen –, um die Tilgung der Forderung zu erzielen. Der Gesetzgeber verwendet Worte, wie „Der Gläubiger hat das Recht aufzurechnen", was einigermaßen die theoretische Konstruktion bestimmt hat. Dasselbe Modell der Aufrechnung wurde dann im Zivilgesetzbuch (ZGB) vom 23. April 1964 aufgenommen, das 1965 in Kraft getreten ist. Die Regelung der Aufrechnung blieb unverändert.

Wenn man theoretisch die zwei Modelle der Aufrechnung betrachtet, deren Vorbild die französische und deutsche Regelung waren, scheinen die Unterschiede grundsätzlich zu sein. In der Tat gehen sie aber nicht so weit; sie werden eher eine Tendenz zum Verwischen zeigen. Dazu tragen sowohl die Deutung der Aufrechnung *ipso iure,* verwendet von französischen Gerichten, als auch manche Elemente der gesetzlichen Regelung der Aufrechnung infolge der Willenserklärung bei. Die französische Rechtslehre und Rechtsprechung betonen, dass es, obwohl die Aufrechnung *ipso iure* erfolgt, in der Zivilprozessordnung keine einzige Vorschrift gibt, die das Gericht verpflichtet die Aufrechnung zu berücksichtigen. Deswegen gibt es heute im französischen Recht keine Zweifel, dass der beklagte Schuldner, der die Aufrechnung beanspruchen will, spätestens in der Berufungsschrift auf diese Tatsache Bezug nehmen muss. Darüber hinaus trägt der Beklagte, der die Einrede erhebt, die Last, dem Richter gegenüber den Stand der Forderungen zu beweisen. Folglich bedeutet die „automatische" Aufrechnung eine seriöse Aktivität des Beklagten. Das Gericht prüft nicht, ob die Forderung des Beklagten durch Aufrechnung getilgt wurde.[6] Andererseits bestehen in der französischen Rechtslehre keine Zweifel, dass der Interessierte auf Aufrechnung verzichten, also gewissermaßen die Gesetzwirkung aufheben kann. Im Modell der gesetzlichen Aufrechnung *ex lege* bleibt den Beteiligten eine gewisse Freiheit überlassen, wie sie über die Tilgung der Forderungen entscheiden. Das Verwischen der Unterschiede zwischen diesem Aufrechnungsmodell und dem Modell der Willenserklärung wird dadurch begünstigt, dass die Gesetzgebungen, die, dem deutschen Rechtsmuster folgend, die zweite Rechtskonstruktion aufnehmen, die rückwirkende Kraft der Willenserklärung über Aufrechnung anerkennen, also die Aufrechnungswirkung mit Beginn der Aufrechnungsphase und nicht mit dem Datum der Abgabe der Willenserklärung oder gar ihrer Zustellung an den Empfänger verbinden.

Eine These über das dritte Modell der gesetzlichen Aufrechnung bietet eine Analyse des französischen Rechts. Unter den Voraussetzungen der Aufrechnung kraft des Rechts finden wir, unter anderen, *„liquidité"* der Forderung, also ihren

---

[6] Charakteristisch ist hier das Fragezeichen im Titel des Kapitels über Aufrechnung *ex lege* im Buch von Ph. Malaurie, L. Aynés, Cours de droit civil, Les obligations, Paris 1998. Die Autoren gaben die Überschrift: „De plein droit?", S. 643.

unbestreitbaren Charakter, verstanden als Präzisierung der Rechtsgrundlage und der Höhe der Ansprüche (*créance certaine et liquide*).[7] Gerade diese gesetzliche Voraussetzung bewirkt, dass der Aufrechnungsmechanismus, vorgesehen im Napoleonischem Kodex, in zahlreichen Fällen nicht wirksam werden kann. Dann bleibt dem auf Erfüllung der Leistung Beklagten, der gegenseitiger Gläubiger ist und dessen Anspruch keinen unbestreitbaren Charakter hat, der Weg der Gegenklage, die man als gerichtliche Aufrechnung bezeichnet. Nach klassischen Prinzipien des französischen Rechts soll die Gegenklage mit der Hauptklage eng verbunden sein (*connexité*). Die französische Zivilprozessordnung geht im Art. 70 von diesem Prinzip bei Klage auf Aufrechnung jedoch ab, und besagt, dass sie auch bei unzureichender Verbindung berücksichtigt wird, es sei denn, der Richter hält es für eine übermäßige Verzögerung der Entscheidung.[8] Gleichzeitig hat die Gesetzgebung gesprochen, dass die gerichtliche Aufrechnung auf dem Weg der Gegenklage von der Seite erfolgt, deren Forderung die Voraussetzungen der gesetzlichen Aufrechnung noch nicht ganz erfüllt, insbesondere die Voraussetzung der „*liquidité*".[9] Folglich ist – gemäß der von der Rechtslehre vertretenen Ansicht – ein neuer autonomer Weg der Aufrechnung entstanden, bezeichnet als *compensation judiciaire.*[10] Die Aufrechnung stützt sich zwar auf Verfahrensvorschriften, ist jedoch nur schwer als Prozessmittel der Verteidigung des Beklagten anzusehen; in der Tat fungiert sie als materiellrechtliches Institut.[11] Einerseits, was bereits erwähnt wurde, muss der Beklagte aktiv werden, um die Aufrechnung *ex lege* zu erreichen, andererseits bedarf es nun keiner besonderen Formalitäten, um die Gegenklage zu erheben. In dieser

---

7 Laut Lexique de termes juridiques, R. Guillien, J. Vincent, Dalloz 1985, S. 137, ist *liquidité* eine der Voraussetzungen der Zwangsvollstreckung; „*Conditions pour saisir: en principe, un créancier ne peut déclancher une procédure de saisie que si la créance est certaine (ayant une existance actuelle et incontestable), liquide (estimée en argent), exigible (non affectée d'un terme suspensif)"*.

8 Art. 70 spricht: „*Les demandes reconventionelles ou additionelles ne sont recevables que si elles se rattachent aux prétentions originaires par un lien suffisant. Toutefois, la demande en compensation est recevable meme en absence d'un tel lien, sauf au juge à la disjoindre si elle risque de retarder à l'excès le jugement sur le tout"*.

9 Zum Beispiel das Urteil von Kassationsgericht vom 14. Juni 1989: "*La compensation judiciaire peut s'opérer au moyen d'une demande reconventionnelle formée par la partie dont la créance ne réunie pas encore tout les conditions de la compensation légale"*, JCP 1989, IV, 302.

10 Vgl. F. Terré, Ph. Simmler, Y. Lequelle, Droit civil, Les obligations, Paris 1996, S. 1035; B. Starck, Obligations..., S. 144, 149; Ph. Malaurie, L. Aynés, Cours ..., S. 644, 645.

11 Deswegen haben verschiedene Autoren deutliche Zweifel, ob die gerichtliche Aufrechnung wirklich ein selbständiger Weg, unterschiedlich von Aufrechnung *ex lege* ist. Vgl. N. C. Ndoko, Les mystères de la compensation, RTDciv. 1991, Nr 11-12. Der erste Teil hat den charakteristischen Titel: "*La prétendue autonomie de la compensation judiciaire"*, S. 661.

Situation wird ein vorsichtiger Beklagter – ohne die Gewissheit zu haben, dass die Voraussetzungen der automatischen Aufrechnung erfüllt sind – statt sich dadurch zu verteidigen, dass die Aufrechnung erfolgt ist, die Aufrechnung beim Gericht beantragen. Die Verschmelzung der beiden Mittel ist so weit gegangen, dass das Kassationsgericht die Urteile der Berufungsgerichte annulliert, die keine Aufrechnung wegen Fehlens der Voraussetzungen für automatische Aufrechnung berücksichtigt haben, ohne die Möglichkeit der gerichtlichen Aufrechnung zu prüfen.[12] Schließlich verpflichtet also das Geltendmachen der Aufrechnungseinrede durch den Beklagten selbst aufgrund des Zivilrechts das Gericht zur eventuellen Aufrechnung der Forderungen. Das Gericht beschließt im Urteil nicht die Aufrechnung, sondern ermöglicht lediglich die gesetzliche Aufrechnung. In der französischen Rechtslehre wurde folgendes Beispiel des Verfahrens dargestellt: Beim Prüfen der Klage auf unbestreitbaren Anspruch (*liquide*) und Gegenanklage, die dieses Merkmal noch nicht hat (z.B. Schadenersatzklage), stellt das Gericht in erster Linie die Begründetheit der Gegenklage und Höhe der eventuellen Forderung fest. So verleiht das Gericht der Forderung aus der Gegenklage den unbestreitbaren Charakter (*rend liquide*), was wiederum Erfüllung der gesetzlichen Voraussetzungen bedeutet und folglich den Aufrechnungsmechanismus in Gang setzt. Nach der Beurteilung der französischen Juristen ist dieser besondere Weg als Verfahrensinstrument nur schwer anzuwenden; zwar erfolgt die Aufrechnung im Gericht, jedoch die Ursache ist ausschließlich der Umstand, dass die Feststellung der Erfüllung der restriktiven Voraussetzungen der automatischen Aufrechnung ohne gerichtliche Beteiligung in der Praxis ein ernstes Problem darstellt. Die Voraussetzungen sind aber die selben wie in den Vorschriften des Zivilrechts, und die Rolle des Gerichts besteht in ihrer Feststellung.[13] Für eine gewisse Sonderung der beiden Aufrechnungswege (gesetzlich und gerichtlich) zeugt die Auseinandersetzung in der französischen Rechtslehre, ob die gerichtliche Aufrechnung rückwirkende Kraft hat, ab dem Zeitpunkt als sie möglich wurde (wie die gesetzliche Aufrechnung) oder aber erst künftig, nach dem Gerichtsurteil.[14]

Die Präsentation der gerichtlichen Aufrechnung, die nach der französischen Zivilprozessordnung fungiert, jedoch als Institut des materiellen Rechts angesehen wird, hat uns in Richtung des *common law* – Systems geführt, das die Aufrechnung als Institut des Prozessrechts betrachtet. Da dieser Bericht grundsätzlich Aufrechnung als eine der Tilgungsarten der Obligationen, also der Surroga-

---

[12] Urteil vom 10. April 1973, herangezogen von N. C. Ndoko, Les mystères..., S. 669, als Abbildung der ständigen Tendenz.

[13] Das Verfahren und sein Charakter, zitiert nach H. L. J. Mazeaud, F. Chabas, Obligations...., S. 1188. Die Autoren stellen die Bezeichnung selbst in Frage: *compensation judiciaire*; nach ihnen entspricht die Bezeichnung nicht dem Rechtsinstitut.

[14] Unterschiedliche Meinungen stellt Ph. Malaurie, L. Aynes, Cours..., S. 645 dar. Heute überwiegt die rückwirkende Auffassung der gerichtlichen Aufrechnung.

te ihrer Erfüllung, zum Thema hat, ist hier kein Platz für eine Analyse der Verfahrensmaßnahmen. Es ist aber nicht möglich, das System, in dem – wie im römischen Recht - die Entwicklung der Aufrechnung mit dem Prozess zusammenhängt, zu verschweigen. Außerhalb des Prozesses kann die Aufrechnung nach dem Konkursrecht stattfinden. Das ist ein Institut des materiellen Rechts, das schon in den Rechtsschriften über Konkurse zu Beginn des 18. Jahrhunderts zu finden ist. Im englischen Recht wird auch im großen Umfang die vertragliche Aufrechnung zugelassen, die freilich außergerichtlichen Charakter hat.

Generell genommen ist die Wirkung, die die Aufrechnung auf dem europäischen Kontinent hat, im *common law* nur durch eine Einrede im Prozess (*set-off*) oder aber eine besondere Gegenklage (*counterclaim*) zu erzielen. Die beiden Prozessmaßnahmen haben sich entwickelt, aber sind heute hauptsächlich durch den Judicature Act von 1925 gestaltet. Die dem Beklagten zustehende *set-off* - Einrede, falls vom Gericht berücksichtigt, führt zur Abweisung der Klage oder zur Verurteilung des Beklagten zur Zahlung der Differenz zwischen der Klage und der Gegenklage auf Aufrechnung. Da *set-off* eine Einrede bleibt, bewirkt sie keine Folgen der Gegenklage; daher ist es nicht möglich, dass ihre Erhebung ein Urteil bewirkt, das die Forderung dem Beklagten zuspricht. Dank der Gegenklage, *counterclaim*, können in einem Verfahren die Streitansprüche beider Seiten untersucht werden; Voraussetzung ist hier jedoch der Zusammenhang zwischen den Klagen des Beklagten und des Klägers. Im Verfahren werden gesonderte Urteile gefällt, wobei der beklagte gegenseitige Gläubiger, dessen Forderung höher als die Forderung des Klägers ist, ein Urteil erhalten kann, das zu seinen Gunsten den ganzen Betrag zuspricht. Ferner kommt es zur Anrechnung der zugesprochenen Beträge, und folglich kann die Vollstreckung nur die Person führen, der der Überschuss zusteht.[15]

Die Darstellung verschiedener Mechanismen der gesetzlichen Aufrechnung erlaubt uns eine These zu formulieren, dass, wenn auch die theoretischen Unterschiede unter den Konzepten der europäischen Gesetzgebung wahrgenommen werden, ihre praktische Bedeutung nicht überschätzt werden darf. Denn erstens, infolge der Evolution des französischen Rechts gibt es heute keine Konstruktion der Aufrechnung, laut der die Tilgung der Forderungen absolut getrennt von der Willenserklärung einer der Seiten ist.[16] Zweitens, von grundsätzlicher Bedeutung für die Wirksamkeit der Aufrechnung ist immer der Umstand, ob die gegenseitigen Gläubiger sich einig sind in Bezug auf die Erfüllung ihrer gesetzlichen Voraussetzungen. Der Realwert der beiden traditionellen Mechanismen der Aufrechnung ist gering, wenn die andere Seite die Erfüllung der gesetzlichen Vor-

---

[15] S. Martin Leake, R. R. A. Walker, Law of Contracts, London 1931, S. 779 – 793; G.C. Cheshire, C. H. S. Fifoot, The Law of Contract, London 1969, S. 445, 446; M. Wolf, Die Aufrechnung im internationalen Privatrecht, Dortmund 1989, S. 49-59.

[16] So auch M. Wolf, Die Aufrechnung.... S. 104. Die Schlußfolgerung hat der Autor aus der rechtsvergleichenden Analyse, darunter auch des angloamerikanischen Rechts, gezogen.

aussetzungen in Frage stellt. Weder die Aufrechnung kraft des Gesetzes noch die konstitutive Willenserklärung über Aufrechnung schützen nämlich die beiden Seiten vor dem Prozess, wenn sie nicht darüber einig sind, dass die gesetzlichen Voraussetzungen gegeben sind. In dieser Situation muss die „Tatsache" der Tilgung der Forderungen vom Gericht festgestellt werden. Diese praktische Bemerkung lässt eine vorsichtige Schlussfolgerung formulieren, dass der Unterschied zwischen dem kontinentalen System, das die Aufrechnung als materielles Rechtsinstitut betrachtet und der prozessrechtlichen Auffassung im *common law* keine tiefe Kluft bedeutet.

## III. Voraussetzungen der Aufrechnung

Die Funktion, die der Aufrechnung im Rechtsverkehr zukommt, insbesondere die Zahlungsfunktion und die Vollstreckungsfunktion, bestimmen eindeutig ihre Voraussetzungen. Daher formulieren die Gesetzgeber sehr ähnliche Voraussetzungen, deren Erfüllung die Tilgungsmöglichkeit der Forderungen durch Aufrechnung bedingt. Gleichzeitig, weil die Aufrechnung die reelle Erfüllung der Leistung ersetzt, sind die Gesetzgeber gegen ihre Anwendung, wenn das der Rechtsschutz der beiden Seiten oder eines Dritten erfordert. Folglich kann man von positiven und negativen Voraussetzungen sprechen. Die Erfüllung der positiven ist notwendig für die Aufrechnung und das Vorhandensein einer negativen schließt ihre Wirksamkeit aus.

Die positiven Voraussetzungen der gesetzlichen Aufrechnung sind im allgemeinen: die Gegenseitigkeit der Forderungen, die Gleichartigkeit der Leistungen und die nur vom Willen des Gläubigers abhängige Möglichkeit der Zwangsvollstreckung der Forderung. Die letztere wird in den Gesetzgebungen unterschiedlich ausgedrückt. Im französischen Recht wird sie durch entsprechende Deutung des Termins *„exigibilité"*, als Voraussetzung der Aufrechnung im Art. 1291 Abs. 1 franz. CC genannt. Im deutschen Recht dienen dazu mindestens zwei Voraussetzungen: die Fälligkeit (§ 387 BGB) und die aus § 390 BGB resultierende Vollwirksamkeit, auch als Durchsetzbarkeit der Forderung oder Freiheit von Einreden bezeichnet.[17] Wichtig ist die Bemerkung, dass unabhängig davon, wie viele Bedingungen der Gesetzgeber formell auch nennt, sie immer so gestaltet werden müssen, dass sie die Verwirklichung des Anspruchs unter Anwendung des staatlichen Zwangs sichern.

An dieser Stelle ist der Unterschied in der Gestaltung der Voraussetzungen der Aufrechnung *ex lege* und der Aufrechnung infolge der Willenserklärung zu

---

17 K. Larenz, Lehrbuch...., S. 258, nimmt als Bedingungen des aktiven Anspruchs: Gültigkeit, Fälligkeit und Durchsetzbarkeit an; W. Fikentscher, Schuldrecht, 9. Auflage, Berlin 1997, S. 202, spricht nur von Durchsetzbarkeit und Erfüllbarkeit; J. Gernhuber, Die Erfüllung und ihre Surrogate, Tübingen 1983, S. 226-229, zählt Durchsetzbarkeit und Freiheit von Einreden auf.

betonen. Im ersten System wird eine Symmetrie zugrunde gelegt: beide Forderungen müssen alle Voraussetzungen der Aufrechnung erfüllen. Bei der Aufrechnung infolge Willenserklärung genügt es, dass die Voraussetzungen von der Forderung des Aufrechnenden, also der aktiven Seite, erfüllt werden. Die Begründung ist einfach: der Aufrechnende zahlt seine Schuld und zieht seine Gegenforderung ein; jeder hat das Recht seine Naturalobligationen zu zahlen, dagegen kann niemand eine solche Schuld einziehen, die noch nicht fällig oder schon verjährt ist. Folglich wird erwartet, dass die Forderung der Aktivseite die Bedingungen der Fälligkeit und Klagbarkeit erfüllt. Der zweite Unterschied in der Gestaltung der gesetzlichen Aufrechnung besteht darin, dass bei der Aufrechnung kraft des Rechts eine zusätzliche, schon erwähnte Bedingung erforderlich ist, und zwar dass beide Forderungen unbestreitbar und im Geld ausgedrückt sind (*liquidité* – Art. 1291 abs. 1 franz. CC). Ohne diese Voraussetzung wäre es schwierig, die Aufrechnungsfolgen zeitlich zu bestimmen.

Es ist zu erwähnen, dass ebenfalls die Voraussetzungen im *common law* ähnlich sind, obwohl sie generell genommen restriktiver sind. Erstens, die Aufrechnung im englischen Recht bezieht sich lediglich auf Geldleistungen. Zweitens, da die Operation im Prozess erfolgt, bewirkt das die strenge Einhaltung der Bedingungen: 1) Gegenseitigkeit, da sich nur der Beklagte und nur gegen den Anspruch des Klägers verteidigen kann, 2) Fälligkeit, 3) Vollstreckbarkeit der Forderungen beider Seiten. Sollte die Forderung des Klägers nicht fällig und vollstreckbar sein, so würde sie vom Gericht nicht untersucht; somit würde jedwede Verteidigung des eventuellen Beklagten gegenstandslos.

Der polnische Gesetzgeber hat bei der Einführung der Aufrechnung kraft Willenserklärung ihre Voraussetzungen auf vier beschränkt. Diese wiegen nicht gleich viel, obwohl sie vom Gesetzbuch formell gleichwertig betrachtet werden. Aus Art. 498 § 1 ZGB geht hervor, dass alle Voraussetzungen beide Forderungen betreffen. Das Gesetz erfordert neben der Gegenseitigkeit und Gleichartigkeit auch noch, dass "beide Forderungen fällig sind und vor Gericht oder einem anderen Staatsorgan geltend gemacht werden können". Trotz dieses Wortlauts wird allgemein angenommen, dass die Fälligkeit und Klagbarkeit nur die aktive Forderung betrifft. In der Lehre betont man mit Recht, dass das Bewusstwerden der Aufrechnungsfunktionen das System der Voraussetzungen der Aufrechnung verstehen lässt.[18] Diese Aufrechnungsfunktionen bewirken eben die differenzierte Bedeutung ihrer Voraussetzungen. Gegenseitigkeit und Gleichartigkeit der Leistungen betreffen beide Forderungen und werden als natürliche oder eigentliche Voraussetzungen der Aufrechnung betrachtet. Die Fälligkeit und Klagbarkeit dagegen sind nur von der Forderung des Aufrechnenden zu erfüllen.

---

[18] Vgl. L. Stępniak, Potrącenie w systemie polskiego prawa cywilnego, Ossolineum 1975, S. 21, 22.

Ohne auf die nähere Darstellung der einzelnen Voraussetzungen der Aufrechnung einzugehen, sind hier jedoch die vom Gesetzgeber zugelassenen Abweichungen in ihrer Erfüllung zu erwähnen. Die grundlegende, man kann sagen natürliche Voraussetzung der Aufrechnung, auch bei der verträglichen Aufrechnung, ist zweifellos die Gegenseitigkeit der Forderungen, nach dem römischen Prinzip *compensatio ex iure tertii nequit.* Es ist charakteristisch, dass trotz der grundsätzlichen Bedeutung der Gegenseitigkeit allgemein Ausnahmen eingeführt werden, darunter betreffen die wichtigsten Abtretung und Bürgschaft. Bei der Abtretung lässt man zu, dass der Schuldner der abgetretenen Forderung gegenüber dem Übernehmer mit einer Forderung aufrechnen kann, die ihm gegenüber dem Abtretenden zusteht. Selbstverständlich werden in der Gesetzgebung verschiedene Voraussetzungen für die Aufrechnung in solchem Fall genannt, was sowohl mit dem angenommenen Aufrechnungsmechanismus als auch mit der andersartigen Regelung der Abtretung zusammenhängt.

Im französischen Recht, angesichts der Aufrechnung *ex lege*, wenn die Aufrechnungsphase vor der Abtretung begonnen hat, fehlt theoretisch der Abtretungsgegenstand, denn die Forderungen werden mit der Aufrechnungsphase getilgt. Der Gesetzgeber regelt jedoch die Lage des Schuldners für den Fall der Abtretung. Wie bekannt, ist nach dem Napoleonischem Kodex die Abtretung nur soweit vollwirksam, als sie unter Zustimmung des Schuldners erfolgt. Von dieser Zustimmung hängt auch die Möglichkeit ab, dass sich der Schuldner gegenüber dem Übernehmer auf die Aufrechnung beruft, die gegenüber dem Abtretenden erfolgt ist. Hat der Schuldner in die Abtretung eingewilligt, so ist die Einrede nicht mehr möglich. Die Forderung des Schuldners gegen den Abtretenden dem Übernehmer entgegenzustellen ist nur möglich, wenn der Schuldner in die Abtretung nicht eingewilligt hat, sondern über diese lediglich in Kenntnis gesetzt wurde. Diese Möglichkeit beschränkt sich auf Forderungen, die später als die Notifikation sind (Art. 1295 franz. CC). Am Rande sei bemerkt, dass die Regelung der Abtretungsfolgen ein weiterer Beweis dafür ist, wie irreführend ein theoretisches Bild der automatischen Aufrechnung sein kann.

Die Rechtsordnungen, in denen die Abtretung nicht von der Einwilligung des Schuldners und nicht einmal von der Kenntnis abhängig ist, schützen den Schuldner im größeren Umfang. Die Gesetzgeber gehen davon aus, dass die Möglichkeit der Schuldenzahlung durch Aufrechnung ein wesentliches, für den Schuldner zweifellos günstiges Element seiner Lage ist. Daher schützen sie die schon gegenüber dem Abtretenden erworbene Aufrechnungsmöglichkeit und sogar seine Hoffnung auf künftige Aufrechnung. Ein Beispiel ist hier die Lösung im deutschen Recht (§ 406 BGB). Das polnische Recht, nach dem deutschen Vorbild, nimmt grundsätzlich an, dass der Schuldner ein Recht auf alle Einreden hat, die er gegenüber dem Abtretenden zum Zeitpunkt der Kenntnisnahme der Abtretung hatte (Art. 513 § 1 ZGB). In einem separaten Paragraphen betont der Gesetzgeber die Zulässigkeit der Aufrechnung, wobei er sie erst dann geltend machen lässt, wenn die Forderung des Schuldners nach der Kenntnisnahme der Abtretung fällig wurde, wenn nur die Fälligkeit früher als die Fälligkeit der abzutretenden Forderung war (Art. 513 § 2 ZGB).

Eine gemeinsame legislatorische Idee liegt auch den Regelungen zugrunde, die zugunsten des Bürgen die Tatsache berücksichtigen, dass dem Hauptschuldner gegenüber dem Gläubiger die fällige Forderung zusteht. Die Idee kommt in Art. 1294 Abs. 1 franz. CC zum Ausdruck, der direkt erlaubt, dass der Bürge dem Gläubiger zur Aufrechnung das entgegenstellt, was der Hauptschuldner aufrechnen konnte. Es ist wieder zu bemerken, dass, falls die Aufrechnung wirklich *ex lege* erfolgte, völlig abgesehen von dem Willen der Seiten und sogar bei Unkenntnis des Schuldners, diese Bestimmung einfach überflüssig wäre. Eine andere, für den Bürgen aber ebenfalls günstige Lösung nimmt die deutsche Gesetzgebung an; in § 770 II BGB wurde dem Bürgen die Einrede gegenüber dem Gläubiger eingeräumt. Der Bürge darf die Befriedigung verweigern, solange dem Hauptschuldner die fällige Forderung gegenüber dem Gläubiger zusteht. Der polnische Gesetzgeber nimmt hier die Lösung des französischen Rechts an, d.h. sowohl im Obligationsgesetzbuch (Art. 260) als auch im Zivilgesetzbuch (Art. 883 § 1) wird dem Bürgen die Möglichkeit der Aufrechnung der dem Hauptschuldner zustehenden Forderung gegeben. In der Rechtslehre vermerkt man aber eine gewisse Inkonsequenz der Regelung aufgrund der Konstruktion der Aufrechnung, die ein Recht ist, das der Person zusteht, die zugleich Gläubiger und gegenseitiger Schuldner ist. Gleichzeitig sind die Juristen der Meinung, dass die Akzessorität der Schuld des Bürgen gegenüber der Hauptforderung ausreichend den Inhalt von Art. 883 § 1 ZGB rechtfertigt. Sie betonen auch, dass diese Lösung von der Rechtmäßigkeit diktiert ist.[19]

Wenn man kurz die negativen Voraussetzungen präsentiert, sind gleich aus unserem Interessenbereich die Sondervorschriften bezüglich Konkurs auszuklammern. Obwohl die Einschränkungen und Ausschluss der Aufrechnung gegenüber dem Insolventen allgemein gültig sind und in Polen heute die Hauptrolle spielen, würde ihre Darstellung eine besondere Erörterung der Konkursfragen in einzelnen Systemen erfordern.[20] Daher konzentrieren wir uns auf die Ausnahmen von der allgemeiner Regelung der Aufrechnung im Zivilrechtskodex.

Selbstverständlich werden die negativen Voraussetzungen verschieden gestaltet, die Gründe jedoch, aus welchen die Gesetzgeber Ausschließungen anwenden, sind sehr ähnlich. Einerseits wird die Möglichkeit, die reale Leistungserfüllung zu vermeiden, von der Gesetzgebung als Privileg des Schuldners betrachtet, und somit ist in gewissen Situationen der Schuldner der Entlastung

---

19 Vgl. L. Stępniak, Potrącenie... S. 33 ff.; A. Szpunar, Zbezpieczenia osobiste wierzytelności, Sopot 1997, S. 108.

20 Im polnischen Recht wird die Frage im Konkursrecht von 1934 geregelt, dessen Art. 32 - 37 der Aufrechnung gewidmet sind.

durch Aufrechnung der Forderung nicht würdig. Es geht hier insbesondere um das Beheben des Schadens aus vorsätzlicher unerlaubter Handlung (§ 393 BGB) und um die Rückgabe der Sache, die dem Gläubiger rechtswidrig entzogen wurde (Art. 1293 Abs. 1 franz. CC, Art. 125 Abs. 1 schweiz. OR). Andererseits nehmen die Gesetzgeber den Wert wahr, den für den Gläubiger die wirkliche Leistungserhaltung darstellt und nehmen an, dass in manchen Fällen eben diese Form der Befriedigung notwendig ist. Folglich schützen die Gesetzgeber im allgemeinen die Forderungen in dem Umfang, in welchem sie aus humanitären Gründen nicht pfändbar sind (§ 394 BGB) oder wirksame Leistung erfordern (Art. 125 Abs. 2 schweiz. OR), oder aber die Unterhaltsforderungen und Forderungen aus einem Arbeitsverhältnis (Art. 1293 franz. CC) gewährleisten.

Die polnische Gesetzgebung hat anfangs, im Obligationsgesetzbuch von 1933, den Ausschluss der Aufrechnung nach dem Vorbild des französischen und schweizerischen Rechts geregelt. Art. 259 des Gesetzbuches hat die Tilgung der Forderungen auf die zur Aufbewahrung gelassenen, geliehenen oder willkürlich weggenommenen Sachen, Forderungen auf Unterhalt und nicht verpfändbaren Forderungen sowie Forderungen nach Lohn bis zu genannter Höhe mittels Aufrechnung ausgeschlossen. Heute werden diese von Art. 505 ZGB geregelt, laut dem nicht aufzurechnen sind: unpfändbare Forderungen, Forderungen nach Unterhaltsleistungen, Forderungen aus unerlaubten Handlungen und solche, für die durch Sondervorschriften die Aufrechnung ausgeschlossen ist. Bei den letzteren sind die Einschränkungen des Art. 89 des Arbeitskodexes von Bedeutung. Erwähnenswert ist auch, dass Art. 504 ZGB die Aufrechnung limitiert, um den gleichen Zutritt der konkurrierenden Gläubiger zum Vermögen des Schuldners zu sichern; hier geht es um Regeln der Aufrechnung der von Dritten beschlagnahmten Forderung.

Die Präsentation der Einschränkungen der Aufrechnung wäre nicht komplett, wenn nur der Wortlaut der Vorschriften betrachtet wird. Es entstehen nämlich zwei Fragen: erstens, ist das Verzeichnis der deutlich vom Gesetzgeber genannten Ausnahmen vollständig, oder gibt es noch andere Ursachen, und zweitens, ist das Ausschließen der Aufrechnung kraft verträglichen Vereinbarung möglich?

Zu der ersten Frage ist zu betonen, dass in der polnischen Rechtslehre die Diskussion über eine zulässige Aufrechnung im Verhältnis Bank – Bankkunde im Gange ist. Einerseits schließt das Gesetz selbst die Aufrechnung nicht aus, andererseits „durch den Bankkontovertrag verpflichtet sich die Bank dem Kontoinhaber gegenüber zur Verwahrung seiner Geldmittel“ (Art. 725 ZGB). Auf der Suche nach der Lösung dieser Frage sollte man die fremden Lösungen in Betracht ziehen. Nach dem Wortlaut des Art. 1293 Abs. 2 franz. CC und Art. 125 Abs. 1 schweiz. OR ist die Aufrechnung ausgenommen bei Forderungen zur

Rückgabe hinterlegter Sachen.[21] Das deutsche Recht sieht diese Ausnahme nicht vor. Es gibt jedoch eine verbreitete Überzeugung, dass die Vorschrift überflüssig ist, wenn der Ausschluss der Aufrechnung aus der Natur und dem Zweck der Obligation hervorgeht, insbesondere wenn das Rechtsverhältnis auf Vertrauen beruht oder eine der Seiten zu besonderer Sorgfalt gegenüber dem Vertragspartner verpflichtet ist.[22] Der Bankvertrag gehört zweifellos zu den Rechtsverhältnissen aufgrund eines besonderen Vertrauens, was gegen die Zulassung der Aufrechnung spricht. Meiner Meinung nach kann heute, angesichts der Verpflichtung der Unternehmer, ihre Verrechnungen über Bankgeschäfte abzuwickeln, den Banken nicht die unbeschränkte Freiheit zugebilligt werden, zur Befriedigung ihrer Ansprüche mit Kundenforderungen aus einem Bankkontovertrag aufzurechnen. Dies wäre eine deutliche Begünstigung der Banken. Eine Differenzierung ist notwendig. Es scheint, dass die erste diesbezügliche Entscheidung des Obersten Gerichts vom 23. Februar 2001 ein Schritt auf dem rechten Wege ist.[23] Das Gericht hat in der Entscheidung die Aufrechnung bei Termineinlagen zugelassen. In der Begründung ist eine Suggestion enthalten, das die Bewertung anders wäre, wenn es um Sparkonto oder Kontokorrent ginge. Dieser Standpunkt ist grundsätzlich zu billigen; es ist zu erwarten, dass die Rechtssprechung konsequent sein wird und die Aufrechnung der Bankforderungen mit Kundenforderungen aus Kontokorrentvertrag nicht zulässt.

Wir haben bisher über gesetzliche Ausnahmen gesprochen. Es ist jedoch zweifellos, dass die Vertragsparteien an realer Erfüllung der gegenseitigen Leistungen interessiert sein können und – folglich - die Zulässigkeit der Aufrechnung, sogar der *ex lege*, ausschließen. Der Umfang und die Form der Ausschließungen sind verschieden und werden an dieser Stelle nicht analysiert. Es scheint notwendig, auf die beschränkte Ausschließungsfreiheit, eingeführt mit der Richtlinie 93/13 der EG über unerlaubte Klauseln in Verbraucherverträgen vom 5. April 1993 (OJL 95/29), hinzuweisen. Es ist zu betonen, dass der polnische Gesetzgeber im Rahmen der Anpassung des polnischen Rechts an die EU- Standards im Gesetz vom 2. März 2000 (Dz. U. Nr. 22, Pos. 271) Vorschriften über Klauseln, die einen Rechtsmissbrauch gegenüber dem Verbraucher bedeuten (sog. unerlaubte Vertragsbestimmungen), zum Zivilgesetzbuch eingeführt hat. Darunter befindet sich der Art. $385^2$ ZGB, der grundsätzlich ein Verzeichnis der unerlaubten Klauseln aus der Richtlinie ist. Folglich besagt der Art. $385^2$ P. 3 ZGB, dass unerlaubt die Bestimmungen sind, die „ausschließen oder wesentlich

---

[21] In der Tat ist die Sache der Aufrechnung im Verhältnis Bank – Bankkunde viel komplizierter, obwohl die schweizerischen Juristen das Gelten von *„l'aura sacre du depot*" betonen. Vgl. P. Engel, Traite des obligations en droit suisse, Neuchâtel 1973, S. 456.

[22] Beispielsweise K. Larenz, Lehrbuch....., S. 261; J. Gernhuber, Die Erfüllung ...., S. 257; R. Stürner in: Jauernig, BGB, 9. Auflage, München 1999, S. 373, 374.

[23] II CKN 403/00, OSN 2001, Nr. 10, Pos. 155; Billigungsglosse von J. Majewski, PPW 2001, Nr.11, S. 22.

einschränken die Aufrechnung der Verbraucherforderung gegen eine Forderung der anderen Partei".

## IV. Prozessuelle Einrede der Aufrechnung

Die bisherigen Erwägungen haben gezeigt, dass die Unterschiede zwischen zwei grundsätzlichen Formen der gesetzlichen Aufrechnung in der Praxis verwischt sind. Ähnlich sind auch die Voraussetzungen der Aufrechnung und ihre Wirkung. Man muss sich auch damit zufrieden geben, dass die Wirksamkeit der außergerichtlichen Aufrechnung, ob *ex lege* oder kraft Willenserklärung, bedeutend von der Annahme durch die Gegenpartei abhängig ist. In der Praxis kommt es oft vor, dass die eine Partei ihren Anspruch geltend macht, obwohl die andere von der Tilgung durch Aufrechnung überzeugt ist. Daher ist sehr wichtig für das gesamte Bild der Aufrechnung, die Rechtslage des Beklagten zu bestimmen. Meiner Meinung nach ist diese Frage – aus der praktischen Sicht – von entschieden größerer Bedeutung als die geringen Differenzen in der Gestaltung der Voraussetzungen für Aufrechnung.

Unser Interesse gilt hier nicht der Widerklage, da in diesem Falle der Kläger seine Forderung direkt geltend macht, also die Aufrechnung nicht zu gebrauchen beabsichtigt. Wir konzentrieren uns auf die Situation, wenn der Beklagte lediglich Klageabweisung fordert (ganz oder teilweise), weil – wie er behauptet - eine Tilgung der Forderung durch Aufrechnung erfolgt ist. Der Beklagte erhebt also die Aufrechnungseinrede, von Natur aus ein Mittel der Verteidigung und nicht der Geltendmachung der Ansprüche. Der Rechtscharakter der Einrede lässt ernste Zweifel aufkommen. Ohne auf die prozessrechtlichen Erwägungen einzugehen, erwähne ich hier nur die wichtigsten Unterschiede bei der Betrachtung der Einrede in verschiedenen Rechtsordnungen.

Nehmen wir zuerst die Feststellung, dass die rechtliche Natur der Aufrechnungseinrede keine Zweifel im französischen Recht aufkommen lässt: sie ist reines Verteidigungsmittel des Beklagten. Die Stellung des französischen Rechts hängt durchaus nicht damit zusammen, dass dort die Aufrechnung *ex lege* erfolgt. Wir machen darauf aufmerksam, das in der Gegenwart die französischen Gerichte die Aufrechnung von Amts wegen nicht berücksichtigen; der Interessierte muss durch die Einrede das Gericht auf die Tilgung der Forderungen hinweisen. Der Unterschied gegenüber dem deutschen, schweizerischen oder polnischen Recht kommt erst bei der gerichtlichen Prüfung der wirksamen Verteidigung des Beklagten zum Vorschein und ist darauf zurückzuführen, dass im französischen Recht die gesetzliche Aufrechnung nur die Forderungen aufgrund eines bestimmten Titels und von bestimmter Höhe betrifft (*liquidité*). Das Gericht prüft natürlich im Verfahren, ob zwischen der in der Klage genannten Forderung und der Forderung des Beklagten die Aufrechnungslage aufgetreten ist, jedoch ist – angesichts der gesetzlichen Erfordernisse der Liquidität der aufzurechnenden Ansprüche - die Aufgabe des Gerichtes einfach. Sie erfordert kein Beweis-verfahren zur Feststellung des Bestehens und des Umfangs der Forderung. Die Prüfung der Einrede erinnert also nicht an ein „Geltendmachen" des Anspruchs, daher taucht der Gedanke, die Einrede als ein Mittel ähnlich der Widerklage anzusehen, nicht auf. Folglich kommt hier das Prinzip voll zur Anwendung, dass „der für die Klage zuständige Richter auch für die Prüfung der Einrede zuständig ist" (*Le juge de l'action est juge de l'exception*).

Die Frage des rechtlichen Charakters der Einrede ist im deutschen Recht aufgetaucht und hängt nicht so sehr mit dem Aufrechnungsmechanismus (erforderliche Willenserklärung) zusammen als mit der Tatsache, dass unter den materiell-rechtlichen Voraussetzungen der Aufrechnung das Erfordernis der Liquidität der Forderung nicht vorhanden ist.[24] Gleichzeitig gibt es im Prozessrecht keine Einschränkungen, wenn es um die Zulässigkeit der Einredeformulierungen geht. Folglich hat der Aufrechnungsberechtigte, gegen den der gegenseitige Gläubiger Klage erhoben hat, die Wahl, ob er die Einrede erhebt oder aber die Widerklage. Mit der Einrede können sogar solche Forderungen zur Aufrechnung gestellt werden, deren Rechtsgrund erklärungsbedürftig ist. Angesichts einer derartigen Regelung ist der Zweifel begründet, ob die Einrede auch tatsächlich ausschließlich das Verteidigungsmittel des Beklagten ist. Schon fünf Jahre nach Inkrafttreten der deutschen Zivilprozessordnung, im Jahre 1884, ist eine Monographie von Schollmeyer erschienen „Die Compensationseinrede im Deutschen Reichs-Civilprozess", in der der Autor den Charakter der Einrede als reines Verteidigungsmittel bestreitet und zu ihrer Bezeichnung den Begriff der „unentwickelten Widerklage" formuliert. Der Begriff fungiert auch gegenwärtig im deutschen Recht.

Die Einrede als Form der Geltendmachung der Ansprüche findet ihre Begründung in einigen Vorschriften der deutschen Zivilprozessordnung. So erlaubt § 145 Abs. 3 ZPO, die Einrede zu gesonderter Prüfung auszugliedern, wenn die Ansprüche zueinander in keinem Zusammenhang stehen; § 302 ZPO sieht die mögliche Sonderentscheidung über die Hauptklage unter zeitweiliger Nichtbeachtung der Einrede vor (sog. Vorbehaltsurteil), was eine Ausnahme von dem allgemeinen Prinzip bedeutet, dass das Gericht über die Einreden nicht gesondert urteilt; § 322 Abs. 2 ZPO verbindet die Rechtskraftwirkung mit dem Urteil, dass die Gegenforderung nicht besteht, was wiederum gegen das Prinzip verstößt, dass die Urteile in den präjudiziellen Fragen die Rechtskraftwirkung nicht gebrauchen.[25] Die Ähnlichkeit der prozessuellen Lösungen hinsichtlich Einrede und Widerklage bewirkt, dass die Rechtssprechung und die Rechtslehre generell den Standpunkt vertreten, dass die Einrede nur vor dem zuständigem Gericht erhoben wird, d.h. wenn das Gericht für Prüfung der Klage und der Einrede zu-

---

[24] Charakteristisch ist, dass laut Art. 120 Abs. 2 schweiz. OR "Der Schuldner kann die Aufrechnung geltend machen, auch wenn eine Gegenforderung bestritten wird".

[25] G. Wagner, Die Aufrechnung im europäischen Zivilprozess, IPRax 1999, Nr. 2, S. 68.

ständig ist. Also falls beispielsweise die Klage vor einem deutschen Gericht und der Gegenanspruch vor einem ausländischen Gericht oder Schiedsgericht erhoben ist, so ist das Prüfen der Einrede im Rahmen des Prozesses unerlaubt. In gewissen Fällen der Aufrechnungseinrede hat das Gericht das Verfahren einzustellen und dem Beklagten eine Frist zu geben, in der dieser den Gegenanspruch vor dem zuständigen Organ geltend macht.[26] Wenn es um die Gerichtszuständigkeit geht, wird die Einrede im deutschen Recht ähnlich wie die Widerklage betrachtet. Es wird jedoch vorausgesetzt, dass die Aufrechnung im Prozess keine Rechtshängigkeit der Gegenforderung begründet.[27]

Zusammenfassend kann man sagen, dass wenn auch die Qualifikation der Einrede im deutschen Recht nicht eindeutig ist, die angeführten Vorschriften, insbesondere § 322 Abs. 2 ZPO, mit der Einrede ein gewisses Prozessrisiko verbinden. Die unbegründete Einrede hat bestimmte negative Konsequenzen für den Beklagten, was den Missbrauch in dem Bereich ausschließen soll, d.h. die Einreden ausschließlich zur Verlängerung des Verfahrens zu nutzen.

Angesichts der dargestellten Regelungen erscheint die Lösung des polnischen Gesetzgebers ungewöhnlich liberal. Der Ausgangspunkt ist die Erwähnung, dass das polnische Zivilgesetzbuch die gesetzliche Aufrechnung nicht auf die sicheren Forderungen von festgelegter Basis und Höhe beschränkt sowie die Bedingung des nahen Zusammenhangs der Ansprüche auf Aufrechnung nicht einführt. Hier ist es auch zu erwähnen, dass das polnische Zivilverfahrensgesetzbuch keine Vorschrift enthält, die – nach dem Vorbild der oben angeführten deutschen Vorschriften – die Aufrechnungseinrede der Widerklage ähnlich stellen wurde. Es wurde zwar in den dreißiger Jahren des 20. Jahrhunderts ein Vorschlag gemacht, ins Gesetz eine Vorschrift über die Rechtskräftigkeit des Urteils über das nicht Existieren der aufzurechnenden Forderung nach Vorbild des § 322 Abs. 2 ZPO aufzunehmen, der aber abgelehnt wurde. Die Zivilverfahrensgesetzbuch von 1932 hat nur die gesonderte Verhandlung „über einen Anspruch, den der Beklagte zur Aufrechnung stellt" vorgesehen, vorausgesetzt, dass er in keinem Zusammenhang mit dem Anspruch des Klägers steht (Art. 239 § 2). Das Gericht konnte dagegen kein Urteil über ausschließliche Ansprüche des Klägers unter Vorbehalt der Modifikation wegen der späteren Prüfung der Einrede fällen. Das heute geltende Zivilverfahrensgesetzbuch von 1964 enthält nicht einmal eine dem Art. 239 § 2 des ehemaligen Rechts ähnliche Vorschrift. Das polnische Recht – sowohl Zivilgesetzbuch als auch das Zivilverfahrensrecht - sehen also keine Einschränkungen vor, wenn es um das Erheben der Einrede der Aufrechnung geht, sowie keine besondere Betrachtung der Einrede angesichts anderer

---

26 Mehr darüber bei G. Wagner, Die Aufrechnung.....; vgl. auch R. Stürner in: Jauernig, BGB, S. 375, 376.

27 R. Stürner in: Jauernig, BGB, S. 376, und ebenda zitierte Rechtsprechung.

prozessualen Einreden.[28] Folglich steht der Beklagte, sobald ihm die Aufrechnung zusteht, vor der Alternative: entweder Widerklage oder Nutzen des Gestaltungsrechts und Erhebung der Einrede. Der Gesetzgeber schränkt die Entscheidungsfreiheit des Beklagten nicht ein.[29] Folge dieser Rechtslage ist die Situation, dass einer eingeklagten sicheren Forderung zur Aufrechnung als Einrede eine Forderung entgegengestellt wird, deren Grund zweifelhaft ist. In der Praxis missbrauchen die Beklagten das ihnen zustehende Rechtsmittel - und erheben - um Zeit zu gewinnen - sogar völlig unbegründete Einreden. Diese „Verteidigung" kostet nichts (Einreden sind gebührenfrei) und ist mit keinem Risiko verbunden.

Die kritische Bewertung des Sachverhaltes liegt der Anschauung zugrunde, die die Einrede als Mittel der Geltendmachung des Beklagtenanspruchs im Prozess qualifiziert. Diese Anschauung vertreten die meisten Prozessualisten.[30] Die Vertreter der materiellen Rechtslehre sind generell der Meinung, dass die Aufrechnungseinrede ausschließlich Verteidigungsmittel des Beklagten ist.[31] Selbstverständlich bestimmt die Stellungnahme viele Fragen näher, nämlich: Zuständigkeit des Gerichts, Rechtshängigkeit (*litis pendente*), Rechtskraftwirkung (*rei iudicatae*), und Unterbrechung des Verjährungslaufes.[32]

Obwohl ich von der Notwendigkeit der Einschränkung der Einredenfreiheit überzeugt bin, schließe ich mich den Stimmen der Zivilisten an, die aufgrund der gültigen Vorschriften keine Anwendungsmöglichkeit - oder Deutungsmöglichkeit - dieser Einschränkungen sehen. Ich finde, dass sie einen legislativen Grund haben müssen; der Formalismus des Prozessrechts ist zweifellos die Garantie der richtigen Verwirklichung des subjektiven Rechts. Um zu beweisen, dass ohne entsprechende Regelung die Folgen der Einrede nicht den Folgen der Gegenanklage gleichgestellt werden können, nehmen wir ein Beispiel. Eine

---

28 Gewisse Einschränkungen gibt es in Sonderverfahren wie dem Urkundenprozess, in dem der Anspruch spätestens bei der Einrede der Zahlungsaufforderung erhoben wird und so wie der Hauptanspruch dokumentiert werden muss (Art. 493 ZVG). Auch in dem vereinfachten Verfahren werden nur die Forderungen aufgerechnet, die im Verfahren geltend gemacht werden (Art. 505 und ff. ZVG).

29 Die Einzelfragen der zeitweisen Beschränkung der Widerklage lasse ich ausser Acht; nach Art. 204 § 1 ZVG, kann die Widerklage „nicht später als in der ersten Verhandlung oder in der Einrede bei Kontumazurteil" erhoben werden.

30 Beispiel: W. Siedlecki, Potrącenie w procesie cywilnym, RPEiS 1968, Nr. 2; J. Krajewski, Z zagadnień potrącenia w procesie cywilnym, NP. 1972, Nr. 4; A. Kuźniar, Funkcje zarzutu potrącenia w procesie cywilnym, Pal. 1974, Nr. 4-5.

31 Beispiel: L. Stępniak, Potrącenie...; A. Torbus, Roszczenie nadające się do potrącenia jako warunek dopuszczalnosci powództwa wzajemnego, Ehrenbuch zu Ehren von Prof. K. Korzan, Katowice 2001.

32 Art. 123 §1 P. 1 ZGB besagt, dass „Die Verjährung wird unterbrochen: 1. durch jede unmittelbar zur Geltendmachung, (...), eines Anspruchs vorgenommene Handlung vor Gericht (...)".

wichtige Wirkung der Gerichtsentscheidung ist die Rechtskraftwirkung und der Ausschluss der erneuten Erhebung desselben Anspruchs vor dem Gericht. Manche Prozessualisten möchten diese Wirkung mit der Einrede verbinden. Da jedoch das Recht keine gesonderte Entscheidung zulässt und das Gericht sich im Urteil nicht auf den Anspruch in der Einrede bezieht, wie kann denn der Umfang der Rechtkraftwirkung in Bezug auf diesen Anspruch festgelegt werden? Meiner Meinung nach kann die Urteilsbegründung allein nur eine schwache Basis der Schlussfolgerungen werden, in welchem Umfang das Gericht die Behauptungen des Beklagten berücksichtigt hat und in wie weit sie abgelehnt wurden.

Das Oberste Gericht hat sich in der besagten Frage indirekt mehrere Male geäußert, indem es konsequent die Stellung einnahm, dass die Einrede, obwohl sie nicht auf einem unbestreitbaren und sicheren Anspruch beruhen muss,[33] ein Verteidigungsmittel des Beklagten ist. Im Urteil von 25. Juni 1997[34] hat das Oberste Gericht erklärt, dass die Einrede der Aufrechnung ungehindert anerkannt werden kann, wenn der Beklagte in einem anderen Verfahren gegen den Kläger eine Forderung erhoben hat. Es hat angenommen, dass beide Verfahren gleichzeitig laufen können. Betont wurde lediglich die "merkbare Inkonsequenz im Handeln des Beklagten", der „sich dem Risiko der Klageabweisung aussetzt, wenn vor dem Verhandlungsschluss festgelegt wird, dass die Forderung durch Aufrechnung mit Gegenforderung getilgt wurde". Im Urteil vom 6. September 1983[35] hat das Oberste Gericht ausdrücklich anerkannt, dass „im anderen Verfahren kann der Gläubiger also seine Forderung geltend machen, sowohl hinsichtlich des Überschusses über den getilgten Teil (den er der Aufrechnung nicht unterzogen hat) als auch hinsichtlich des vom Gericht nicht berücksichtigten aufzurechnenden Teils". Den Gedanken finden wir auch in der These des Beschlusses des OG vom 20. November 1987[36], die lautet: „Die Nichtberücksichtigung der Einrede der Aufrechnung vom Gericht verhindert nicht die spätere Klage auf den Einredegegenstand". In den Begründungen hat das Oberste Gericht betont, dass „Gegenstand der Entscheidung ist der Anspruch des Klägers und nicht des Beklagten erwähnt in seiner Einrede der Aufrechnung". Weiter erzählt das Gericht, dass der Inhalt des Urteils in der Sache, in der die Einrede der Aufrechnung erhoben wurde, „keine negative Entscheidung über die Einrede enthält".

---

33 Zum Beispiel Urteil vom 25. Juni 1997 III CKN 116/97, OSN 1997, Nr. 11, Pos. 184.

34 III CKN 116/97, OSN 1997, Nr. 11, Pos. 184.

35 IV CR 260/83, OSN 1984, Nr. 4 , Pos. 59.

36 III CZP 69/87, OSN 1989, Nr. 4, Pos. 64; in der Begründung ist der Gedanke entfaltet: der Gläubiger „kann in neuer Klage sowohl seine Teilforderung geltend machen – im Umfang, der die Höhe vom Kläger im rechtskräftig geschlossenem Vefahren verfolgt, übersteigt und dadurch in diesem Teil keiner Aufrechnung und Tilgung unterliegt (die unverbrauchte Forderung), als auch die Forderungen zum im vorangehenden Verfahren nicht berücksichtigten Teil geltend machen".

Man kann also glauben, dass, trotz der Kritik seitens der Prozessualisten, in der Rechtsprechung des Obersten Gerichts die Meinung tief verankert ist, die Einrede der Aufrechnung ausschließlich als Verteidigungsmittel des Beklagten zu betrachten. Als vollbegründet sind dagegen die Postulate *de lege ferenda* anzusehen, denn die wechselnde Situation macht neue Regelungen im Zivilverfahrensgesetzbuch erforderlich.

## V. Schlussfolgerungen

Die bisherigen Erwägungen haben gezeigt, dass die Unterschiede zwischen zwei grundsätzlichen Formen der gesetzlichen Aufrechnung in der Praxis verwischt sind. Es scheint, dass die kontinentalen Rechtsordnungen – obwohl mit verschiedenen Instrumenten – eine gemeinsame Idee verwirklichen. Das bedeutet, sie ermöglichen die außergerichtliche Tilgung von Forderungen, ohne reale Leistungen zu bringen. Gleichzeitig bin ich überzeugt, dass man, um ein gesamtes Bild der Aufrechnung in jedem Rechtssystem zu bekommen, man die Lösungen des Zivilrechts und Zivilverfahrensrechts parallel studieren muss. Das erfordert aber eine viel tiefere Analyse.

## Summary: Set-off in Comparative Law

Today the usefulness of an universal application of set-off is undisputed. This, however, does not tell anything about the mechanism and the prerequisites of the set-off in different legal systems.

Although there are provisions on legal set-off independent of the intention of one party in almost all civil codes one may speak of two or even three systems of legal set-off by law (*ipso iure*), also called automatic set-off, (2) set-off by virtue of a declaration of intention by one of the creditors, and (3) set-off on the basis of a decision of a court of justice. The first solution was adopted by the Code Napoleon of 1804. In order to emphasize the automatism the French legislators used three different formulations in Art. 1290 CC. The set-off occurs at the time when it becomes possible. The same mechanism was adopted among others in Belgium, Spain, Italy and Austria. The legal set-off by virtue of a unilateral legal act of the creditor appears for the first time in the German BGB. § 388 BGB says that the set-off takes place by virtue of a declaration of the creditor vis-à-vis the other party. This pattern has been adopted by the Swiss legislation. The Polish legislators chose the same solution (Art. 498 ZGB of 23 April 1964). The first type of legal set-off was developed in French law. It is based on procedural provisions, but functions in fact as an institute of substantive law (*compensation judiciare)*.

After a review of the various mechanism of legal set-off it is possible to set up the thesis that, although one can ascertain theoretical differences between the concepts of European legislators, one should not overestimate their practical importance. For, firstly, there is today – due to the development of French law – no constructions of set-off which separates the discharge of the claims absolutely from the intention of one of the parties. Secondly, the legislations requiring a declaration of intention recognise the effect of this declaration retrospectively. Consequently, they connect the discharge of the reciprocal claims with the beginning of the set-off phase and not with the time when the declaration is made.

The function of payment and the function of execution which are inherent to set-off determine its prerequisites. In general they are: the reciprocity of claims, the similarity (*Gleichartigkeit*, i.e. performances of the same kind) and the possibility of enforcement depending only on the intention of the creditor. The last-mentioned prerequisite found different expressions in the various legislations, for example the requirement that the payment is due, the claim is actionable, that it is not subject to a defence (*Einrede*). It is characteristic, that in spite of the principal importance of reciprocity there are some general exceptions. The most important exceptions concern assignment and sureties. The reasons why legislators exclude the possibility of set-off are also similar. On the one hand the legislators consider this surrogate of performance as a privilege of the creditor. In certain situations the debtor is not worthy of the discharge by a set-off: especially in the cases of obligations to pay damages for an intentional tort or to return something that the creditor has been illegally deprived of. On the other hand the real maintenance of performance (*reale Leistungserhaltung)* is deemed necessary by the legislators. Consequently, they protect in general the claims up to the limit of non-seizability for humanitarian reasons.

The research concerning set-off shows that the differences in substantive law between two principal types of legal set-off are blurred in practice. To get a complete picture of the set-off in each legal system it seems necessary to study also the solutions in the law of civil procedure.

# Sexual Identity and Law - Sex or Gender?

*Dr. Sharon Cowan, University of Warwick*[*]

## Introduction

In this discussion I aim to show that the question of sexual identity in law (and indeed generally) is not at all straightforward.[1] I will demonstrate that questions of sexual identity are complex, and argue that while law tends to look for the absolute truth of someone's sex,[2] the answer to the question as to what sex someone is differs depending on what social or legal context we are in when we ask that question. With this in mind, the following discussion is divided into four main parts. First I will explore what we mean by sex and how that relates to gender. Secondly I will place these complex questions about the definition of sexual identity in the context of English law on transsexuality. Thirdly, I compare issues arising from transsexuality with English law on intersexuality.[3] Finally, I concentrate on recent developments on sexual identity and law in the Canadian context. Unlike English law, Canadian law on marriage has for some time recognised the post-operative sex of transsexuals, and the debates in recent case law have instead related to defining sexual identity in non marriage contexts. The discussion begins with an introduction to the concepts of sex and gender in order to provide a back-drop for my arguments about the legal construction of sexual identity in English and Canadian law.

## 1. Sex and gender - a few words

There has been a well documented move within feminist theory to distinguish between sex and gender (Kessler and McKenna 1985) - **sex** was said to be based on basic biological characteristics - chromosomes, hormones etc., while

---

* Different elements of this paper have been given as presentations at the SLSA conference in Bristol, 2001, and at UBC Law School, Vancouver in 2002, and my ideas have been improved in the light of helpful comments at those times. I would like particularly to thank the Centre for Feminist Legal Studies at UBC for allowing me the space and time to work on these ideas. The work has also benefited from comments given by Simon Halliday and Gillian Calder, to whom I am most grateful. Finally, I am pleased to have been given the opportunity to present these ideas at the Warwick-Giessen colloquium in September 2002, and I thank all those at that meeting who listened and talked with me afterwards.

1 In this paper I refer to sex, gender and sexual identity. I have used sexual identity to mean the way in which one defines oneself as a sexed being. The terms sex and gender are interrogated throughout the discussion.

2 See Foucault (1984: 57-61) for a discussion of sex as the "truth" of oneself.

3 The term intersex is used to refer to those whose biological sex is deemed ambiguous (neither clearly male nor female) at birth. See discussion below.

**gender** was explained as the social manifestations and practices associated with biological maleness or femaleness. Feminists emphasised this distinction because they wanted to demonstrate that differences between men and women which were widely assumed to be natural (for example behaving in a "feminine" manner in terms of dress, language and so on) and which therefore provided the basis for differential treatment, were in fact part of gender roles and therefore socially produced and escapable rather than natural and inevitable. Femininity was a construct while femaleness was biological. That this distinction has become a well known part of mainstream social and legal thinking about sex/gender is demonstrated by the judgement of Dame Butler-Sloss and Lord Justice Walker in the recent Court of Appeal case of *Bellinger v Bellinger*[4]:

> "The words 'sex' and 'gender' are sometimes used interchangeably, but today more frequently denote a difference. Mrs Cox [the lawyer in the case] submitted that gender was broader than sex. Her suggested definition was that 'gender' related to culturally and socially specific expectations of behaviour and attitude, mapped onto men and women by society. It included self-definition, that is to say, what a person recognised himself to be... It would seem from the definition proposed by Mrs Cox, with which we would not disagree, that it would be impossible to identify gender at the moment of the birth of the child."

Despite widespread legal and social reliance on the sex/gender distinction, from the late 1980s onwards some feminists began to argue that this distinction between sex and gender was not quite so clear cut, and in fact moved to question whether it existed at all. Recently then feminist scholars have turned more attention to the question of the social construction of sex (Lacey 1997: 65), now suggesting that the terms sex and gender are interconnected, not only in the sense that female sex is assumed to give rise to a feminine gender but, as is claimed by many recent theorists such as Judith Butler, also because sex itself (the interpretation of bodies) is a social construction. Here the main argument is that sex, or sexed bodies, are produced through discourses about gender and sexuality (Nelson 1999: 337).

Thus, according to Judith Butler,[5] there is no biological pre-existing sex through which gender and sexuality emerge. The sexed body is not a blank page awaiting gender and sexuality to be written in (Butler 1990: 147). Instead, "gender is a performance that *produces* the illusion of an inner sex or essence or psychic gender core" (1991: 28). Rather than argue that sexuality and gender are only important because they relate to sex as the primary and crucial organising principle within society, we might just as easily argue that we should focus on *(hetero)sexuality* as the primary organising principle. In this view, sex and gender are only important because heterosexuality is crucial to producing fami-

4 [2002] Fam. 150, at 160.
5 Following Foucault (1984: 152, 157).

lies and reproducing capitalism. At any rate, what Butler argues is that we should not focus on whether sex/gender or sexuality is more important, but rather on the relationship between these concepts. For her then, sex is socially constructed (1993: 5-6).

What this means in practice is accepting that our definition or understanding of sex (as understood to mean biology, or sexed bodies), and what criteria should be used to decide sex, seem to shift in different contexts, both social and temporal. What I intend to do now is look at "constructions" of sex in England and Canada, in both legal and medical discourse, through a discussion of the treatment of people who are transsexual, and people who are born intersex.

## 2. English law - the legal definition of sex

In England, according to section 11(c) of the *Matrimonial Causes Act 1973*, parties to marriage must be respectively male and female, otherwise the marriage is null and void.

English law does not, therefore, recognise the post-operative sex of a transsexual for the purposes of marriage; a post-operative female transsexual cannot marry a man since she is regarded, despite surgery, as being biologically male. This was confirmed by the case of *Corbett v Corbett*[6] which laid down a biological test for sex in the area of marriage.

*Corbett* is the case that has historically informed Commonwealth judicial decisions on this subject, including Canada and Australia, both of which have subsequently reformed their law in this area. At the moment, the UK is one of only four countries in Europe (alongside Albania, Andorra and Ireland) that does not legally recognise the post-operative sex of transsexuals. It seems this is about to change as part of a forthcoming announcement from the Lord Chancellor,[7] and in response to a very recent challenge to the law in this area by way of the decision of the European Court of Human Rights in *Goodwin v UK*.[8] However until the law changes, the case of *Corbett* is still the leading case on the legal definition of sex in the UK. It continues to be authoritatively cited, as in the recent English cases of *Bellinger*, and *W v W* which I will examine shortly. It seems important then to discuss briefly the law as applied in *Corbett* in order to demonstrate how its principles have been influential on the development of English law on sexual identity.

6 (otherwise Ashley) [1970] 2 All E.R. 33.

7 See Claire Dyer "Sex change victory after 30 years" Guardian, 10 December 2002.

8 (2002) 35 E.H.R.R. 18. The judges held that by refusing to recognise the post-operative sex of transsexuals, the UK was violating Articles 8 (the right to respect for private life) and 12 (the right to marry and found a family) of the European Convention on Human Rights.

*Corbett v Corbett*

April Ashley was registered as a boy at birth, but at the age of 35 underwent sex reassignment surgery, lived as a woman and married a man. However, the relationship failed and her husband tried to have the marriage annulled on the basis that the marriage was void since, he argued, April Ashley was not really a woman. The judge, Mr Justice Ormrod, held that the decision as to the validity of the marriage turned on the "**true sex**" of the parties. Since April was a boy **at birth**, she remained a man despite the reassignment surgery. The judge laid down a biological test for sex, stating that there are three things to consider in this respect - chromosomes, gonads and genitals. If they are congruent - that is, if each lines up as being male at birth, the individual is deemed to be male, and remains male even after sex reassignment. If these three factors are not congruent, that is if they don't line up together, it was held, priority is to be given to genital factors. Thus the court decided that sex is fixed at birth at the latest and surgery could not change one's "true sex". As was stated by counsel for the respondent in *Corbett*, the law knows only two sexes.

Contrary to opinion in a previous case,[9] Mr Justice Ormrod decided that sex with a person who has a surgically constructed vagina, is not ordinary and complete intercourse. The implication then is that a male to female transsexual cannot ever, as a woman, consummate a marriage. There are several things to notice about the judgment at this point. Firstly, Ormrod J made it clear he was not deciding the legal test for sex per se, but rather the meaning of male and female **in marriage cases**. This left open the way for courts in other areas of, for example criminal law, to interpret this decision as only referring to marriage, and therefore as distinguishable.

Ormrod J states that although April Ashley may be of female gender psychologically, to argue that she should be treated as a woman in marriage is to confuse sex with gender. He says very clearly, "Marriage is a relationship which depends on sex not gender. Since the basis of sexual difference in marriage is biology rather than psychology, she cannot ever legally marry a man. As Katherine O'Donovan points out, sex is therefore not a matter of choice in law; rather it is an essential biological characteristic (1993: 50). Again the distinction is made between natural, biological sex and socially produced gender.

This is the legacy of *Corbett*. Although this was a decision of the High Court, and therefore was of persuasive rather than binding authority in future High Court cases, *Corbett* became the referent for subsequent cases dealing with the issue of how to decide the sexual status of post-operative transsexuals

---

9 *SY v SY* [1962] (a case involving a woman with a vagina which was surgically lengthened to enable her to take part in sexual intercourse), where the court said by way of observation that a woman with a surgically constructed vagina probably could consummate a marriage.

in English law. The case has never been overruled by a domestic court, though it has been challenged by the recent decision of *Goodwin v UK*. And although Ormrod J explicitly referred to the fact that this decision was made in the context of marriage law only, a challenge to this decision in other areas of law was not faced until the case of *R v Matthews* [1997], some 27 years later.[10]

*R v Matthews*[11]

This fairly recent Crown Court case in English criminal law held that a post-operative male to female transsexual with a surgically constructed vagina could be raped *per vaginam* and was therefore for the purposes of this area of law a woman.

The issue of the rape of a transsexual person has also been raised in other countries. For example, in Australia legislation was passed in 1991 stating that in the context of rape law, vagina includes a surgically constructed vagina (Sharpe 1998: 31). In Canada, sexual assault law is gender-neutral, and sexual assault can be committed through the penetration of any orifice by any object or body part, and thus includes the penetration of a surgically constructed vagina.[12] Recent UK government proposals contained within the White Paper on Sexual Offences have suggested that the law in England will soon be changed to explicitly include those with surgically constructed vaginas within the category of possible rape victims.[13] It is unclear as yet whether or not "vagina" will be interpreted so as to include those which are surgically constructed. Therefore transsexuals will be deemed to be women for the purposes of this law, or whether the surgically constructed vagina will be specifically legislated for so as to provide for a specific category of transsexual rape victims. However the recent European decision of *Goodwin v UK* has been applied in an employment discrimination context in a way that suggests that male to female transsexuals will be considered to be women rather than a special category in themselves.[14]

At any rate, the logical implication of the English case of *Matthews* is that since a post-operative transsexual woman can be raped, it should be the case that a marriage can be consummated even if the wife has a surgically constructed vagina. This question was not explicitly raised in the case, however, and had not been raised subsequently until the case of *W v W*, discussed be-

---

10 The question as to the legal sex status of transsexuals was raised in a criminal law context by the case of *R v Tan* [1983] Q.B. 1053, where the court relied on *Corbett* and defined the transsexual male to female in the case as being legally male.

11 (1997) Crim. L.R.

12 Canadian Criminal Code paragraphs 271-3. This position of gender neutrality is also reflected in the treatment of transsexuals in Canada, as discussed below, whereby law does not try to fit transsexuals within the either male or female binary equation, but rather takes a more "gender neutral" view of transsexuality.

13 See details of the proposed Bill at www.protectingthepublic.homeoffice.gov.uk.

14 *Chief Constable of West Yorkshire v A (No. 2)* Times, 14 November 2002.

low.[15] By implication this conflicts with *Corbett*. It also shows that questions to do with sexual identity have historically been given different consideration depending on the area of law in which they are asked.

How has *Corbett* affected subsequent transsexuality cases? The most recent UK case is *Bellinger*.

*Bellinger v Bellinger*[16]

Mrs Bellinger was registered as male at birth and at the age of 20 married a woman. The relationship dissolved four years later. After eight years of counselling, Mrs B underwent male to female sex reassignment surgery, and three months later in 1981 married a man with whom she is still currently living. In order to clarify the legal status of her marriage, and her own sexual identity, Mrs B applied to the court for a declaration that she is validly married to her husband. The court held that in line with section 11(c) of the 1973 Act, parties to a marriage have to be male and female. The criteria for deciding the sex of a transsexual, the High Court said, was the test applied in *Corbett* - chromosomal, genital and gonadal, and Mrs Bellinger's petition was dismissed. This case was appealed in 2001 and the Court of Appeal affirmed the decision of the lower court. The appeal to the House of Lords is due to be heard in January 2003. However this may be circumvented by the Lord Chancellor's forthcoming announcement about reform in this area.

While the judge in *Bellinger* follows the decision in *Corbett*, he is sympathetic to the campaign for a change in the law relating to transsexual marriage and sexual status. All three Court of Appeal judges also said that there was "momentum for change" in the legal stance towards transsexuals, and that the government should move swiftly to produce a consultation paper on changes to the law.[17]

The regulation of sexual identity in England has been inconsistent; a transsexual woman is recognised as a woman for some purposes (e.g. rape) but not for others (e.g. marriage, or birth certificate changes). Medically speaking, a transsexual's post-operative sexual identity is recognised across the board - no exceptions are made, for example, in the context of marriage. The question

---

15 Forthcoming changes to English law that will validate the post-operative sex of a transsexual, discussed above, suggest that for the purposes of marriage law, a male to female transsexual will be deemed able to consummate a marriage.

16 [2002] Fam. 150 (Ct of Appeal); [2001] 1 F.L.R. 389 (High Court). The discussion here focuses on the decision of the High Court unless otherwise stated.

17 They referred to the Home Office Report of the Interdepartmental Working Group on Transsexual People, published in April 2000. There was in addition a consultation paper published by the Scottish organisation "Equality Network" on proposals for legal recognition of transsexuals, published in September 2002. There has therefore been some consultation on the issue, but the suggestions of the working group have not as yet been implemented.

arises here then - if medicine allows a change in an individual's sexual identity to be generally applicable, why doesn't law? Is it because law has a vested interest in maintaining certain kinds of sexual identities or (heterosexual) families?[18] Is "sex" a medical question or a legal question? It appears that judicial decisions around sexual identity are a mixture of both. While it may seem as though law has more power to define a person's sex than medicine, both in terms of the practical decisions made in marriage and birth certificate cases, and in terms of the symbolic power which law gives to sexual difference. At the same time however we see within the cases on transsexuality that law is simultaneously turning to medicine to provide definitions of sex, in order that these can be co-opted or utilised by law.[19]

Recent research (accepted by court in *Bellinger* and in *W v W*)[20] has suggested that sexual identity may not be determined before or at birth, but is rather a process that continues in the brain even after birth. Indeed, further experiments on the brain, it was stated, may "reveal further indications of gender". While there is still an obvious reliance on biology and medicine here, it seems that Ormrod J's test of sex = sex at birth rather than gender, may be being undermined.

Clearly then there have been developments in medical knowledge and opinion since *Corbett*, as acknowledged in *W v W* (discussed below) and *Bellinger*, and reflected in *Goodwin v UK*, which demonstrate that the *Corbett* test is no longer appropriate in cases involving the determination of sexual identity.

I turn now look at the legal status of those who are born intersex in the UK, as this serves to show up some continuities and some contradictions in the legal (and medical) decisions around sexual identity.

## 3. Intersexuality in English Law

First of all I want to discuss what is meant by intersex. The term hermaphrodite has been used in the past to describe such individuals, but the term intersex has now been adopted by those in the medical profession and those themselves born intersex.[21] The roots of the word hermaphrodite are from Greek my-

---

18 Sharpe (2001) argues that legal acceptance and acknowledgement of transsexual identities only takes place within a heterosexual framework – i.e. only those transsexuals who have surgery and conform to gender expectations of their assigned sex, including forming heterosexual relationships, can legitimately be accepted in their new sexual identity.

19 Some theorists characterise these dialogues as kinds of power struggles between law and medicine. See for example Smart (1989).

20 Charles, J in *W v W* refers to research by Professor Gooren, reported in *Nature*, November 1995, vol. 378, p. 68.

21 See for example the website of the UK Intersex Society – www.ukia.co.uk, and that of the Intersex Society of North America – www.isna.org.

thology and there is much written on the history of hermaphrodites.[22] Here though I simply want to emphasise that as far as science, and particularly medicine, is concerned, we have moved from a pre-19th century perspective of there being one sex, where female genitalia was seen as merely a less developed form of male genitalia, to a post-19th century belief in the existence of two clear and distinct sexes (Laqueur 1990). Those who fall outside this clear binary system are termed to be hermaphrodite, or more commonly now, intersex.

So how do these questions of the legal status of sex affect those who are born intersex? There is not much in the way of documented legal disputes involving intersex individuals.[23] However, the question was discussed in a recent UK case about a woman who was born intersex who came before the court to have her sex decided for the purposes of marriage.

*W v W*[24]

In this recent High Court case, W (the wife) was registered as male at birth, despite being of indeterminate sex. W behaved and dressed like a girl and at puberty developed breasts and female body shape. Her adoptive father, who had always wanted a boy, forced her (aged 15) to take testosterone injections, which failed to have effect. When threatened with further injections W ran away. From her late teenage years she dressed and behaved as a woman. In her thirties she had hormone treatment and later gender reassignment surgery. Her first marriage was annulled on the grounds that the parties were not respectively male and female, as required by s11(c) of the *Matrimonial Causes Act 1973*. When her second marriage failed, W issued a petition for divorce while her husband sought a decree of nullity on the grounds that W was not female. W fought this petition because, she said, she was female and wanted to be recorded as such on her birth certificate, and to be allowed the legal right to remarry as a woman.

In *W v W* it was held that both physical and psychological factors should be taken into account when deciding whether someone is male or female. Expert medical opinion in the case was that considering all the evidence, if a decision had to made as to W's **biological** sex status, it would be (albeit borderline) male. The court however stated that the decision as to which sex an individual should be assigned should not be based purely on the basis of which side of the male/female dichotomy the genitals features fall - even where those genital features line up with other factors such as gonads and chromosomes. While W seemed to be marginally more biologically male than female, the court accepted that her bodily habitus and gender orientation were female. W was in fact

22 See for example Foucault's Introduction to Hercule Barbin (1980), and Judith Butler's (1990) comments on this; Thomas Laqueur (1990); Alice Dreger (1998); Anne Fausto-Sterling (2000).

23 Although see Campbell (1998).

24 [2001] Fam.111.

physically "inter-sex", but for the purposes of marriage, said the court, W was a woman.

The judge in this case, Charles J, quotes at length from *Corbett*, and comes to the conclusion that the biological test laid down in that case is not satisfied here, because the three biological considerations - gonads, genitals and chromosomes - are not congruent. He does not explicitly disagree with the decision in *Corbett*, but rather distinguishes *W v W* from *Corbett* on the basis that *Corbett* was about transsexuality, whilst this is a case about a person who was born intersex. This case was also decided four days before the first instance decision in *Bellinger*. While it was thought that *W v W* would have an impact on transsexuality cases, it was distinguished by the judges in *Bellinger* and *Corbett* was applied instead.

There are several interesting points about the judgment in *W v W*. Firstly (and as *Matthews* would suggest), Charles J held that after surgery, W **was** capable of consummating the marriage even though her vagina was surgically constructed. Charles J also stated that the capacity of a person to consummate a marriage *as* a male or female was not a decisive factor in deciding whether the person *is* a male or female for the purposes of marriage. In this case, W (the wife) could not have had sexual intercourse at all without surgical intervention. Therefore, simply because W could not consummate the marriage as a woman without first having some sort of surgery did not mean that she was not a woman for the purposes of marriage. This reasoning leads to two interesting conclusions: one, that although this is not a transsexual case, Charles J is saying that someone with a constructed vagina is capable of consummating marriage - clearly contrary to Ormrod J's opinion in *Corbett* - which has implications for future transsexuality cases; and two, that Charles J clearly considers the legal meaning of "woman" in marriage to be independent of whether or not the "woman" in question can have penile-vaginal penetrative sexual intercourse, thus moving away from relying on a purely reproductive and biological definition of woman.

Secondly, it is interesting that while in terms of biological factors W was found "on balance" to be male, the court held that she was female. Evidently then it is not merely biological factors that should now be taken into account. Charles J did not expressly contradict *Corbett* here, but rather distinguished *Corbett* on the grounds that *W v W* was not a case about a transsexual, and therefore he was not bound by *Corbett* or by purely biological considerations. Charles J maintained that the *Corbett* test in fact is not satisfied because the three factors normally taken into account (gonads, genitals and chromosomes) are not congruent. Following *Corbett*, if these factors are congruent, the biological test is appropriate and sex is fixed at birth. However, if the factors are not congruent the biological test is not appropriate, as in *W v W*, and different conclusions result - that is, sex need not be considered as fixed at birth, and psychological characteristics can be considered. Clearly then the way in which we decide a person's sex for the purposes of the law depends upon what test we use. The implication is, again contrary to *Corbett*, that there is no once and for all truth of sex. Sex is not an immutable essence but differently constructed depending on context.[25]

So are those born intersex male or female? Charles J says that we could come to the conclusion that those who do not satisfy the biological test in *Corbett* are neither men nor women, but he himself does not support this view. This is because to support such a view would create a third category "the boundaries of which would not be clear."[26] Charles J is here demonstrating law's discomfort with unclear boundaries, especially in the area of sex. He maintains that sex can be decided with the "benefit of hindsight",[27] and that this is simply a case of W being mistakenly registered as a boy at birth. Charles J clearly wants to come to a definite conclusion about W's sex for the purposes of marriage, and here he decides that she is a woman. There is still evidence therefore of his reliance upon biology.

However, **at the same time** as this "what is the true sex?" position is adopted, Charles J recognises that in this case W "true" sex is inter-sex, but that she has to be assigned a sex for the legal purpose of marriage. It seems here that Charles J acknowledges that there is no objective and conclusive reality of sex which is generally applicable, and thus again implicitly contradicting the view in *Corbett* that there is a "truth" of sex. Perhaps most revealing, and with a surprisingly social constructionist tone, Charles J says of the categories of sexual identity: "As I have said in my judgement, care should be taken with the use of the labels or descriptions "inter-sex" or "physical inter-sex" and it is more important to have regard to the factors which lead them to be being applied or possibly applied."[28]

It would seem that the judge here tries to achieve the desired result by any means possible (and thus an internally inconsistent argument). On the one hand he has recourse to biology and a hindsight view of W's **real** sex, yet on the other and simultaneously, he rejects traditional sex categories in three ways: the recognition that her physical sex is not sufficient to define her as either male or female; the realisation of the unsatisfactory nature of sexual identity labels; and the acceptance that W's psychology also has to be taken into account. This in my view shows the tension between law's need for clear bounded sexual identity categories, alongside the realisation that these categories and their boundaries are inadequate to describe the spectrum of human sexual identities.

---

25 Sharpe (2001) has a slightly less optimistic view of the implications of the decision in *W v W*.

26 [2001] Fam. 111, at 144.

27 [2001] Fam. 111, at 132.

28 [2001] Fam. 111, at 146.

It is also worth pointing out here that if the UK were to allow same sex marriage these issues would not be as important, since it would not matter in marriage case which sex a transsexual or intersexual person truly was. It may however still be important for individuals to be able to have their birth certificate reflect what they identify as being their true sex. Hopefully this will soon be the position for English law, as prompted by the decision in *Goodwin v UK*.

## 4. Canadian discussions of sexual identity – what makes a woman?

First, the issues of deciding sex for the purposes of marriage no longer arises in a Canadian context. This is because by way s.36 of the *Vital Statistics Act 1990*, if a person has surgery to change their anatomical sex, they can apply to have their birth certificate changed to reflect their post-operative sex. The *Corbett* situation does not occur. Where the issues of deciding sex have come up in Canada in recent years are within a human rights context and relate to cases about for example, deciding whether a transsexual male to female can use women's bathrooms in public places;[29] or whether male to female transsexual can be allowed to volunteer in a rape crisis centre, or lesbian drop in centre; and whether a convicted male to female transsexual should be incarcerated in a male or a female prison.

In the 1999 case of *Mamela v Vancouver Lesbian Connection*,[30] the court held that by not allowing Mamela, a (pre-operative) male to female transsexual, to participate as a volunteer in the drop in centre, Vancouver Lesbian Connection was discriminating against her on the grounds of sex. The earlier case of *Sheridan v Sanctuary Investments Ltd. (No. 3)* found that discrimination against a transsexual is *by definition* discrimination on the basis of sex.[31] According to the judge in *Sheridan*:

> "In my view… I am satisfied that discrimination against a transsexual constitutes discrimination on the basis of sex. Whether the discrimination is regarded as differential treatment because the transsexual falls outside the traditional man/woman dichotomy… or because male-to-female transsexuals are regarded as a subgroup of females (and vice versa)… the result is the same: transsexuals ex-

---

29 As in *Sheridan v Sanctuary Investments Ltd.* (No. 3) (1999) 33 C.H.R.R. D/467 (B.C.H.R.T.).

30 36 C.H.R.R. D/318 (B.C.H.R.T.).

31 The courts came to the same conclusion in the English case of *P v S and Cornwall County Council* [1996] All E.R. (EC) 397, although on the slightly different basis that a transsexual suffers because they are compared with those in the sex they are deemed to belong to before surgery.

perience discrimination because of the lack of congruence between the criteria that determine sex."[32]

In *Mamela*, the court accepted the petitioner's self-identification as a transsexual lesbian female, who does not identify as a woman because she thinks that "woman" is a political construct which is always defined in relation to man. The court does not question this self-identification, and unlike the British courts, does not spend any time debating the meaning of these terms "lesbian" or "female", much less woman. The case turns on a finding of fact that M is a transsexual. There is no verbal gymnastic process whereby law tries to fit M into either the male or the female category. She is defined as a transsexual and is treated according to her membership of that category. Her sex, in the traditional binary sense, is not defined.

In the case of *Kavanagh v Canada*,[33] the court did discuss the question of what it means to "live as a woman" and the context of this question is that of trying to find a place for a pre-operative male to female transsexual within the prison system. In this case, the court concedes that neither male nor female prisons are appropriate for Kavanagh because she falls outside the traditional male/female dichotomy, and as such her placement in either prison would cause problems. Equally inappropriate is a dedicated unit for male to female transsexuals (due to their small number within the system). The lesser of two evils, they conclude to house Kavanagh within a male prison but to give her extra support and attention. The court here seems to accept again that to try to fit transsexuals within the male/female binary is extremely difficult, both practically and conceptually, and perhaps not appropriate.

More recently the case of *Nixon v Vancouver Rape Relief Society*[34] has brought these questions of categorisation strongly into the forefront. Kimberly Nixon, a male to female transsexual, brought an application to the Human Rights Tribunal that she had been discriminated against on the grounds of sex by Vancouver Rape Relief (VRR). She had tried to volunteer as a helper at VRR's counselling service for rape victims and had been turned away. VRR tried to justify its actions on the basis that she was not a woman, in the sense that she had lived some of her life as a man, and therefore had not undergone the social and lived experience of being treated as a woman living under patriarchy. She would not therefore, they argued, be able to relate properly to women rape victims coming to VRR for advice. Women in a rape crisis centre, they submitted, need a safe and unambiguous space, and this could not be the case if counsellors were transsexual women.

---

32 (1999) 33 C.H.R.R. D/467 (B.C.H.R.T.) paragraph 93. Section 13 of the 1996 Human Rights Code protects against discrimination in employment, and section 8 protects against discrimination in relation to accommodation, services or facilities.

33 [2001] C.H.R.D. No. 21 (Q.L.).

34 [2002] B.C.H.R.T.D. no. 1 (Q.L.).

Interestingly however, in contrast to the legal situation in the UK, both parties accepted that sex and gender exist along a continuum.[35] The arguments of counsel for Rape Relief acknowledged that "…it is common ground that sex and gender falls along a continuum and is not binary, thus raising the question of which distinctions on that continuum are non-discriminatory."[36]

Importantly then, Nixon was accepted legally as a woman – the question posed by VRR was whether or not she had the qualifications as a woman to provide the services required by VRR clients. They claimed a bona fide occupational requirement that their volunteers have life-long experience of being a woman. Using a social rather than a biological argument, the implication of the VRR submissions to the court was that Nixon was not "woman enough."[37] This argument was ultimately rejected by the court.

In the end the court held that VRR had discriminated against Nixon on the basis of sex, and she was awarded damages for injury to dignity.[38] However the argument in this case centred upon "what makes a woman". Polarised views were adopted and the case rather unfortunately split the Canadian legal (and other) feminist communities down the centre. However the tribunal member, while dealing with the issue of discrimination, does not really give any guidance as to **how** we should decide an individual is male or female, or in fact under what circumstances it may be important to make that judgement in the first place. The finding is that Nixon is transsexual and has suffered discrimination on the grounds of sex. And while it is accepted in the case by all the parties and the judge, that sex and gender exist on a continuum, we are no closer to knowing when it will be important to defend clear binary male/female boundaries of sex (as was suggested in *Kavanagh*) and when it is unimportant as to whether an individual fits our traditional man/woman categories. As Christine Boyle, co-counsel for Nixon said, "which distinctions on that continuum are non-discriminatory?"[39]

## Conclusions

These discussion demonstrates that this is a complex and difficult area, and that there may be no way of effectively judging once and for all a person's sex-

---

35 Paragraph 13.

36 See the argument of co-counsel Christine Boyle, cited on Vancouver Rape Relief's website at www.rapereliefshelter.bc.ca.

37 While this is clearly a social argument, it is so deterministic about what it means to have social experience of being brought up as a woman, that it may as well be based on biological considerations. This point was made in the judgement - see *Nixon v Vancouver Rape Relief Society* (2002) B.C.H.R.T.D. 1 para 202.

38 Kimberly Nixon was awarded $7,500 (Canadian), the highest amount ever awarded by the tribunal.

39 See footnote 36.

ual identity. English law has historically been reluctant to accept the post-operative sex of transsexuals, though this position seems about to change. Canadian law for some time seems to have avoided the question of the "true" nature of sex in marriage cases, but rather has had to address difficult questions of what exactly it means to be woman in society, and whether there are any circumstances under which it will be important (litigious) as to which category an individual is assigned. While English law has grappled with questions of sex, Canadian law has concentrated on questions of gender. Although the two jurisdictions seem to be dealing with sexual identity from different perspectives, the underlying issue appears to come down to the same question * what makes a woman?

Two general issues are raised by these developments. First, whether someone is considered legally male or female may depend on the context (jurisdiction, area of law and so on) of the question and it also depends on who is asking the question * for example is it medical or a legal question * and for what purpose.

Secondly, while transsexuality and intersex people may challenge our current categories of sex and gender because the individuals do not fit the categories, law may in fact go down the road of further entrenching binary categories of sex, but simply allowing people to choose which one they wish to adopt. The position in Canada and the proposed changes in England, while allowing transsexual people to marry in their adopted sex, still leave intact the idea that the world of sexual identity is based on a male/female distinction * the perception is still that really there are only two sexes, even if we are always unclear as to how that distinction is to be made. And transsexuals and intersexuals must be assigned to one of those two categories (the most suitable category being the one where their bodies and genders can be matched up) in order to make sense of their identities. This does not challenge the sex/gender dichotomy. Neither, according to Sharpe (2001), does it question the heterosexual framework of families or partnerships. And, not least, this approach does not address the issue of how to deal with a transsexual who does not want or is unable to have reassignment surgery. Is such an individual both male and female? Or neither?

Katherine O'Donovan argues, as was accepted in the cases discussed above, that "even" scientists accept that it is most likely that "sex" is best represented by a continuum rather than a binary (1993: 51). This raises many questions as to whether and when we should be allowed to choose our own sex, and whether we ought to perpetuate firm sexual identity categories at all. The above discussion also highlights the trouble that law has in mediating the tension between the need for clear boundaries around its sexual identity categories, and the overwhelming evidence that such labels and categories are inadequate. At any rate the cases discussed above offer us an opportunity to seriously rethink the way in which we treat sexuality, gender and sexual identity in law.

## Bibliography


*Barbin, H.*: Being the recently discovered memoirs of a nineteenth century hermaphrodite (trans. by Richard McDougall) (New York: Pantheon, 1980)

*Butler, J.* (1990*)*, Gender Trouble: Feminism and the subversion of identity (New York: Routledge)

*Butler, J.* (1991) "Imitation and gender insubordination" in Fuss, D. (ed.) Inside/Out: lesbian theories, gay theories (New York: Routledge)

*Butler, J.* (1993) Bodies that Matter: on the discursive limits of 'sex' (New York: Routledge)

*Campbell, A.* (1998) "Successful Sex in Succession: Sex in dispute – the Forbes-Sempill case and possible implications" Juridical Review 5, 257-79

*Dreger, A.* (1998) Hermaphrodites and the medical Invention of Sex (London: Harvard University Press)

Equality Network (2002) Proposals for the legal recognition of the gender identity of transsexual people in Scotland (Edinburgh: Equality Network)

*Fausto-Sterling, A.* (2000) Sexing the body: Gender politics and the construction of sex (New York: Basic Books)

*Foucault, M.* (1984) The History of Sexuality: An Introduction (London: Peregrine)

Home Office (2000) Report of the Interdepartmental Working Group on Transsexual People (London: Home Office)

*Kessler, S.* and *McKenna, W.* (1985) Gender: an ethnomethodological approach (Chicago: University of Chicago Press)

*Lacey, N.* (1997) 'On the subject of sexing the subject' in Naffine and Owen (eds) Sexing the Subject of Law (North Ryde, NSW: LBC Information Services)

*Laqueur, T.* (1990) Making Sex: body and gender from the Greeks to Freud (Camb, Mass; London: Harvard University Press)

*Nelson, L.* (1999) "Bodies (and spaces) do matter: the limits of performativity" Gender Place and Culture Vol. 6, No. 4, 331-353

*O'Donovan, K.* (1993) Family Law Matters (London: Pluto Press)

*Sharpe, A.* (2001) Transgender Jurisprudence: Dysphoric bodies of law (London: Cavendish)

*Smart, C.* (1989) Feminism and the Power of Law (London: Routledge)

# Contract Law and the Inclusion of Terms and Conditions in the Case of Trading via Commercial Internet Platforms

*Prof. Dr. Andreas Müglich, University of Applied Sciences Gelsenkirchen/Recklinghausen*

## A. Introduction

The information society is changing the lifestyle of citizens worldwide and at the same time the fundamental mechanisms of the world economy. E-Commerce is the major catchword that describes this process in particular. One of the main ideas of E-commerce is to ease the flow of goods by breaking the paper bottleneck, by setting up a system of electronic communication, software agents (automated computer systems) act autonomously to locate goods and services. But the term e-commerce should not be mixed up with the broader category of electronic business. The latter category encloses not only questions of the formation of contracts but also consists of services such as online support, account maintenance, operation of database services (selling information), commodities by means of computer telecommunications networks and others which are connected with commercial transactions. Thus the notion of the term Electronic Business is broder than the understanding of E-commerce. Therefore e-commerce is mostly defined as:

> "The purchase of goods, services or other financial transactions in which the interactive process is mediated by information or digital technology at both, locationally separate ends of the interchange."[1]

Various estimates suggest that about 80% of the total E-commerce value is allocated in the business-to-business segments.[2] But not only the movement of goods and transportation services will increase to a great extent. At the same time E-commerce will also change business practices. Online-marketplaces will create new types of tradingtools and supply chain communities. Some predictions are assuming that online-marketplaces will also alter the relationship between seller and buyers. But nevertheless it is doubtfull if E-commerce really raises legal issuses which are novel. This paper examines the question whether the existing law is flexible enough to deal with such issues.

---

1 ACEA discussion paper: e-commerce, freight distribution and the truck industry, p. 5 (http://www.acea.be/ACEA/e-commerce_-_freight_distribution_and_the_truck_industry.pdf).

2 Auswirkungen neuer Informations- und Kommunikationstechniken auf Verkehrsaufkommen und innovative Arbeitsplätze im Verkehrsbereich; Bericht der Bundesministerien für Verkehr, Bau- und Wohnungswesen, Wirtschaft und Technologie, Bildung und Forschung 2001, p. 15.

## I. Reasons for making use of Internet Trading Platforms

Some phenomena which are associated with e-commerce, simplified business transactions in part. The role of geographic distance in forming business relationship is reduced and the barriers to entry into the retail business are lower. Platform operators usually offer their customers a standardized solution package geared to the needs of a customary user. These tools should help him to place his procurement and collaboration processes with suppliers and engineers on a completely electronic level. Users of Commercial internet platform are expecting, that they as suppliers can meet the decision-makers of potential customers in strategic sourcing, thus receiving the opportunity of being taken into consideration when spot buys or long-term contracts are awarded. Buyers and product engineers receive an overview of the capacities and production features of vast numbers of suppliers and can make pretty easily a comparison. Through electronic cooperation with the suppliers, it will be easier for the users to work out product specifications with the supplier online or to take a new technological product by the manufacturer into account.

On the other hand manufacturing companies will receive access to supplier and vendor pools and gain the opportunity to process sourcing more effectively. The enormous complexity of production operations has caused a number of changes. One of those is the increasing usage of computers and information processing. One benefit of this process is, that buyers receive through electronic sourcing solutions, which are part of this development, an efficient tool to reduce expenses for materials. On average, this means approximately a saving of around 5-40% on material costs as well as a shortening of the sourcing cycle between 20-60%. The solutions for sourcing and procurement thus offer the users of a business-to-business-marketplace the opportunity of acquiring, specifying, and negotiating products and contracts online together with their vendors and subsequently processing them per basic agreement.

Through electronic sourcing solutions and marketplaces, suppliers will encounter enterprises with a high degree of mass production and construction, because many of those companies mainly will put their engineering and sourcing in the near future to tender via particular eMarketplaces.

## II. How do internet platforms work?

Contract relations in the field of business-to-business transactions are comparable with running a ménage à trois. First a company has to become a member of the platform. This relationship has to be distinguished form the business relations between the users among each other.

Any application for affiliation in an electronic marketplace requires the conclusion of a so called "user contract" or "membership agreement". This contract rules the relationship between the operator of the platform and the single user who is often called "member". In most cases it is a mixed contract and mainly a kind of licence-agreement, which enables the member to use the trading tools of the eMarket, for example procurment and auction tools, electronic agents or information boards. The operator usually will screen the applicant prior to the conclusion of the membership agreement and will make a reservation which allows him to reject the application. The application form is tied with terms and conditions which are connected with the "user contract". There will be no admission to the eMarketplace without acception of those terms by the applicant. The following wording is typical:

> "The platform operator reserves the right, in its absolute discretion and without giving reasons, to reject any application. ... The acceptance of the application for admission will become effective for the user only when the operator has sent a corresponding written admission confirmation per e-mail, mail or fax to the user and the latter logs in for the first time on the marketplace using the log-in and password submitted with the written admission confirmation and accepts the user terms and conditions."

The outcome is, that the operator is not obliged to accept any application and mustn't give any explanation. Operators therefore are entitled to deny the application only on suspection of a supposed risk of insolvency.

The true "user agreement" has to be separated from the contractual relationship between the users as such. But nevertheless there are some cross connections. The platform is only useful if the offers and requests for trading are provided accurately and in good faith. The operator has to take measures to ensure that the accessible information is not forged or stolen, that the authenticity of the acting users is guaranteed and that the customes are bound by the concluded contracts. For that reason the "user agreement" contains a number of obligations which have retrospective effects. For example:

- the information contained in the application has to be accurate;
- the user is obliged to inform the platform operator of all future changes in the information provided;
- the platform operator is entitled to verify the authenticity of the request and the identity of the person making it.

Some terms and conditions of use are containing to some extent regulations with respect to contracts between buyer and supplier. Buyers have the opportunity to open requests for quotes and auctions and to invite suppliers based on individual criteria to make binding offers. In these cases the question arises how the existing lack of contractual agreements can be filled.[3] Next to that only a short line of e-marketplaces enables users the application of their own terms and conditions beside the terms and conditions of the membership contract.

---

[3] Wiebe, MMR 2001, 109 at 110, comment on decision OLG Hamm 14. Dec. 2001.

In the result of that some specific legal questions arise. The following analysis will concentrate on the problems of

- is a product description or request for quote a binding offer or only an invitation to treat?
- is it possible to apply the terms and conditions of the internet platform to the contract between the users of the eMarketplace?
- which requirements must be met in the case of inclusion of terms and conditions between commercial contractors?

## B. Electronic Contracting

Does trading with the help of an electronic marketplace rise new legal questions, or is it a delightful new playground for old games.[4] The answer depends on whether the existing contract law is flexible and likely to accommodate "new" internet trading practices. Purchasing procedures will mostly fall into two categories: negotiated contracts and auctions. At first glance not all cases of negotiated contracts seems to be suitable for online contracting. Especially complex projects involve a variety of specific questions which are to be discussed. However more and more complex supply chain systems are connected with electronic trading platforms. Through this way electronic contracts became part of modern electronic purchasing systems.[5]

A contract is defined as an agreement between two or more parties that is binding in law, which requires that the parties must have reached an agreement (offer and acceptance). The question is whether the traditional rules of contract law are able to establish the facts which are necessary to conclude a contract. This might be doubtful, because the specific nature of internet raises more conflicts than any other inventive process of modernizing commerce. It is border- and timeless and its intangible character leaves the contracting parties unsure whether common law is able to offer legal answers. Some of those were answered in the meantime by a series of legislative initiatives.[6]

### I. Product description or request for quote - binding offer or invitation to treat?

One of those questions is the judgement of the display of goods in e-commerce shops or online trading platforms. Has this action to be sorted out as an advertisment, an invitation to tender or is it a binding offer?

---

4 See *Sommer*, Against Cyberlaw, 15 Berkely Tech L.J. 1145 at 1231 (2000).

5 E.g. Volkswagen AG with VW Group Supply.com.

6 E.g. in Germany.

*a. European perspective*

As far as the German Civil Code is applicable to the question whether an offer on a internet platform is binding has to be answered with respect to §§ 145 ff. BGB. § 145 BGB contains the basic principle, that the offeror is bound on the basis of a promise which is capable of acceptance. This obligation is not existent in the case the bindung character was excluded in a previous explicit statement.[7]

Additional difficulties arise, where the concurrence of offer and acceptance is important in order to ascertain whether a valid contract has been formed and when the contract was concluded. This may be vital if the parties are contracting between different jurisdictions by fax, telex, e-mail or through Internet or other forms of instantaneous communications.[8] The regulations in §§ 145 ff. BGB are dispositive, so that the contracting parties can find other arrangements. Merely using the word offer or invitation to treat does not mean it has that effect legally. The deciding factor is the legal meaning or construction as it would have appeared to a reasonable man but not the wording used by the contracting parties (objective approach).[9] Only the real nature of the phrase counts and not the language used.[10] Invitations to treat (invitatio ad offerendum) are a collection of disparate instances of situations which can trigger an offer. Their purpose is to solicit an offer or to initiate negotiations.

*1. Advertisements*

Throughout all European jurisdictions, advertisements of goods for sale are usually construed as invitations to treat.[11] But also an advertisement can be construed as an offer, if it offers a reward for the return of lost property. English contract law describes such cases as unilateral contracts, which means, that one party binds itself by a conditional promise leaving the other party free to perform the condition or not.[12] Circulars, catalogues and price-lists distributed by trader will therefore normally be regarded as invitations to treat.[13] Otherwise the supplier could only protect himself by merely stating that the offer was open

---

7 E.g. "freibleibend".

8 E.g. English contract law; *Applebey*, Contract Law, Chap. 3.2.

9 E.g. English precedent; *Spencer v. Harding* (1870) L.R. 5 CP 561; *Duxbury,* Contract Law, 4 th. London, p. 2.

10 German courts make reservations on that rule, if only commercial parties belonging to the same business branch are involved; *BGH* VersR 2002, 122 at 124.

11 *RGZ* 133, 391; same in Scandinavian countries *Ring/Ring-Olsen*, Einführung in das skandinavische Recht, p. 218.

12 *Carlill v. Carbolic Smoke Ball Co.*, C.A. [1893] 1 Q.B. 256.

13 Palandt – *Heinrichs*, § 145 BGB MN 2; *Grainger&Son v. Gough* [1896] A.C. 325; *Partridge v. Crittenden* [1968] 2 All E.R. 421.

only while stocks last, or that they were on offer on a "first come, first serve" basis.[14]

*2. Display of goods*

Goods on display in shop windows[15] or supermarkets are invitations to treat, not an offer.[16] Instead the customer makes the offer when he takes the article to the cash-desk to pay for it.[17] Under contract law, shops are not bound to sell goods at the price indicated and a customer cannot demand to buy a particular item on display. If a shopkeeper offers goods or services for sale to the public, he has the intention not to commit himself, because for example he hasn't enough goods on stock to fulfil his contractual obligations.[18]

The customer is informed that he may himself pick up an article and take it to the shopkeeper with a view to buy it.[19] It is necessary to fix the moment at which the contract is concluded. The contract is concluded when the shopkeeper or the store's employee accepts the offer by the buyer. Usually he expresses his willingness to sell, when he puts the goods through the machine to tread the bar code and record the sale at the check out. From this point the ownership passes to the buyer.[20] This rule is based largely on practical convenience, business practice and common sense.[21]

*3. Auction Sales*

The auctioneer's request for bids is an invitation to treat and the single bid is an offer[22] Sometimes auctions take place with a reserve price. If the higest bid does not reach this price, the auctioneer can withdraw the lot.

*b. Efforts for adjustment of contract law to digital demands*

The usage of advertisements, displays and auctions in an offline situation is likely similar to the electronic process of selling through eMarketplaces (website stores etc.) or electronic mail systems, so that the common contract rules could also be applied to online contracts in general too. In the meantime the finding is undisputed, that contract statements can be transmitted online. At the same time

---

14 *Applebey*, Contract Law, Chap. 3.6.

15 *Fisher v. Bell* [1961] 1 Q.B. 394 at 399; *BGH* NJW 1980, 1388.

16 BGH NJW 1980, 1388.

17 *Pharmaceutical Society of Great Britain v. Boots Cash Chemists Southern Ltd* [1953] 2 Q.B. 796 at 801; *Fisher v. Bell* [1961] 1 Q.B. 394; *Upex,* Davies on Contract, 8. ed., p. 9.

18 *Weber*, E-Commerce und Recht.

19 *Pharmaceutical Society of Great Britain v. Boots Cash Chemists Southern Ltd* [191] 2 Q.B. 796 at 801.

20 *Applebey*, Contract Law, Chap. 3.4.

21 *Applebey,* Contract Law, Chap. 3.4.

22 *§* 156 BGB; *BGHZ* 138, 339 at 342; *Payne* v. *Cave* [1789] 3 Term Rep 148; sec. 57 (2) Sale of Goods Act 1979.

it is more and more recognized, that most of the existing legal framework fits to online contracts. This development has been promoted fundamentally by the UNCITRAL Model Law on Electronic Commerce.[23] Article 11 (1) states:

> "In the context of contract formation, unless otherwise agreed by the parties, an offer and the acceptance of an offer may be expressed by means of data messages. Where a data message is used in the formation of a contract, that contract shall not be denied validity or enforceability on the sole ground that a data message was used for that purpose or stored by electronic, optical or similar means, including electronic mail."

An increasing number of states have already adopted this model law, to adjust their contract law to the needs of electronic commerce. Australia, Bermuda, Colombia, Ecuador, France, Hong Kong Special Administrative Region of China, India, Ireland, Philippines, Republic of Korea, Singapore, Slovenia, the States of Jersey and, within the United States of America, Illinois have based legislation on the UNCITRAL Model Law on Electronic Commerce. Furthermore the Canada Uniform Electronic Commerce Act 1999 and the U.S. Uniform Electronic Transactions Act 1999 have been influence by the UNCITRAL Model Law.[24]

The European Commission has also initiated a bundle of lawmaking processes in respect to electronic commerce.[25] Fields which are concerned are the treatment of contracts and formal contract requirements, digital signatures, legal effectiveness and validity on account of their having been made by electronic means[26]; required information about the technical steps to follow to conclude the contract, technical means for identifying and correcting input errors prior to the placing of the order;[27] general informations to be provided, as the name of the service provider, geographic address at which the service provider is established, his electronic mail address, information concerning trade or public registration etc.[28] and commercial information which enables the user to identify the communication clearly as commercial as well as the natural or legal person on whose behalf the commercial communication is made;[29] the liability of intermediary service providers for the information transmitted, caught or hosted[30] etc.

---

23 UNCITRAL Modal Law on Electronic Commerce, www.uncitral.org/english/texts/electcom/ml-ec.htm. Form requirements, writing and signature requirements are not discussed in that paper. S.g. UNCITRAL draft model law on electronic signatures (A/CN.9/446; para. 212).

24 http://www.uncitral.org/en-index.htm.

25 See *Lindholm/Maennel*, Directive on Electronic Commerce (2000/31/EC), CRi 2000, 65 at 68.

26 Art. 9 Directive on electronic commerce.

27 Art. 10 Directive on electronic commerce.

28 Art. 5 Directive on electronic commerce.

29 Art. 6 Directive on electronic commerce.

30 Art. 12 – 14 Directive on electronic commerce.

Both, the UNCITRAL Model Law and the European directives intend to remove still existing legal barriers to the use of electronic commerce. The concept is to develop international standardized trade law instruments.

## II. Standard terms and conditions

### *a. Definition of offer and acceptance through terms and conditions*

Despite the efforts of states and intergovernmental organizations in contract practise, commercial trading partners often try to find contractual solutions to transborder and other legal obstacles of electronic commerce.

Some standard business terms therefore define requests for quotes and auction bids only as invitations to treat, thus they cannot be regarded as binding offers pursuant to § 145 BGB.

Despite these regulations the contracting parties in the field of commercial transactions are able to establish separate agreements which deviate from the above mentioned principles or put them into concrete terms. For example:

> "Suppliers have the possibility to select buyers according to individual criteria and to make binding offers to their requests for quotes. ... The offers of a supplier are binding and irrevocable declarations to enter a contract based on the buyer's request for quotes. ...
> A buyer is free to select whether and if so which of the received offers he wants to accept."

This example of terms and conditions used by an eMarketplace operator illustrates, that the presentation of goods and services through a internet platform should have merely the effect of an invitation to treat.

Another common eMarketplace trading tool are electronic auction sales. The auctioneer who offers goods for sale is merely inviting the potential bidders to make offers to buy them. Usually the request for bids is an invitation to treat.[31] He isn't obliged to accept such an offer. The consequence is, that the potential buyer makes the offer when he bids. Similar to § 156 BGB, Section 57 (2) Sale of Goods Act 1979 (England) states that "a sale by auction is completed on the fall of the auctioneer's hammer or in any customary manner". But there is no auctioneer's hammer with online auctions. This problem is solved by setting a closing time for the auction on the website by which all bids must be placed. The highest bid at the time the auction closes is bound to contract unless the reserved price has not been reached.[32]

Some terms and conditions of internet platform operators are different. Auction platforms which are accessible solely to commercial members sometimes

---

[31] *Payne v. Cave* (1789) 3 Term Rep 148.
[32] *Chissick/Kelman*, Electronic Commerce, Chap. 2.40.

try to avoid in most cases the binding effect of the fall of the hammer. For example:

> "Within the scope of auctions, suppliers also remain bound by their respective offers for an additional 30 days after the expiration of the auction period or possibly extended period set by the buyer, unless the parties have agreed otherwise. § 156 BGB is expressly excluded."

Auctions which are serving commercial purposes, are similar to procurement procedures. The supplier with the highest or lowest bid (reverse auction) makes an offer to the auctioneer so that the contract is not completed with the fall of the hammer respectively the closing time of the auction. The auctioneer is not bound to the best bid, unless the parties reached a corresponding agreement.

The contracting parties have to keep in mind, that the offer must be distinguished from all other statements made in the process of negotiating. Only an offer is capable of being accepted. In order to determine the existence of an offer the courts consider among other circumstances the intensions of the parties, the facts of the individual case, custom or trade practices and surrounding circumstances.

In a recent case the BGH[33] (online auction) decided, that even the placement of goods to be auctioneered through an internet platform could meet the conditions of a binding offer, if the offerer would accept the highest bid.[34] If the wording of a party is not clear, the courts are entitled to use the standard business terms and conditions for purposes of interpretation and construction of the statement (offer). The main condition is, that the offer must be intended to be legally binding.[35] However, standard business terms and pre-established statements as offer or acceptance have to be distinguished. On the basis of the recent jurisdiction it can be assumed, that a binding offer can be expressed through the switching on of an offer on an internet platform. Standard business terms applied to the user agreement can be used in this respect as a basis for the interpretation and construction of such pre-established statements. Furthermore the interpretation or contract gap filling can be based on the expectations and the common sense of the contracting parties which is connected with the usage of the internet platform.

In practice, general statements can only scarcely be made at this point because the online auction systems differ. Decisions have to be made by a case to case analysis.

Messages which were mailed in the course of bidding or negotiation are reaching the offerer or offeree only through the platform messaging system. The

---

33 *BGH* CR 2002, 213 – 216.

34 *BGH* CR 2002, 213 at 215.

35 *Ibid.*

platform operator therefore acts as a reception agent according to § 164 III BGB[36] and is not a party of the contract concluded between the users of the platform. According to german law the contract is complete when the message (offer, acceptance) arrives at the offerer/ offeree unlike the Anglo-American law which applies the postal rule. The postal rule means that communication occurs as soon as the letter is posted.[37] But the postal rule is kept within strict confines and applies only to postal services when the post is the proper method of communication. The Distance Selling Regulations 2000[38] only applies to contracts between seller and suppliers and consumers made exclusively by means of distance communication. These regulations do not apply to non-consumer contracts, commercial services, auctions etc. Commercial traders are entitled to derogate from those rules or to agree supplementing provisions. The freedom of contracting is only limited through §§ 310 I, 307 BGB (review of subject matter). Solely invalid are those provisions in commercial standard business terms, if they, contrary to the requirement of good faith, place the contractual partner of the user at an unreasonable disadvantage (§ 307 I BGB). Such an unreasonable disadvantage is for example assumed if a provision cannot be reconciled with essential basic principles of the statutory rule from which it deviates, or if it restricts essential rights or duties resulting from the nature of the contract in such a manner that there is a risk that the purpose of the contract will not be achieved (§ 307 II BGB).

*b. Application of the platform terms and conditions to the contract between its users?*

Usually standard business terms are contractual terms which have been pre-established for a multitude of contracts one party to the contract (user) normally presents to the other party upon the conclusion of the contract (§ 305 I BGB). They are only incorporated into the contract, if the user, during the conclusion of the contract, in brief

1. expressly draws the other party's attention to them and
2. gives the other party, in a reasonable manner, the possibility of gaining knowledge of their content and if the other party agrees that they are to apply (§ 305 II BGB).

These regulations also applicable to standard business terms which are used to business or legal persons (§ 310 I BGB). § 307 I and II BGB nevertheless applies to the extent that this results in the invalidity of the contractual provisions

---

36 *BGH* CR 2002, 213 at 214.

37 *Adams v. Lindsell* (1818) 1 B & Ald. 681; *Applebey*, Contract Law, Chap. 4.11.

38 85/577/EC.

referred to in §§ 308 and 309 BGB; due regard has to be directed to the particular customs and practices applying in business transactions.

Non of these requirements are fulfilled, if parties contract through internet platform apart from the case of using their own standard business terms and conditions. More and more internet trading platforms allow their users to fall back on additional agreements of standard business terms.

Actually there is a dispute in German law literature if the standard business terms agreed to in the user contract can also be used for contractional obligations between users of an internet platform although none of the contract parties presented the terms upon the conclusion of the contract between the users.[39] The BGH took no stand on that controversy. Some votes have criticized the BGH for not making a comment on that question and expect further uncertainties concerning the formation and interpretation of contracts concluded through internet trading platforms.[40] It's to be expected, that the dispute is merely academic, because the e-marketplace operators will react to the BGH-decision and it is to be expected that they will fit the wordings of the trading system screens and the contract terms and conditions to make clear whether the tender is only an invitation to treat or a binding offer.

### c. *Requirements for inclusion of standard business terms between commercial contractors?*

Terms and conditions may play a considerable role in the course of the handling of mass business transactions and the design of contractual obligations and liability according to customs and business practices. With the online-business two procedures predominate with regard to the introduction of terms and conditions.

In the majority of the cases the opportunity of accepting terms is opened to the user, by clicking a text (for example AGB) or an icon, transmitted by means of a hyperlink directly to a website which contains the wording of the standard business terms.[41] A second option is the download and printout of the standard business term as a PDF file.[42]

---

39 *Wiebe*, Vertragsschluss bei Online-Auktionen, MMR 2001, 109; *Spindler*, Vertragsabschluss und Inhaltskontrolle bei Internet-Auktionen, ZIP 2001, 809; *Sester*, Vertragssschluss bei Internet-Auktionen, CR 2001, 98; *Rüfner*, Virtuelle Marktordnungen und das AGB-Gesetz, MMR 2000, 597; *Ulrici*, Zum Vertragsschluss bei Internet-Auktionen, NJW 2001, 1112; *Grapentin*, Vertragsschluss bei Internet-Auktionen, GRUR 2001, 713.

40 *Wiebe*, Rechtsverbindliches Angebot in Online-Auktionen, MMR 2002, 216.

41 For example t-online.iloxx.de; e-komplett.de; fas-web.de; cargex.de; lagerflaeche.de; benelog.com.

42 FrachtenboerseOnline der RAG Verkauf; contingate.com.

Regularly the use of the platform is based on the previous registration of the user. With the online application the operater already points out, that the applicant has to accept the terms and conditions for the usage of the platform. The question whether the terms and conditions were included into the contract is decisive. This basic principle doesn´t count, when the terms and conditions are used towards a business person (§ 14 BGB; legal definition).

The German Act to modernization of the Law of Obligations doesn´t change the pattern of the former § 24 AGBG.[43] Although § 305 II BGB (former § 2 AGBG) is not applicable to business transactions, the courts regularly demand, that the contracting party can or could understand the intention of the user which leads to the inclusion of the standard business terms. As little as a conclusive behavior can create a "silent" statement.[44] The demand for a reduction of the content of terms and conditions used in the internet for purposes of better understanding and readability doesn´t fit to commercial transactions.[45] A reasonable express reference to the terms and conditions leads also to the validity of the incorporation through a hyperlink.[46] The requirement of presentation is already met, if the user enables the other party gaining knowledge of content of the terms and conditions upon request.[47] The option to print the terms and conditions must not be guaranteed.

Since a home page with brochures and/or product offers in catalogs is comparable, the reference on AGB must be presented clearly even in the financial traffic since brochures in the first place inform about the range of facilities of the home page operator and few about content of contract and general business conditions. Therefore a not misleading indication of the validity of general business conditions is necessary on the home page.[48] This reference must be positioned, where user usually seek to find conditions and information on the contract handling. Through frame-contract the validity is supposed to be arranged as general business conditions for a large number of single contracts to be closed one day, for example freight contracts. It has to be ensured during the organization of the home page and input masks to attach the expression unmisleadingly, that the inclusion will registers not only the basic contract "frame-contract", but also the

---

43 BT-Drs. 14/6040, p. 160.

44 *BGH* NJW 1992, 1232; Palandt – *Heinrichs*, § 24 AGBG MN 3 und § 2 AGBG MN 22 f.; *Kamanabrou*, Vorgaben der E-Commerce-RL für die Einbeziehung von AGB bei Online-Rechtsgeschäften, CR 2001, 421 at 424.

45 *OLG Köln* CR 1998, 244 ff.; *LG Ravensburg* CR 1992, 1472 at 1473; *LG Aachen* NJW 1991, 2159 at 2160.

46 *OLG Köln* NJW-RR 1998, 1277 at 1278; *Köhler/Arndt*, Recht des Internet, 134.

47 *BGHZ* 102, 293 at 304.

48 Ulmer/Brandner/Hensen/Schmidt - *Ulmer*, AGB-Gesetz, Kommentar, § 2 AGBG MN 80a.

following final contracts.[49] The bare indication of general business conditions does not suffice in that case.[50]

If the at the beginning of a business partnership introduced business terms and conditions, change in facts and needs require an adjustment of the terms and conditions in the course of the business relation, the question of variation of contract arises because a variation must be accomplished through offer and acceptance (§§ 145, 146 BGB). The alteration of business terms and conditions has to be incorporated into the contractual relationship in the same manner.[51] An unconditional change by the user is not valid.[52] Clauses for alteration of standard business terms are only held valid if the other party has the right to contradict.[53]

Naturally also foreign users have the opportunity of access to internet platforms. For many reasons electronic commerce business merchants may not wish to deal with all customers from all jurisdictions (for example import/export restrictions or different understanding of formation of contract). If the vendor intends to accept orders only from customers based in special countries, a note on the website has to state that intention. Choice of Law and Jurisdiction Clauses can seize the applicable law and specify the jurisdiction. Jurisdiction deals with issues of forum, whereas applicable law deals with the legal principles the aforesaid forum applies. In German law Art. 27, 28 EGBGB governs the choice or determination of applicable law and jurisdiction. In the absence of a choice of law, the contract is governed by the law of the country most closely connected to the contract or the habitual residence or, in the case of a body corporate or unincorporated, its central administration.[54] The latter will apply in most cases to the platform operator.

To my knowledge disputes between online contractors are settled mostly through arbitration, which is assosiated with the tendency to avoid court rulings and in result, to consolidate legal rules of electronic commerce "to keep open the legal sky".

## C. Summary

The legal framework possesses the flexibility to deal with this new commercial medium. Recent landmarking efforts have completed the ability of the law to govern online transactions. The question is if the law can cope with transactions in the fast developing and virtual word of cyberspace. Some uncertainties

---

49 *BGHZ* 117, 190 at 198.

50 *BGHZ* 117, 190 at 195.

51 *OLG Frankfurt/M.* VersR 1998, 1540 at 1541; Ulmer/Brandner/Hensen/Schmidt - *Ulmer*, AGB-Gesetz, Kommentar, § 2 AGBG MN 64.

52 *BGH* VersR 1971, 1116 at 1117.

53 *OLG Köln* CR 2001, 514 (515).

54 See *Rühl*, Rechtswahlklauseln in AGB, 1999; *Schröder/Wenner*, Internationales Vertragsrecht, p. 57 ff.; *Martiny*, in: Reithmann/Martiny, Internationales Vertragsrecht, p. 45 ff.

will arise from the fact, that the parties must rely on their standard terms and conditions and the court´s interpreation of the law. The standardization of European contract law will ease the handling of electronic commerce through internet platforms.

# Conclusion of Contracts on the Basis of Use of Electronic Commerce - Some Comparative Legal Problems of the Russian Legislation

*Dr. Kamil Arslanov, University Kazan*

Problems of electronic commerce, especially regarding to questions of process of the conclusion of contracts in the electronic form, are topical for the Russian private law system. Legal basis of electronic commerce in its modern form have been incorporated by acceptance of the Civil Code of the Russian Federation,[1] though even in days of existence of Soviet Union a number of acts on electronic commerce has been accepted. Here it is possible to mention the Instructive guidelines (Instructivnje ukazanija) of the State Arbitration of the USSR from June, 29, 1979 № I-1-4 «use as proofs on arbitration affairs of the documents prepared with the help of electronic-computer facilities».[2] Thus even before acceptance of the First part of the Civil Code of the Russian Federation,[3] but already after the beginning of reforming of the Russian legal system, in judiciary practice there were numerous disputes over use of the electronic digital signature. These disputes have led finally to acceptance of the «Pismo» (Letter) of the Supreme Arbitration Court of the Russian Federation from August, 19, 1994 № S1-7/OP-587 «About separate recommendations accepted at meetings on judicial - arbitration practice»,[4] where in section IV the Court analyzes a

---

1 A first part of the Civil Code of Russian Federation from November, 30, 1994 № 51-FZ («Rossiiskaj gazeta» 8.12.1994; «Sobranie zakonodatelstva Rossiiskoi Federazii» 5.12.1994, № 32, an item 3301). A second part – from January, 26, 1996 № 14-FZ («Rossiiskaj gazeta» 6 (7,8).2.1996; «Sobranie zakonodatelstva Rossiiskoi Federazii», 29.1.1996, № 5, an item 410). A third part – from November, 26, 2001 № 46-FZ («Rossiiskaj gazeta» 28.11.2001; «Sobranie zakonodatelstva Rossiiskoi Federazii» 3.12.2001, № 49, an item 4552).

2 The text of Instructive guidelines was published in «Sistematisirovannji sbornik instruktivnjh ukazanii Gosudarstvennogo arbitrazha pri Sovete Ministrov SSSR», Moskwa, 1987. Specificity of the Russian law system is the edition through the highest judicial instances (the Supreme Court and the Supreme Arbitration Court of the Russian Federation) special generalizations of practice of both subordinate instances and own judiciary practice, which accepts forms of decisions of plenums of such instances, circulars of presidiums of the courts. The general tendency in jurisprudence and practice of Russia shows, that the decisions of highest judicial instances have an effect of judicial precedent (look, for example, prof. V.V. Jarkov's opinion in the textbook «Arbitrazhnji prozess (Arbitration process)», Moskva: Jurist, 2000, p. 241; see also «Sudebnaja praktika kak istochnik prava (Judiciary practice as a source of Law)», Moskva: Jurist, 2000.

3 Further: CC.

4 «Bulleten Vjsshego Arbitrazhnogo Suda Rossiiskoi Federazii (The Bulletin of the Supreme Arbitration Court of Russian Federation)», 1994, № 11.

question, if the circumstances of a case could be verified by proofs made and signed with the help of electronic-computer facilities in which the system of the digital (electronic) signature is used.

Last years in the Russian legislation there were essential changes by way of fixation of separate aspects of the electronic conclusion of contracts. First of all it concerns acceptance of the Federal Law Act from January, 10, 2002 № 1-FZ «About the electronic digital signature».[5] Besides it is necessary to pay attention for sphere of the electronic form of the conclusion of contracts to the Federal Law Act from February, 20, 1995 № 24-FZ «About the information, informatization and protection of the information",[6] the Federal Law Act from February, 16, 1995 № 15-FZ «About intercommunication»,[7] etc.

By the Order of Parliament (Gosudarstvennaj Duma) of the Russian Federation from June, 6, 2001 № 1582-III GD has been accepted in the first reading the draft of the Federal Law Act № 11081-3 «About electronic trade».[8] Herewith the Russian legislator is guided by the international experience of legal regulation. In the field of electronic commerce most countries orientate themselve on the Model Law On Electronic Commerce Of The United Nations Commission On International Trade Law (UNCITRAL), approved on December, 16, 1996 by the Resolution 51/162 at 85-plenary session of General Assembly of the United Nations. Legislation based on the UNCITRAL Model Law on Electronic Commerce has been adopted in Australia, Bermuda, Colombia, Ecuador, France, Hong Kong Special Administrative Region of China, India, Ireland, Isle of Mann (Crown Dependency of the United Kingdom of Great Britain and Northern Ireland), New Zealand, Pakistan, Philippines, Republic of Korea, Singapore, Slovenia, the States of Jersey (Crown Dependency of the United Kingdom of Great Britain and Northern Ireland), Thailand, and, within the United States of America, Illinois. Uniform legislation influenced by the Model Law and the principles on which it is based has been prepared in Canada (Uniform Electronic Commerce Act, adopted in 1999 by the Uniform Law Conference of Canada) and in the United States (Uniform Electronic Transactions Act, adopted in 1999 by the National Conference of Commissioners on Uniform State Law) and enacted as law by a number of jurisdictions in those countries.[9]

---

5 «Rossiiskaja gazeta» 12.1.2002; «Sobranie zakonodatelstva Rossiskoi Federazii» 14.1.2002, № 2, an item 127.

6 «Rossiiskaja gazeta» 22.2.1995; «Sobranie zakonodatelstva Rossiskoi Federazii» 20.2.1995, № 8, an item 609.

7 «Rossiiskaja gazeta» 23.2.1995; «Sobranie zakonodatelstva Rossiskoi Federazii» 20.2.1995, № 8, an item 600.

8 It is not accepted till now in final edition.

9 See the information about status of the Model Law using an official internet site of The United Nations Commission On International Trade Law: www.uncitral.org.

In spite of the fact that from the moment of introduction of the First part of the Civil Code of the Russian Federation over 7 years have passed, the electronic variant of the conclusion of contracts has not got accustomed in Russia to the full. It can be connected with rigid orientation of subjects of the Russian market to traditional ways of the conclusion of contracts, fear of mistakes and a deceit, including fears of infringements of intellectual property rights.[10]

In the present abstract it was supposed just to chalk out those questions which are determined by the Russian specificity of electronic commerce. These questions are connected to participation of foreign subjects in juridical relation.

Let's note, that the Russian legislation reveals the following groups of questions in conjunction with an electronic commerce:

The order of application of the law to contracts made by way of use of electronic facilities, including a network of the Internet. A question on a place of conclusion of contracts.

Here there is a question of a collision of the legal regulations when representatives of the different legal systems take part in contractual relations, and also in case of the conclusion of contracts through parties which though are representatives of one country, but they are staying in the different countries. This question is resolved in the Third part of CC where has found the regulation of the international private law (section VI: articles 1186-1224).

The Russian legislator does not provide special rules for electronic transactions, having limited to the general regulation.

The legal status of individuals (physical persons) and collective entrepreneurs (corporations) is defined by the law of the country where the person is registered or founded (articles 1201, 1202 CC). If the person is not registered, the rule about application of the law of a place of the basic realization of enterprise activity is applicable (close 2 of article 1201 CC).

The parties of the contract have the right to choose the law applied to their contract. However, if from set of circumstances of the affair existing at the moment of a choice of the law follows that the contract is really connected only to one country, this choice of the parties cannot infringe on imperative norms of the country to which the contract is really connected (item 5 of article 1210 CC). At absence of the agreement of the parties about the law of contract to the contract is applied the law of the country to which the contract is most closely connected (item 1 of article 1211 CC). Thus – if other does not follow from the law, conditions or an essence of the contract or set of circumstances of an affair – by the law of the country to which the contract is most closely connected is implied the law of the country where there is a residence or the basic place of activity of

---

10 The problem of mutual relation of electronic commerce and protection of the right of participants of a civil juridical relations is not alien to other legal systems. See, for example, Hoeren, Thomas, E-Business und die Rezession: Was wird vom elektronischen Handel bleiben? NJW 2002, 37.

the party which carries out the performance having crucial importance for the contents of the contract (item 2 of article 1211 CC). Such is the law of the country of the seller, donator, lender, carrier, forwarding agent, insurer, agent, guarantor, licensor, etc.

To the obligations arising from unilateral transactions – if other does not follow from the law, conditions or an essence of the transaction or set of circumstances of an affair – is applicable the law of the country where there is a residence or the basic place of activity of the party which is taking up the obligations under the unilateral transaction (article 1217 CC).

Taking into account that Internet-services generally involve consumers, the Russian legislator has provided guarantees of their rights. The choice of the law applying to the contract which party is the physical person using, getting either ordering or having intention to use, get or order movable things (works, services) for the personal, family, domestic and other needs which have been not connected to realization of enterprise activity, cannot cause deprivation of such physical person (consumer) of protection of his rights given by imperative norms of the law of the country of a residence of the consumer, if one of the following circumstances (item 1 of article 1212 CC) took place even: (1) conclusion of the contract was preceded in this country with the offer addressed to the consumer, or advertising and the consumer has made in the same country actions necessary for the conclusion of the contract; (2) the contractor of the consumer or the representative of the contractor has received the order of the consumer in this country; (3) order for purchase of movable things, performance of works or rendering of services is made by the consumer in other country which visiting has been initiated by the contractor of the consumer with a view of prompting the consumer to the conclusion of the contract.

At absence of the agreement of the parties about applicable law and at presence of the circumstances which have been mentioned above, to the contract with participation of the consumer the law of the country of a residence of the consumer is applicable (item 2 of article 1212 CC). Thus the rules established by items 1 and 2 of article 1212 CC, are not applied: (1) to the contract of transportation; (2) to the contract about performance of works or about rendering of services, if work that should be executed or services should be rendered extremely in other country than the country of a residence of the consumer. These withdrawals are not distributed to contracts on rendering for a total price of services on transportation and accommodation (irrespective of inclusion in a total price of cost of other services), in particular on contracts in sphere of tourist service.

According to article 1209 CC, the form of transactions submits to the law of a place of its fulfilment; thus the transaction accomplished abroad cannot be recognized as void owing to non-observance of the form if requirements of the Russian legislation (item 1) are observed. The form of foreign-economic transactions, even one of which parties is the Russian legal person, submits irrespective of a place of fulfilment of this transaction to the Russian legislation (item 2).

The questions of application of the law considered above to concluded contracts (articles 1210-1212 CC) concern only (1) interpretation of the contract; (2) rights and duties of parties of the contract; (3) performance of the contract; (4) consequences of default or inadequate performance of the contract; (5) termination of the contract; (6) consequences of invalidity of the contract (article 1215 ГК).

Therefore the concept «a place of fulfilment of the transaction» is important. Fulfilment of the transaction is understood as giving to it of a validity. In other words, "fulfilment of the transaction" is connected to the moment of the beginning of its action. Adhering consensual systems of the conclusion of the contract the Russian legal system as well as the majority of the European countries resists here to the «mail-box theory» of Anglo-American legal family.

The Russian law contains requirements of the written form concerning some kinds of contracts. These are contracts for the sums over 10 minimal sizes of a payment (for January, 2003 – 10 × 100 = 1.000 roubles[11]); contracts in which at least one of the parties is a corporation (article 161 CC); contracts of rent of vehicles (articles 633, 643 CC), etc. Non-observance of such requirement entails impossibility to refer to a testimony confirming the transaction and its conditions (article 162 CC).

The general norm determining the form of the contract, and the electronic contract in particular, is the article 434 CC. So, according to item 2 of this article, the written contract can be made by drawing up of one document signed by the parties, and also by an exchange of documents using of the post, cable, teletype, telephone, electronic or other connection facilities allowing authentically to establish that the document proceeds from the party of the contract. Thus, the Russian legislator has considered that the written form is observed in case of an opportunity of an authentic establishment of that corresponding electronic messages proceeded from the parties of the contract. The authentic establishment of such fact can be connected to a question on the electronic digital signature.

The necessary essential element of any written document is the signature of the person or the signature of persons who make it. The signature in such document replaces the expressed consent of the person in the oral transaction.

Article 160 CC contains in item 2 a position according to which the use at fulfilment of transactions of the electronic-digital signature or other analogue of the autographic signature is supposed in cases and in the order, stipulated by the law or by the agreement of the parties. Such law is already mentioned above:

---

11 See the Federal Law Act from June, 19, 2000 № 82-FZ «About the minimal size of a payment» («Rossiiskaja gazeta» 21.6.2000; «Sobranie zakonodatelstva Rossiskoi Federazii» 26.6.2000, № 26, an item 2729).

Federal Law Act from January, 10, 2002 «About the electronic digital signature».

As it was marked in the report «E-commerce in Russia: opportunities for growth and development» prepared by the American Chamber of Commerce in Association with the Russian Chamber of Commerce and Industry (March, 2000),[12] three variants of sophistication are currently employed in Western Europe and North America to define electronic signature. The first variant provides that all electronic signatures should satisfy legislative requirements about the signature. The second variant provides that the electronic signature has a validity only, if it (1) really belongs to the person using it; (2) can be verificated; (3) is exclusively under the control of the person using it; and (4) it is connected to the information in such a manner that in case of change of the information the signature loses its force. The third variant establishes that requirements about legality of the signature are observed only with the electronic digital signatures made using of public key cryptography technology that satisfy legal signature requirements. The Russian legislator has chosen the third variant of the signature, i.e. – as it was specified in the report mentioned above – the most strict.[13]

Modern legal practice shows the necessity of the international legal unification in the field of electronic commerce by virtue of it's transboundary character. Adoption in the middle of 90th years of XX centure of the special Model Law On Electronic Commerce Of The United Nations Commission On International Trade Law demonstrates a urgency of electronic commerce for the international economic order. The orientation of leading legal systems on Model Laws allows to speak about gradual creation of the mechanism of uniform application of norms about electronic commerce in national legislations.

---

12 Referring to: Thomas J. Smedinghoff and Ruth Hill Bro, Moving with Change: Electronic Signature Legislation as a Vehicle for Advancing E-Commerce, originally published in: The John Marshall Journal of Computer and Information Law, Vol. XVII, No. 3, Spring 1999 at 723.

13 See also «Pismo» (Letter) of the Supreme Arbitration Court of the Russian Federation from June, 7, 1995 № S1-7/oz-316 «About the Federal Law Act "About the information, informatization and protection of the information"» («Bulleten Vjsshego Arbitrazhnogo Suda Rossiiskoi Federazii», 1995, № 9).

# The European Court of Human Rights: Which Way Next?

*Loveday Hodson, University of Warwick*

*'At any rate – we have to give the personal opportunity to the individual to establish the dignity of the individual human spirit and to prevent injustice.'*[1]

## Introduction

The European Court of Human Rights ['the Court' or 'ECtHR'] now has an enormous workload, far greater than could have been envisaged when it was established in January 1959. There has been a consistently dramatic rise for several years in the number of individual applications that the Court is receiving, and it is fair to say that the Court is now buckling under their weight. The issue of this increase in applications to the Court was highlighted at the European Ministerial Conference on Human Rights, held in Rome in November 2000 to celebrate the 50th anniversary of the signing of the European Convention on Human Rights ['the Convention' or 'ECHR'].[2] One thing that became clear at this meeting was that there was concern about the capacity of the Court to deal with the increasing number of applications. This prompted the Committee of Ministers to establish an Evaluation Group ['the Group'] to examine the problem and to consider possible solutions. The *'Report of the Evaluation Group to the Committee of Ministers on the European Court of Human Rights'*[3] ['the Report'] has now been published, and the Committee of Ministers is currently considering its suggestions.

The question now facing the Council of Europe, and indeed all those who take an interest in the working of the Court, is therefore; 'Which way next for the European Court of Human Rights to deal with this increase in individual applications?'. What is clear is that this is not simply about solving a practical problem; this question also raises philosophical issues about what the role of the Court ought to be. It is, of course, unarguable that the increase in the number of member states to the Convention[4] and an increased awareness amongst the people of Europe of its' provisions have both contributed to this situation. But I would argue that it has primarily arisen as a result of the gradual strengthening of the role of the individual applicant within the Strasbourg machinery. This is

---

1 Council of Europe, *'Collected Edition of the Travaux Preparatoires of the European Convention on Human Rights'*, (The Hague: Nijhoff, 1975) Volume 2, p. 200, *per* Sir Maxwell-Fyfe, United Kingdom.

2 87 UNTS 103; ETS 5; UKTS 38 (1965), Cmnd 2643.

3 Council of Europe, Strasbourg, September 2001. A copy of the report is available online at http://cm.coe.int/stat/E/Public/2001/rapporteur/clcedh/2001egcourt1.htm.

4 Forty-four States have now ratified this treaty.

the result of a persistent philosophical commitment to providing a place for *all* people to be heard who claim to have had their human rights violated. Indeed, the establishment of a right of individual petition is seen by many as being the true achievement of the drafters of the Convention.[5] Any solution to the current problem will, therefore, inevitably have to be evaluated in light of this historic commitment.

## Where Did it All Begin? The Triumph of Liberal Individualism

To put the current problem in perspective, it is useful initially to take a brief historical view of the Court and its foundations. The look to where we are going often requires consideration of where we have come from. It goes without saying that the story of the Convention begins with the end of the 1939–1945 War, which had rocked Europe to its foundations. As part of the process of rebuilding the region, the Council of Europe was formed to promote peace and security. The Consultative Assembly of the Council of Europe adopted on the 8th September 1949 Recommendation 38, which asked that the Committee of Ministers arrange for the drafting of a convention for the purposes of ensuring effective enjoyment of human rights. This Resolution included a draft convention that listed twelve basic freedoms and also included a proposal for the establishment of a commission and a court of justice, with individuals being granted access to take their complaints to the commission. This suggestion was something of a novelty in international law experience, something that the drafters of the Convention were well aware of.[6]

The novelty of the suggestion to include an individual application procedure in the Convention meant that it was not accepted without hesitation. It was immediately clear that not all delegates drafting the ECHR saw the participation of victims in the procedures of an international tribunal as a desirable means of securing human rights. One of the drafters of the ECHR who was adamantly against the proposal was the delegate of the United Kingdom in the CA, Sir David Maxwell-Fyfe, whose objections to such a system were mostly based

5 See, for example, B. Dickson, 'The Council of Europe and the European Convention' in B. Dickson (ed.), *'Human Rights and the European Convention'*, (London: Sweet & Maxwell, 1997) at p. 8.

6 *Op. cit.* n. 1, volume 6 p. 132, 'The third revolutionary reform, is that we shall be introducing at last into this thing called international law, this right of individual appeal which takes the supervision of the respect for human rights out of the field of inter-state politics and offers the possibility to the injured individual himself, at least to inform public opinion by means of a Commission of Enquiry of the most serious abuses of which he may have been the victim in violation of the undertakings assumed by this Convention.' *Per* Mr. Rolin, Belgium.
For an extensive reference to contemporary and modern references to this subject see M. Shaw, *'International Law'*, (Cambridge: Cambridge University Press, 1997, 4th ed.) fn. 228 at p. 182.

upon practical considerations.[7] One of his concerns was the likelihood of a *'shoals of applications'* being made by disgruntled individuals, an argument supported by the Norwegian delegate who argued that the procedure could be used to render the Council of Europe impotent.[8]

However, it was clear that it was not simply practical considerations that were causing some of the drafters to hesitate in accepting this idea. The Belgian delegate in the Consultative Assembly also said that to create a court to which an individual could bring her State would be to look for verdicts *'which would have a particularly degrading character'*.[9] Some States were clearly anxious about ceding sovereignty in such a way. Those against the proposal were concerned that applications could be 'politically inspired' and open to abuse by those on the extreme right and left of the political spectrum seeking to challenge and embarrass the Governments of the day.[10] Mr. Ungoed-Thomas of the United Kingdom, said to the Consultative Assembly:

> ...it is difficult to believe that there will not be brought before the Court cases which are largely influenced by perfectly genuine but political feelings...The action which is proposed to be taken in allowing individuals to bring countries before the Court is, in my view, a retrogressive and an anti-democratic action.[11]

Those against the procedure felt that other Member States were the best complainants in such cases. Given the political climate of the time, it is understandable that such fears were voiced.

However, those expressing these notes of caution were swimming against the tide of opinion within the Council of Europe. It became clear that for many of the drafters the crucial *raison d'être* of the Convention was to ensure to individuals protection from the State where necessary. The Second World War had provided them with enough evidence that even in Europe, *'where the fundamental rights of freedom were thought to be secured to man, those rights were first undermined and then brutally trampled down'*.[12] In 1949 the victorious States in the Council of Europe were able to explain the War as having been a battle between totalitarianism and liberal democracy. In essence, the delegates showed a tendency to distinguish between democratic and totalitarian regimes in the following way: *'we believe that the State exists for the individual, while they believe that the individual exists for the State*[13]'. The protection of individuals' rights and fundamental freedoms therefore came to be connected with the pro-

---

7 Ibid., volume 1, p. 120.
8 Ibid., volume 2, p. 190, *per* Mr. Sundt, Norway.
9 Ibid., volume 2, p. 144, *per* Mr. Rolin, Belgium.
10 Ibid., volume 2, pp. 188-190.
11 Ibid., volume 2, p. 168.
12 Ibid., volume 1, p. 66, *per* Mr. Kraft, Denmark.
13 Ibid., volume 2, p. 90, *per* Mr Sweetman, Ireland, CA.

tection of liberal democracy and central to the liberal philosophy of the Council of Europe States.[14] The Greek representative summed up the mood of the majority of the Consultative Assembly:

> Man is an end in himself! The City and the State are so many organs constituting the means of preserving his dignity, of ensuring the pacific development of his personality and of guaranteeing for him humane living condition.[15]

To the majority of the drafters, therefore, it seemed to follow logically that the individual should play a central role in any enforcement mechanism established under the treaty. Furthermore, fears of an unmanageable number of claims being presented to the Court were held to be unfounded and exaggerated. In fact there was a clear feeling that the right-minded States of the Council of Europe would not be at risk from human rights applications anyway.

The result of these debates was a compromise by which individual states were given the option of whether or not to accept the individual application procedure in relation to the applications to the European Commission of Human Rights [ECmHR or 'the Commission']. But only Member States and the Commission could refer case to the Court that was also established.[16] So it was after a comparatively short gestation period that the Convention entered into force on 3 September 1953 after being ratified by the necessary ten states. The competence of the Commission to receive individual applications took a while longer to become a reality. Sweden was the first country to recognise the Commission's competence in this respect in February 1952, followed by Ireland and Denmark a year later. In September 1953 the CA adopted a Recommendation urging all Member States to ratify the Convention and to accept the optional jurisdiction. Finally by July 1955 the Commission became competent to receive individual applications. It would not be until January 1959, with the necessary eight States had recognised the Court's compulsory jurisdiction, that the European Court of Human Rights was established in Strasbourg. However, despite conditions being attached to the right to individual petition, it is generally recognised that it was no small achievement under the international law of the day to secure to individuals recognition as actors under an international law regime at all.[17]

---

[14] See Article 1 of the Statute of the Council of Europe. Article 8 also provides that violation of this provision can lead to suspension or expulsion from the organisation. This Statute was signed by the Governments of Belgium, Denmark, France, Ireland, Italy, Luxembourg, the Netherlands, Norway, Sweden, and the United Kingdom.

[15] *Op. cit.* n.1 volume 1, p. 56, *per* Mr. Antonopoulos, Greece.

[16] Former Article 44 of the Convention.

[17] See, for example, p. van Dijk and G.J.H van Hoof, *'Theory and Practice of the European Convention on Human Rights'* (The Hague, London and Boston: Kluwer Law International, 1998, 3rd ed.), pp. 44-45.

*The Rise and Rise of the Individual in the Strasbourg Machinery*

If there was some reluctance at the time of the drafting of the Convention towards the idea of the right to individual petition, the position of the individual has since gone from strength to strength. Since 1950 there has been an increasing acceptance of the role of the individual in the Strasbourg proceedings, and with this better access for victims of human rights violations to the organs of the ECHR. In recent years, as we shall see, the individual application procedure has become a compulsory part of the Convention machinery. Consideration will now be given to the steps that were taken towards this end.

As mentioned above, under the original terms of the Convention individuals had no standing to refer their cases to the Court. It was also clear that individual applicants were not formally parties to their cases. On a literal interpretation of the Convention victims were simply there to help the Commission to reach their decision on whether the state in question had complied with the terms of the ECHR. In fact there was not even a requirement under the Convention that applicants be given a copy of the Commission's Report. However, 'the formal exclusion of the applicant was attenuated in the practice adopted by the Commission and the Court'.[18]

The position of the victim was, somewhat unsurprisingly, raised in the very first case that came before the Court, *Lawless v Ireland (No.1)*.[19] The preliminary question for the Court to address was whether, given the official position of the applicant, his views could be put before the Court. The Commission had attempted to ameliorate the position of the applicant by sending to him a copy of its report and inviting his observations. These observations were then incorporated into the final Report sent to the Court. The Irish Government raised objections to this practice, saying that it was incompatible with the supposed objectivity of the Commission's Report and also with Article 44 of the Convention. The Court, clearly mindful of the right to fair trial contained in the ECHR itself, said that it:

> ...must bear in mind its duty to safeguard the interests of the individual, who may not be a party to any court proceedings, and whereas the whole of the proceedings in the Court, as laid down by the Convention and the Rules of Court, are upon issues which concern the Applicant; whereas, accordingly, it is in the interests of the proper administration of justice that the Court should have knowledge of and, if need be, take into consideration, the Applicant's point of view.[20]

---

18 P. Mahoney, 'Developments in the Procedure of the European Court of Human Rights: the Revised Rules of Court', 3 *Yearbook of European Law* 127-167 (1983) at p. 129.

19 Judgment of 14 November 1960, A. 1.

20 Ibid.

Mahoney also notes that it was often difficult for the Court to get a full and clear picture of the facts without being able to hear one side.[21] The Court consequently decided that the practice of the Commission was not incompatible with the Convention and was, indeed, necessary for it to be an effective mechanism. This was a remarkable show of commitment to the notion of individual justice, as Robertson and Merrills note:

> If in Lawless the Court had decided that the applicant could not see the Commission's report, or that he could not comment on it, a barrier would have been set up between the individual and proceedings in the Court, which would become, as it were, the private affair of the government and the Commission. By rejecting this in its very first case the Court not only laid the foundation for subsequent improvements in the applicant's position, but also showed that it was committed to a conception of the Convention in which the protection of the rights of the individual takes priority over jurisdictional and procedural objections reflecting the traditional attitudes of governments.[22]

In the subsequent case of *De Wilde, Ooms and Versup v Belgium*,[23] the Court was asked by the Commission to hear representations from an applicant's lawyer. The Court did not accept the Belgian government's objection that this was contrary to Article 44 and agreed to hear the representations in question. Ten years after *De Wilde* it was customary for applicants' comments to be transmitted to the Court via the Commission's Report, and for the applicant or her lawyer to attend the hearing pursuant to Rule 29(1).[24] As de Meyer notes these developments *'a certainemant permis de remédier dans un certaine mesure á la situation peu satisfaisante dans laquelle la convention semble avoir place les requérants don't il s'agit, en leur refusant le droit de 'se presenter devant la cour' et de la 'saisir' de l'affaire'*.[25] In respect of the role of the individual, these cases began to mark out a path along which subsequent amendments to the ECHR have followed.

---

21 P. Mahoney, 'Developments in the Procedure of the European Court of Human Rights: the Revised Rules of Court', 3 *Yearbook of European Law* 127-167 (1983) at p. 131.

22 A.H. Robertson and J.G. Merrills, *'Human rights in Europe: a study of the European Convention on Human Rights'* (Manchester: Manchester University Press, 1997, 3rd ed.) pp. 307-308.

23 Judgment of 18 November 1970, A. 12.

24 *Op. cit.* n. 21 at p. 130.

25 J. De Meyer, 'La Situation des "personnes physiques", "organisations non gouvernementales" et "groupes de particuliares" dans la procedure devant la Cour européenne des Droits de l'Homme' *Annales de droit* (Louvain 1974) 65-74 at p. 72.

On 1 January 1983 new Rules of Court came into force that aimed to formalise this de facto position of the individual.[26] The new rules ensured that when a case was referred to the Court the person (or group) who initiated the complaint would be sent copies of the originating document and the Commission's report[27] and was given the opportunity to take part in the proceedings.[28] If the applicant chose to do so she could then become directly involved in the running of the case and would be sent copies of all relevant documents filed[29] and the judgement.[30] She was also given other rights in relation to the running of the case, such as being able to apply for interim orders[31] and to submit a claim for just satisfaction.[32] She would also be legally represented,[33] with legal aid being made available. Mahoney clearly felt that these developments signified a greater trust in the individual application procedure:

> The original 1959 Rules of Court, in making possible the limited degree of participation that they did, should not be underestimated, having regard to this context of caution towards the role of the applicant. The subsequent evolution in practice was slow and empirical, being based on the fruits of a patient evaluation of experience; more importantly perhaps, it was accompanied by a change in attitude on the part of all concerned, Governments included, as to the best way of enforcing human rights within the Convention system.[34]

However, 'it was apparent that everything which could be done to improve the applicant's position, short of amending the Convention, had been done'.[35] It was to this that attention next turned.

*Protocols 9 & 11*

By 1986 the Committee of Ministers had said that the question of the *locus standi* of individuals should be looked at in the context of reforming the procedures of the Strasbourg machinery.[36] In October 1990 Protocol 9 was adopted by the Committee of Ministers at their 446[th] meeting and opened for signature, ten

---

26 Pursuant to Article 55 the Court has the power to adopt its own Rules of Procedure. It had first indicated that it might do so in 1974. For more details see generally P. Mahoney, *op. cit.* n. 21.

27 Rule 33 (1) & (2).

28 Rule 33 (3) (d).

29 Rule 37 (4).

30 Rule 54 (4).

31 Rule 36 (1).

32 Rule 49 & 53 (1).

33 Rule 30.

34 For more details see generally P. Mahoney, *op. cit.* n. 21 at p. 132.

35 A.H. Robertson and J.G. Merrills, *op. cit.* n. 22 at p. 307.

36 Third medium-term plan (1987-1991) adopted by the Committee of Ministers on 20[th] November 1986.

signatures being required before it entered into force. The most essential part of the Protocol was that it amended Article 44 of the ECHR, thereby giving individuals and non-governmental organisations standing to refer their cases directly to the Court. The only caveat was that under the new Article 48 (2), a panel of three judges vetted any cases referred by individuals.

An unsurprising consequence of these changes was the marked increase in applications to the Strasbourg organs. A need was soon perceived to alter the ECHR enforcement procedures to accommodate this increase in work. The system as it was then contained significant elements of over-lap and repetition and could be accused of being unnecessarily complex. At the 89th session of the Committee of Ministers, in November 1991, the ministers instructed that priority be given to the streamlining of the ECHR procedures. The drafting of a new protocol was soon under way. The text of Protocol 11 was opened for signature on 11 May 1994, and came into force in November 1998. The most significant changes it introduced are as follows:

- There is a single full-time Court and no Commission.[37]
- The Court has mandatory jurisdiction to receive applications from 'any person, non-governmental organisation or group of individuals claiming to be the victim of a violation by one of the High Contracting Parties of the rights set forth in the Convention…'.[38]
- Each registered application is dealt with judicially. It is initially dealt with by a judge rapporteur, whose role is to channel the application to a Committee of three judges (who can declare it inadmissible unanimously) or to a Chamber of seven judges (if it warrants closer examination) for an admissibility decision.
- The powers of the Committee of Ministers are abolished, apart from the supervising of the Court's judgments.[39]

It is fair to say that these changes made a reality of the practical, moral and philosophical commitment to the individuals' role identified by the majority of the drafters of the Convention in 1949.

## So Where Did it all go Right? The Evaluation Group's Report 2001

A commitment to the individual within the Strasbourg machinery is therefore a key foundation of the ECHR system, and as such its influence cannot be overestimated. But it is undeniable that it has brought with it many problems, problems that have been considered by the Evaluation Group. One might say

---

[37] Article 19 onwards.

[38] Article 34. Although under Article 56 (4) states are able to make a declaration that the right to individual application does not apply to the citizens of its' overseas territories.

[39] Article 46 (2).

that the Court has become a victim of its own success. The rhetoric of individualised justice has had an enormous impact on the popular consciousness in Europe. The Court has come to be seen as an institution for individuals. There is now a great awareness of, and faith in, the Strasbourg machinery. That was bound to happen in an institution that has stood the test of time and, if anything, opened its doors wider to the victims of human rights violations. And, of course there is the issue of the opening up of the Convention to the countries of Eastern Europe. There are now 44 Member States to the Convention, with Bosnia-Hertzegovia ratifying this year. At the time that the Report was written, the combined population of the member states was 772 million.[40] Even when Protocol 11 was being drafted, this increase in membership was not envisaged. The sheer (increasing) volume of applications that the Court now receives forces one to consider whether this commitment to providing individualised justice is both realistic and desirable. It is its' increasing appearance of impracticality that has forced the issue on to the agenda at Strasbourg.

The statistics provided by the Court in relation to provisional applications give one an idea of the scale of the problem:

> The annual number of provisional applications grew from 4,044 in 1988 to 20,538 in 1999, to 26,398 in 2000 (that is, by some 553% over the full period and by some 28% in the last year). In the first seven months of 2001, 20,739 provisional applications were received; if the same rate were maintained, provisional applications in 2001 would total 35,553, an increase of nearly 35% over 2000.
>
> The annual number of applications registered grew from 1,013 in 1988 to 8,402 in 1999, and then to 10,486 in 2000 (that is, by some 935% over the full period and by some 25% in the last year). In the first seven months of 2001 7,909 applications were registered; if the same rate were maintained, registered applications in 2001 would total 13,558, an increase of more than 29% over 2000.[41]

In fact the number of registered applications in 2001 was 13,858. The following diagram gives an illustration of how dramatic the increase in applications has been:

40 *Op. cit.* n. 3, p. 18.

41 Ibid., para. 25 p. 23

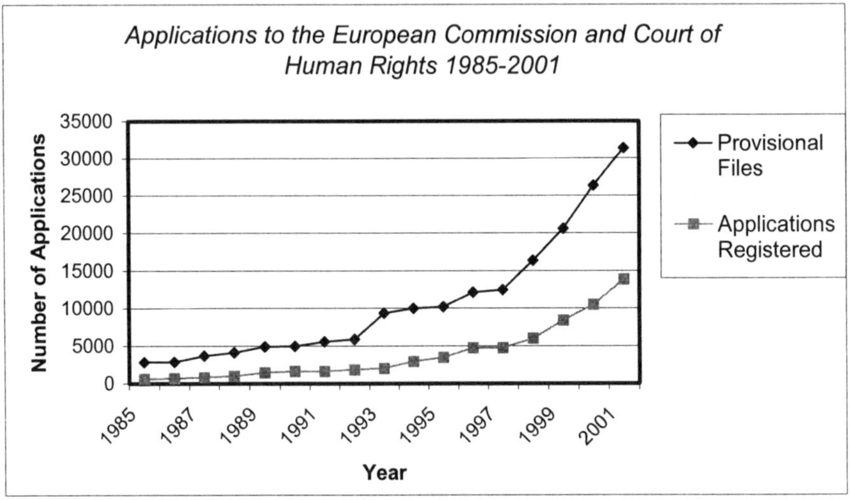


The growing number of applications made to the Court has caused serious problems. One of the most obvious is the delay in dealing with applications. Many cases are not being completed within three years (with five to six years being far from unusual), when the Court has set ideal target for dealing with cases as two years. Of course it also inevitably means that the budget of the Court has increased. The Report states that the proportion of the Council of Europe's budget that is taken up by the Court has increased continuously, with the percentage figure of the Council of Europe's budget taken up by the Court growing from 10% in 1989 to 16.5% in the draft budget for 2002.[42] Along with this have also come the associated problems of staff shortages, an increase number of languages in which the Registry must work,[43] and a lack of space in the purposely-designed building that has only been occupied by the Court only recently. The Council of Europe's internal auditor's conservative estimate was that there would be a 100% increase in applications between 2000 and 2005. These lead to the rather bleak conclusion being made in the Report that:

> '...immediate and urgent action is indispensable if the Court is to remain effective. If no steps are taken, the situation will simply deteriorate, with the Court having no prospect of "catching-up" with its ever-increasing arrears of work. It

---

[42] Ibid., para. 17 p. 19.

[43] Under Rule 34 of the Court's Rules of Procedures, applicants may communicate with the Court in their own language until an application has been declared admissible. In practice, many continue to communicate in their own language after this stage.

will no longer be able to determine all cases within a reasonable time, its public image will suffer and it will gradually lose credibility.'[44]

The 'open-door' policy of the Court to individual applicants brings with it other problems too. In the first place there is the issue of cases being registered that are manifestly ill-founded. Let us assume, to take a very simple example, that we are talking about a complaint involving a violation of the Convention that occurred before it had been ratified by the State in question. Under the procedures at the time of the drafting of the Report, the application would not be initially registered, but rather classified as a 'provisional application'. There would then be correspondence in the applicant's language with a lawyer at the Registry explaining what the problem with the application was. So even those complaints that are not pursued (the Report tells us that roughly 40% of cases are registered[45]) still, of course, have to have a considerable amount of attention devoted to them. And even after that, the applicant could still insist on the filing of their application, meaning that it would require the Court to provide a detailed admissibility decision. The vast majority of registered applications are declared inadmissible or struck off the list; in the year 2000, for example, there were 6,774 such cases. So the notion of individualised justice is encompassing cases that actually fall outside of the scope of the Court's work.

A further problem of treating each alleged violation of the Convention as meriting consideration is the questionable jurisprudential (rather than moral) value in dealing with repetitive cases. A clear finding from the Court of a violation in one case, might very well lead to other victims wanting to pursue a (well-founded) claim based on the same or similar facts. The number of such applications to the Court can and does have serious resource implications. One might ask whether it is sensible for the ECtHR to spend its limited time on such applications. For example, the Court has been particularly troubled by cases involving delay in domestic legal proceedings in Italy, brought under Article 6(1) of the Convention. The amount of work these applications have created in Strasbourg is quite astonishing. The Report tells us:

> Thus, of the total of 21,128 applications registered in the period from 1 November 1998 to 31 January 2001, 2,211 were directed against Italy; of these 1,516 related to the length of proceedings. Again, of the 1,085 applications declared admissible in 2000, 486 concerned Italy and, in 428 cases, related to this same issue. In addition, as at July 2001, there were altogether about 10,000 further provisional applications against Italy falling into this category, of which 3,177 files were ready for

44 *Op. cit.* n. 3 para. 39 p. 34.
45 Ibid., para. 25 p. 23.

registration but could not be processed for lack of human resources in the Registry.[46]

The Registry has analysed the 695 judgments delivered in the year 2000 and categorised them on the basis of their jurisprudential importance. They concluded that 485 were straightforward cases concerning the alleged excessive length of domestic proceedings. Only 94 of the judgments in 2000 were deemed to be 'leading judgments selected for publication'.[47]

## An Evaluation of the Group's Solutions?

In attempting to suggest some solutions to the current crisis facing the Court the Evaluation Group commenced from the following principles:

*a.* There should be no reduction in the substantive rights guaranteed by the Convention and its Protocols.
*b.* The right of individual application, which lies at the heart of the Strasbourg machinery, must be preserved in its essence.
*c.* The Court must be in a position to dispose of applications within a reasonable time but, at the same time, to maintain the quality and authority of its judgments. The latter point goes not only to the credibility and public image of the Court; judgments also often serve as guidelines in the framing of measures to be taken in the respondent State and in other States too.'[48]

It is point *b*, and in particular whether or not the Report has successfully maintained this principle whilst at the same time finding an effective solution to the current problem that has caused the most disquiet amongst commentators.

### *National Measures*

One of the primary solutions that the Evaluation Group was keen to emphasise was a stronger focus on national measures to ensure the protection of rights. Many of these are common-sense suggestions, such as improving education about the Convention. In the Report there is a strong emphasis on the subsidiarity of the Strasbourg system. Again, this appears to be uncontroversial. But what is something of a novelty is that the Report emphasises this as a matter of practicality rather than principle:

> The Court's role must remain subsidiary and it cannot conceivably take over duties and responsibilities incumbent on the Contracting States themselves or act as a first-instance court in respect of a large number of violations of Convention

---

46 Ibid., para. 27 p. 25.
47 Ibid., para. 32 p. 29.
48 Ibid., para. 41 p. 35.

rights alleged to have occurred in a community of almost 800 million individuals.[49]

Presumably using similar logic, the Group notes with approval the fact that the Court has dramatically reduced the number of fact-finding missions that it has embarked on. The Court has done so by finding that a lack of effective investigation at the domestic level is itself a violation of the Convention. But this emphasis on domestic remedies leaves one with a simple and obvious concern: isn't it precisely at times when the domestic remedies have failed that the Strasbourg mechanism should be at its most effective? In the case of a disappearance, for example, is it enough for the Court to find that the lack of investigation is in itself a violation of the right to life? Do we not expect, at times of such fundamental lack of respect for the Convention's right, the Court to step in to conduct a proper investigation? The limitations of simply relying upon the subsidiarity principle are clear and I would suggest that the relationship between Strasbourg and the domestic authorities is more complex than it suggests. In an ideal world there would be no need for external supervision of States human rights record at all; but of course in practice there are times when there is a need for the Court to act in the face of a domestic states inertia or even wilful disregard for the Convention. To rely on arguments of the impracticality of doing so appears to me to be resigned to the fundamental failure of the Strasbourg system.

*Execution of Judgments*

In a similar vein, the Group felt that if the system were working properly then States would simply comply with all adverse judgments and amend whatever legislation or practice it is that offends the Convention. In theory, therefore, there should be no need for 'repetitive' cases. The logic of the Evaluation Group is simple: repetitive cases are indicative of problems at the domestic level and it is therefore the domestic level that should be the target for suggested solutions. The question for the Group therefore became how best to strengthen measures for ensuring compliance with the Court's judgments. The idea of fining States for non-compliance was rejected for the potential injustice it might bring about.[50] One solution suggested by the Group is for the Court to give firmer guidance as to what measures might be taken by the national authorities to remedy the offending law etc, a practice that the Court has began to adopt. Of course this would have to fall short of requiring specific amendments to legislation, for example, but the Group saw the benefit of the Court developing the practice of giving an indication of what may be the best way to comply with judgments.[51] In relation to the position of the individual applicant, this suggestion seems rela-

---

[49] Ibid., para. 47 p. 38.
[50] Ibid., para. 49 p. 39.
[51] Ibid., para. 49 p. 39.

tively uncontroversial. But what would impact on the position of the individual applicant is the Group's further suggestion that pending cases that raise a similar point to that raised by a case already under consideration ought to be able to be 'frozen', pending the outcome of the 'leading' case.[52] Presumably the idea being that those pending will not be in need of a full hearing.

The idea that 'repetitive' cases need not be heard again introduces something of a novelty in to the Convention's mechanisms. It is undoubtedly true that individual applications can be selfish and repetitive, and that hearing each of them can be costly. But experience has shown that it is through these individual narratives that a fuller picture of a State's human rights record emerges. If applications are repetitive, such as in the Italian delay cases, then this is suggestive of a continuing problem. Frequently the State may be facing something of an endemic problem and a host of applications may be seen as unhelpful in such situations. But human rights violations show us when States have failed to achieve the right compromise when faced with such situations. And we come full-circle. For whilst we should be able to rely on States to remedy any violation, these repetitive cases show that, for whatever reason, we cannot always do so. The question therefore is should the Court give voice to each victim of a violation? There are those who say it cannot and, of course, there are those that say it absolutely must. It is simply suggested here that the former position should not be adopted, and the latter rejected, on grounds of expediency. These are important questions of principle, not just practicality.

*Measures Requiring no Amendment of the Convention*

In terms of speeding up the current procedures the Group does make clear attempts not to hinder access of individuals to Strasbourg. For example, the Group rejects both the idea of insisting upon legal representation at all stages of the proceedings and insisting upon the use of one of the official languages of the Court, both of which would obviously be potentially problematic for applicants.[53] However, the Report does make it clear that certain measures ought to be taken to speed up the proceedings. To this end the Court's procedures for handling 'manifestly ill-founded' applications was changed in January 2002. Since that time all application have been registered, so there is no longer a category of Provisional Application. However, once an application is registered, if it is manifestly ill-founded then it will be concluded by a very admissibility decision, in an official language, stating that it is inadmissible but not setting out detailed reasons for this. The clear aim of these changes is to eradicate the lengthy correspondence that an inadmissible case can entail; but from a point of principle their cost is high.

---

52 Ibid., para. 51 p. 40.

53 Ibid., para. 55 p. 41.

The Report also suggests other changes to the current procedures that are cause for concern. The Group shows itself to be strongly in favour of friendly settlements, a procedure currently encouraged and already greatly used in Strasbourg. The Group note the benefit of reaching a settlement for all concerned:

> ...in addition to providing Governments with a means of avoiding excessive publicity and applicants with a means of obtaining an immediate and certain result, the conclusion of a friendly settlement can involve substantial budgetary savings for the Court, especially where a fact-finding mission would otherwise have been necessary.[54]

The Group propose that the Court therefore be even more pro-active in attempting to reach friendly settlements. They suggest this might be achieved by making the applicant incur a penalty in the 'just satisfaction' award if they refuse to accept a reasonable friendly settlement. Perhaps even more disconcerting is the Report's suggestion that the applicant's consent to striking a case off the list could be dispensed with if the refusal of a friendly settlement offer is unreasonable.[55] And in fact this practice has since been adopted by the Court, for the first time in the case of *Akman* v *Turkey*[56] which concerned the fatal shooting of the applicant's son by security forces. There was strong opposition by the applicant in this case to the settlement. It was felt that the settlement was unsatisfactory and that the 'apology' offered by the Government was too vague and did not involve a genuine acknowledgment of guilt. It is highly questionable whether it is desirable for a human rights tribunal to enforce a settlement in a case that involves such a serious violation.

### *Measures Requiring Changes of the Convention*

Further, more radical, measures considered by the Evaluation Group were those that would involve amendments to the Convention. They rejected both the idea of setting up regional human rights tribunals throughout Europe[57] and allowing the Court to give preliminary rulings at the request of national jurisdictions.[58] But the Group were clearly of the opinion that there are two categories of case that do not warrant the Court's attention; those that are manifestly ill-founded and those of minor or secondary importance. The suggestion from the Group is that the Court should have the power to remit back to the domestic authorities those cases raising no substantial issue under the Convention. They also suggest that a two-tier system of dealing with applications be re-introduced, with the preliminary examination of applications being done by an un-elected body of

54 Ibid., para. 62 p. 44.
55 Ibid., para. 62 p. 44-45.
56 Appl. 37453/97, judgment of June 26 2001, unpublished.
57 *Op. cit.* n. 3, para. 83 p. 52.
58 Ibid., para. 84 p. 52.

appointed experts. The idea is that the judges of the Court should be devoting their time to cases that 'raise substantial or new and complex issues of human rights law, are of particular significance for the State concerned or involve allegations of serious human rights violations'.[59] In response to the anticipated criticisms they said:

> To the objection that such a solution would deprive some victims of violation of the Convention of protection, the Evaluation Group would reiterate that the primary responsibility for applying Convention standards lies with domestic courts and authorities. More basically, the Group would reply that the point has been reached at which a difficult choice has to be made: either the Court continues to attempt to deal in the same way with all the applications that arrive (in which event it will slowly sink), or it reserves detailed treatment for those cases which, in the light of its overall object and purpose…,warrant such attention. Not without some soul-searching but nevertheless unreservedly, the Group opts for the second alternative.[60]

As discussed above, offering to refer cases back to the Country of origin is, in certain situations, wildly optimistic. As a coalition of NGOs note in response to the Group's proposals; '…in view of the number and nature of previous adverse Court judgments against certain States, we have serious doubts that some States would be willing and able to establish such systems. The obvious danger arising from these proposals is that applications could be held in limbo and that applicants would be unable to obtain an effective remedy for human rights violations either from the national authorities or the European Court.'[61]

It is questionable too whether it is satisfactory in terms of providing justice for all violations of the Convention to adopt a two-tier system. The rationale behind this suggestion is clear and compelling. However, it must be recognised that would be an obvious move towards a 'Constitutional Court' style-system. It is certainly a significant move away from the hall-mark of the Convention which has been that all applicants can expect to have their complaints fully and independently determined by a judicial body. A further concern this suggestion of the Report raises is for the future development and imaginative interpretation of the Convention's provisions. Let us take the example of same-sex relationships. Under the old two-tier system the Commission made a decision in 1983 that such relationships could not fall within the scope of the right to respect for family life under Article 8.[62] All subsequent applications on this issue were declared inadmissible on the basis of that decision. Clearly that did not allow for social

---

59 Ibid., para. 98 p. 56.

60 Ibid., para. 92 p. 55.

61 *'NGOs response to the Report of the Evaluation Group'*, unpublished, para. 3 p. 2. Copy on file with the author.

62 *X & Y v UK*, 32 DR 220.

and legal developments to be taken into consideration and the issue was never put before the Court until the coming in to force of Protocol 11. Clearly then any re-introduction of a two-tier system would entail the danger of similar stagnation of issues, and the Court not being given the opportunity to consider such important human rights issues.

## Conclusion

This Report is now with the Committee of Ministers for consideration and the Standing Committee on Human Rights are expected to report back in June 2003. Of course it is trite to say that within the Council of Europe nothing has officially been decided yet about the future direction for the European Court of Human Rights. It is possible that the suggestions of the Report could all be ignored, although that seems highly unlikely given the scale of the problem facing the Court. The Registrar of the Court says that despite the feeling of extreme reluctance within the Registry to reduce the right of individual petition, this sits alongside an acceptance that something must be done. Even John Wadham, director of Liberty, acknowledges that the '...statistics certainly do make worrying reading'.[63] The inevitable conclusion is that in the near future we are likely to see significant steps taken backwards away from the commitment to providing justice for all individuals who have had their human rights violated. Many cases involving the violation of human rights may never be heard by a judicial body. The path that the Council of Europe appears to be taking, away from its historic commitment to providing justice in the case of all human rights violations, should be followed with caution. It would certainly be wrong for matters of expediency to determine the future of human rights protection in Europe.

---

63 John Wadham & Tazeen Said, 'What Price the Right of Individual Petition: Report of the Evaluation Group to the Committee of Ministers on the European Court of Human Rights', E.H.R.L.R. 2002, 2, 169-174.

# The Internationalization of Constitutional Law

*Prof. Dr. Brun-Otto Bryde, Universität Gießen,*
*Richter des Bundesverfassungsgerichts*

The Warwick-Giessen-Seminars, which owe so much to Günther Weick's inspiration, have contributed a lot to our understanding of the law of our partners. From the outset these seminars covered all fields of the law. I was always grateful for the chance to present my own current research in the field of constitutional law to a foreign audience, because I have always found it to be a sign of danger when German legal concepts and discussions could not adequately be translated into English. By an extraordinary coincidence my last contribution in this series was a critique of the German Constitutional Court's methodology[1] and I could of course not know at that time that I would participate today as a Constitutional Court Judge myself.

I felt, however, in those past seminars the contribution of constitutional law in an comparative law discourse to be different from private law. I had the impression that it was somewhat less relevant for a foreign audience. Foreign private law has an immediate impact on legal practice as is evident in Günther Weick's main area of specialty, conflicts of law. The movement towards uniform private and commercial law in the last decades especially under the auspices of the European Community, has transformed large parts of the law into transnational law. While I never suffered from an inferiority complex concerning the importance of comparative constitutional law I had to admit that it did not have the same immediate relevance for legal practice but is more of academic interest for our understanding of foreign political and legal systems and - perhaps - as an inspiration for legal and constitutional policy.

This situation has changed. Constitutional law is no longer a parochial subject but has become an international one, the main reason being the development of international human rights law.

In comparative constitutional law, as in general comparative law, one can group different legal systems into "families" even though categorization is more difficult. In this context a distinction which might be unfamiliar is especially fruitful, i.e. the distinction between old and new constitutions. The decisive date for this distinction is not the turn of a century or a war but the creation of the major instruments of international human rights law, the European Convention of Human Rights of 1950 and the international covenants of 1966.

This distinction is important, because in drafting bills of rights after these dates, especially in the worldwide process of reform and democratization in the

---

1 The Role of Constitutional Jurisprudence in German Democracy in: G. Weick (ed.), Competition or Convergence, 1999, p. 23 ff.

1980s and 90s, international human rights treaties provided the main source of inspiration. In Europe the new democracies tried to avoid any possible conflict between their new constitutional law and European human rights law by integrating the Strasbourglaw and jurisprudence into their own constitutional texts.[2] On other continents the UN-treaties were of major importance.[3]

International human rights law influences national constitutional law not only by serving as a textual model. In constitutional systems without a bill of rights the international treaties are sometimes treated as constitutional law to fill this gap in the legal order. An obvious example is Austria, where the constitutional protection of human rights is guaranteed through the ECHR. But we find examples for the incorporation of international human rights law on all continents. In Tanzania, e.g., the courts gave legal force to the invocation of the international human rights treaties in the constitution, which in the view of the drafters probably was mere rhetoric.[4]

Another way in which international human rights law influences national law is the interpretation of national law in conformity with international law. This method is especially popular in Common Law jurisdictions where conferences of high judges approved the Bangalore principles to this effect.[5] This way of incorporation by interpretation has now been put into written law in the British Human Rights Act.[6]

In this family of constitutions whose constitutional law has been influenced by the reception of international human rights law the interpretation of constitutional law is internationalized. Legal doctrine and courts borrow freely from other countries. It is not unusual to cite case law from international courts or from other jurisdictions. A leading case on the freedom of assembly by the Supreme Court in Zambia of 1995 cites case law from Ghana, Nigeria, Tanzania, Zimbabwe, India and the Strasbourg Court.[7]

Interestingly enough, this international process of receiving international human rights law has in return influence on international law. In many countries

---

2 W. Kahl, Das Grundrechtsverständnis der postsozialistischen Verfassungen, 1994, p. 69 ff.

3 Kabudi, Human Rights Jurisprudence in East Africa (VRÜ-Beihefte 15), 1995, p. 25 ff.; Scholler, Die neue äthiopische Verfassung und der Schutz der Menschenrechte, VRÜ 1997, p. 166 ff.; J. Dugard, International Human Rights, in: van Wyk/Dugard/de Villiers/Davis, Rights and Constitutionalism: the New South African Legal Order, 1995, p. 193 ff.; Bryde, Der Verfassungsstaat in Afrika, in: Morlok (Hrsg.) Die Welt des Verfassungsstaates (Kolloquium zum 65. Geburtstag von P. Häberle), 2001, p. 203, 212 ff.

4 Kabudi, op. cit. (Fn. 3), p. 33, 94 f.

5 Kabudi, op. cit. (Fn. 3), p. 28 f.

6 Lord Irvine of Lairg, The Development of Human Rights in Britain under an Incorporated Convention on Human Rights, Public Law 1998, p. 221, 232 ff.

7 Supreme Court of Zambia, Christine Mulundika and 7 Others v. The People 1995/SCZ/25.

constitutional texts that are identical or very similar to the international texts are now the law of the land. That helps to strengthen international law because this way a body of case law and interpretative scholarship is created that could never have arisen on the international level alone.

International human rights law influences national law not only as a model but also because national courts have to take the possibility into account that international courts will declare their judgments unlawful if they deviate from international human rights standards. Especially for the highest tribunals it is an unfamiliar situation no longer to be the highest authority.

This fact has influenced the development of constitutional control in countries without a tradition of judicial review. Obviously the incorporation of the ECHR in Britain through the human rights act was heavily influenced by the wish to stop those cases from reaching Strasbourg. Also in Scandinavia we find the strengthening of constitutional control through the courts to be a result of a dialogue with international courts. A recent doctoral thesis from Giessen clearly established this for Denmark.[8] Similarly, as soon as France had opened the road for individual complaints reaching Strasbourg the French courts, especially the Conseil d'etat became very much more ready to apply the Convention as part of the national law.[9]

A final contributing factor in the internalization of national constitutional law is the fact that judges like to justify their decisions by invoking precedents. In this perspective, drawing on persuasive precedents from international or foreign courts can add legitimacy to judicial decisions. Especially in new constitutional orders in which the courts cannot draw on a body of their own jurisprudence this is helpful. An additional reason might be that in this way they can justify judicial ideas that are unfamiliar, perhaps even unpopular in their own country with an appeal to the authority of prestigious foreign sources.[10]

You will have noticed that until now I have not spoken about German constitutional law. The process I described is an international development in which Germany does not hold a prominent place. An electronic search in the case law of the German constitutional court for citations of the European convention will yield less than 20 hits in the first 104 volumes and other human rights instruments play an even more negligible role in German jurisprudence.

This can partly be explained by the fact that the reasons I just put forward for the reception of international human rights law in other jurisdictions play a lesser role in Germany.

---

8 Mors, Verfassungsgerichtsbarkeit in Dänemark, 2002, p. 98 ff.

9 C. Grewe, Die Grundrechte und ihre richterliche Kontrolle in Frankreich: Grundlagen und aktuelle Entwicklungen, EuGRZ 2002, p. 209, 212.

10 On the role of constitutional courts in constitutional transition cf. Bryde, Constitutional Courts in Constitutional Transition, in: Van Loon/Van Aeken (eds), 60 maaml recht en 1 maal wijn (Liber Amicorum Van Houtte), 1999, p. 235 ff.

The Basic Law of 1949 is an old constitution in my distinction. It does not belong to the family of constitutions that drafted their bill of rights with international human rights law serving as a model.

In addition, the system of fundamental rights protected by the Basic Law is so comprehensive that there is less necessity than in other countries to fill gaps with the help of international documents. This might be an exaggerated claim if you look only at the texts. Especially in the field of procedural law guarantees the ECHR is much more comprehensive. The German Constitutional Court has, however, developed very similar guarantees by interpretation based on the principle of the rule of law enshrined in Art. 20 GG.[11]

Less easy to explain is why the Constitutional Court refrained from drawing on foreign precedents, especially in its early phase. In 1951 the Court was in a very similar position to today's constitutional courts in Eastern Europe. Perhaps it would also have been similarly open to foreign experiences if it could have used foreign models.[12] But the ECHR-organs and the few other European constitutional courts started work at the same time and the US Supreme Court belonged to a very different legal system.

But these reasons alone cannot explain and even less justify why German constitutional law scholarship and jurisprudence show so little interest how disputed issues are discussed in other countries. The reasons for the integration of international human rights law into national constitutional law are present in Germany too even if to a lesser degree.

While in 1949 the drafting of the Basic Law could not benefit from the human rights treaties that came later the universal declaration of human rights was already in existence and it has influenced the wording of Art. 1 subsection 3 which refers to human rights. This could have opened the German fundamental rights discourse much more for the development of international human rights law than it actually did.

I already mentioned that the ECHR is much more differentiated and precise in providing for procedural guarantees. Here the influence is greatest. The Basic law does not spell out, e.g., the presumption of innocence. The Constitutional Court deduces it from the rule of law but because it has no text in the Basic Law it cited the words of the ECHR and drew heavily on the case law of the Strasbourg organs in its jurisprudence.[13] Similarly the principle that court proceedings should be public is spelled out in ECHR and not in the Basic Law where it is

---

11 Right to a fair trial: BVerfGE 57, 250 [274]; right for effective protection through the courts: BVerfGE 88, 118 [123].

12 In 1958 in its leading case on freedom of speech (the Lüth case) the court cites both the French declaration of human rights in French (un des droits les plus précieux de l'homme) and Cardozo in English (the matrix, the indispensable condition of nearly every other form of freedom): BVerfGE 7, 198 [208].

13 BVerfGE 35, 311 (320); 74, 102 (121); 74, 358 (370); 82, 106 (114).

deduced form the principle of rule and law and democracy. Again the Court cites the ECHR in a recent case.[14]

In addition, similar to other countries in Germany too there is an incentive to avoid defeats in international tribunals by bringing the national law into line with international standards from the outset. While the instances where this happens are not many they do hurt. The most prominent example is the length of court proceedings. Strasbourg is much more strict than Karlsruhe in this case[15] and while I find some of the decisions of the European Court doubtful I think the German courts could have avoided the conflict by being more active in developing a similar case law themselves.

Another field where German law is in potential conflict with human rights law is its decision to reserve some fundamental rights (freedom of assembly and basic economic freedoms) to Germans. Fundamental rights reserved to nationals are difficult to reconcile with a conception of basic rights influenced by human rights law.[16] As Germany is under multiple treaty obligations not to discriminate against foreigners such a category of incomplete fundamental rights raises the possibility that a foreigner loses his case in Karlsruhe only to win it in an international forum. International law, e.g. CERD allows a state to restrict access to foreigners but forbids discriminating against those living in the country and admitted to the labor market.[17] The possibility of conflict has however been narrowed down by the jurisprudence of the Constitutional Court. It assumes that the general freedom of action guaranteed in Art 2 subsection 1of the Basic Law protects foreigners who cannot claim the protection of more specific guarantees. As the distinction of a protection under Art. 2 on the one hand and 12 or 8 on the other is negligible the problem might be solved in practice.[18]

Finally, even a Court with much self-confidence like the German Constitutional Court can profit from the additional legitimacy provided by foreign persuasive precedents. When we decided recently against much popular opinion for a Muslim halal-butcher it was helpful to point out that the Austrian Constitutional court had reached the same result on the basis of the ECHR.[19]Also for the difficult task to reconcile our own standards of the rule of law regarding retroactive penalization and the avoidance of impunity for crimes committed in a non-democratic regime international human rights jurisprudence proved helpful.[20]

---

14 BVerfGE 103, 44 (64).

15 Cf. EGMR NJW 1997, 2809.

16 Wallrabenstein, Das Verfassungsrecht der Staatsangehörigkeit, 1999, p. 73 ff.

17 Cf. the opinion of CERD in Habassi/Denmark (Communication No. 10/1997 v. 6.4.1999), CERD/C54/D/10/1997).

18 For a recent example BVerfGE 104, 337 (halal-butcher).

19 BVerfGE 104, 337 (349).

20 BVerfGE 95, 96 (133).

But I do not wish to restrict myself to such pragmatic reasons when I advocate an interpretation of the Basic Law that is open to the international human rights discourse. I think Germany should join the international movement towards an internationalized constitutional law based on human rights. Greater openness towards international discussion of constitutional issues would be helpful for German constitutional law and jurisprudence.

The problem is that not all German lawyers have such a perfect training ground for internationalization as we have in Giessen thanks to the Warwick-Giessen seminars.

# Common Sense v. Legal Expertise A Case Study of Comparative Analysis of Lay Participation in the Former GDR and the FRG*

*Regina E. Rauxloh, University of Warwick*

## Introduction

### 1. Why look at the East?

Whether it is the jury in America, magistrates in England, assessors in Italy or African customary courts: in various criminal justice systems of the world there is some kind of participation of non-legally trained citizens in the process of decision making in criminal cases. The role of laypersons in the criminal trial might be more or less active, but for some reason different legal systems based on very different ideologies seem to have one common notion: that citizens should have a say in criminal justice.

This paper explores two very different legal systems that are based on contrary ideologies, yet come from the same criminal law tradition, i.e. the former German Democratic Republic and the (now reunified) Federal Republic of Germany. How much say do these systems give their citizens in the administration of justice? What are the reasons behind any different or common features?

Of course one could ask, what is the use in looking at a legal system that has been extinguished more than a decade ago and that is not likely to be re-established in a similar form ever again. For me there are three reasons for this historical comparison:

Firstly, I want to take a closer look at the past. A reunification of states also means a reunification of history. The GDR is now part of our common German history and also of our common European history that, unfortunately, is still rather Western centralised even today. GDR history, and even GDR legal history is one of the most fruitful research branches of German history. Nevertheless, much of this history is unfortunately read and written under the light of the present claim of victory of the Western superior system over the "failed" Eastern system.[1] Instead of looking at the GDR legal system with the assumption that all areas are biased, political, and of unlawful injustice, we should instead be open for critique of the "victorious" system at the same time. A such historical comparison may reveal new views on both the GDR and the FRG.

---

* I am grateful to Prof. Lee Bridges, Prof. Upendra Baxi, and Prof. John McEldowney who read an initial draft of this article. The views expressed and any mistakes are attributable to myself alone.

1 Not only is history usually written by the victors but as Markovits puts it clearly: History most of all serves present aims (Markovits 2001, 514).

Secondly, I believe that the comparison with such a different system coming from the same legal tradition can reveal a fresh critically look at our own (Western) assumptions and notions of criminal justice. Even if we do not follow the socialist views of law and society, a new perspective can help to explain our present system. Additionally, it is healthy that we are forced to rethink our assumed basic principles and see if we still can justify our "victorious" system and justify this victory over all branches of legal practice.

Finally, by putting aside the all consuming condemnation of the socialist criminal justice system and trying to be more discerning as well as critical, about the liberal system and West German practice, new perspectives are opened with regards to the development of our system.

Thus examination of lay participation is one attempt at using research in modern legal history to reconsider our historical view of the East German past, rethink our criminal procedures of the present, and draw conclusions for the future.

## 2. The 'people's voice' in Germany

Plato and Aristotle favoured the whole community of citizens (i.e. all free male adults) as constituting the jury trial. Participation in a criminal case was considered as a basic right of each citizen in a democracy.

### *a) Middle Ages*

Interestingly, in the Old German process, too, it was the whole fellowship of free men who would come together to attend the oral and public criminal trial, called thing. The community of free men (Volksgenossen) would decide about a sentence suggested by men who were versed in law. Since any crime was understood as a violation of the tribe there was no difference between private law and criminal law trials. The rules of evidence were strict: the accused could give an oath that he was innocent and oath mates (Eideshelfer) could swear about his good character or that his oath was true, but there were no statements given by eyewitnesses. Besides, there were ordeals that would demonstrate guilt or innocence.[2]

During the second half of medieval times, together with the development of public power criminal law was gradually distinguished from private law and became a public matter. The principle of private action was replaced by the principle whereby only the prosecutor could initiate the action. Now, the judge investigated himself and became prosecutor at the same time - the true inquisition process.[3] Procedures became secret, written and more rational and ordeal was

---

2 Roxin 1998, 520 ff.; Richter 1983, 49.

3 This form of procedure with the judge and prosecutor and even defence counsel in one person lived on until the 18th Century.

replaced by witnesses' statements. The victim developed from accuser to witness, the defendant from subject to object of investigation. The advantage of this was that it stopped the former self-administered justice through feuds. The price for more rational evidence was that the confession became the only absolutely reliable proof, which resulted in the extensive application of torture.

In 1532 (following numerous complaints about biased and cruel justice) the German Reich enacted a Criminal Procedure Code including Criminal Law: the Constitutio Criminalis Carolina (CCC) which was adopted by many German states. This law was based on the scientific methods of the Italian, highly developed law, which had merged Roman and canonical law. With the reception of the scientific Italian law, the law became more and more remote from the people.[4] The CCC discouraged private accusations and strengthened the inquisitorial role of the judge. Although the procedures were written and secret there had to be lay judges present when the judge interrogated the defendant. However, only rarely did lay or professional judges receive adequate legal training and consequently, case files were often sent to the Oberhof (highest territorial court) or law schools, neither of which would have even seen the defendant. However, it was on their recommendations that the sentence was determined. Thus, the investigating institution differed from the deciding body.[5]

*b) The Enlightenment*

With the rise of the absolutist states, laypersons completely disappeared from the jurisdiction. Instead the influence and direct intervention of the absolutist rulers on the professional and state judges increased dramatically.[6] In the 18th Century and especially following the French Revolution, enlightenment movement pressed for rationality, humanity and thus the abolition of inquisition and torture. Public trial, free evaluation of evidence, and the public prosecutor were introduced. Also the constitution of lay participation in the form of juries was demanded. It was hoped that the jury would help to abolish the absolute government's interference in the jurisdiction. The call for procedural reforms could not be separated from political claims and the jury always has been seen as a political device rather than merely an appropriate tool for finding truth in single cases.[7] As a legal instrument it had political importance at the same time.[8] Hence it is not surprising that, right from the beginning the jury was both celebrated and yet condemned at the same time for being an important aspect of representative democracy.[9]

4 Eser 1995, 162.
5 Roxin 1998, 522.
6 Eser 1995, 163.
7 Richter 1983, 53.
8 Vormbaum 1988, 133.
9 Rüping 1976, 270.

In 1798 the jury trial was introduced into Rheinland-Palatine[10] and in 1850-1852 most of the German states introduced new Criminal Procedure Codes with lay participation, prosecutors, public and oral trial and free evaluation of evidence.[11] Shortly after the institution of the jury trial the mixed bench was re-introduced as well.

With the unification of the German Reich and the drafting of a united Reich Judicature Act (Gerichtsverfassungsgesetz) in 1877, the jury could only remain under the compromise of reduction of its jurisdiction.[12] According to the GVG of 1877 most serious crime was decided by the jury that imitated the English model in comprising twelve lay judges, who would decide only about guilt and innocence, while the professional judge bench would issue the sentence.[13] Less serious crime was handled by trials with only five professional judges. Small crime was tried before the lay judge court (Schöffengericht) consisting of two lay judges and one professional where all three decided about guilt and sentence. In all Appeal Courts and in the Supreme Court of the German Reich (Reichsgericht), which heard cases of high treason at first instance, there was no lay participation.[14]

The jury of 1877 excluded expressly women,[15] servants, schoolteachers and de facto those who could not afford loss of earnings.[16]

The jury was considered a democratic achievement, but it gradually became more and more criticised on the continent.[17] This was mainly due to the fact that the jury had to decide without any influence from the professional judges. Since there had to be some legal advice, the judges had to formulate a form of question that was given to the jury. This had to deal with all important considerations.[18] The judge was obliged to explain the questions without giving any indication of his view of the answers, especially with regards to the evaluation of evidence. In contrast to the Anglo-American system where the judge is much less actively involved in the hearing, in the inquisitorial systems the explanations had to be purely academic with no reference to the individual case. Too much was often demanded of the jurors and there have been many misjudgements both in favour and against the defendant. Since the jury's verdict had not to be substantiated there was no possibility to appeal against the decision.[19] Har-

---

10 Because of the French occupation of the left bank of the Rhine (Richter 1983, 53).

11 Richter 1983, 53.

12 Vormbaum 1988, 143. The conservative government favoured a replacement of the jury by a bench of lay judges.

13 Hartung 1970, 601 (The author was himself involved in the Emminger'sche Reform.)

14 Schäfer 1988, Einleitung, Rn. 2.

15 Women were allowed in 1922.

16 Vormbaum 1988, 146.

17 Hartung 1970, 601.

18 Hartung 1970, 605.

19 Hartung 1970, 606.

tung argues that the jury did not work in Germany because it was an English institution related to the English adversary system that was foreign to the inquisitorial system with a less impartial and more active judge.[20]

*c) Lex Emminger*

In the Weimar Republic, the selection of lay judges and jurors was gravely criticised, not at last because the working class was underrepresented.[21] In 1923 the Ministry of Justice of the German Reich (Reichsjustizministerium)[22] formulated a draft for abolishing jury trial. This was strongly opposed by the law commissions of both Reichsrat and Reichstag (especially the Social Democrats) and the abolition was "balanced on a knife-edge".[23] However, due to the political events in mid 1923[24] the government was able to introduce the draft as a decree without the procedure of parliamentary legislation (Notverordnung). On the 4th January 1924 the jury was abolished by the so called Emminger'sche Reform[25] against the strong opposition of Reichtstag and Reichsrat and hence since than it was always held in disrepute.[26] This development had the approval of practising lawyers because of their academic resistance against the opinion of the simple people, bad practical experiences of unjust verdicts, and consciousness of their social rank.[27]

After the new regulation, middle and serious crime was now decided by a mixed bench consisting of three professional and six lay judges at the Regional Court, so-called Schwurgericht. Lay judges even sat in the appeal cases,[28] whereas minor criminal cases now were decided by one single professional judge only.[29]

In 1933 in a re-election of the lay judges all "Non-Aryans" and "people's enemies" were replaced. At the beginning of World War II a decree ended any participation of lay judges.[30]

---

20 Hartung 1970, 609.

21 Rüping 1976, 270; Hitler's trial 1924 was judged by fanatic supporters of him.

22 Under Gustav Radbruch with the support of the Prussian Ministry of Justice.

23 According to Hartung no modification of the Judicature Act by the decree has been examined and discussed so much as the change of jury in lay judges' trial: Hartung 1970, 605.

24 Passive resistance against the French occupation of the Ruhr District, currency reform.

25 So named after the Minister of Justice Erich Emminger (1880-1951).

26 Vormbaum 1988, 141.

27 Vormbaum 1988, 134.

28 However, in practice a professional judge with two lay judges has much more power than three professional judges with a twelve member jury who alone can decide about guilt and innocence and thus (in case of an acquittal) exclude the professionals completely from sentenceing.

29 Hartung 1970, 605. The reason for this was that in the time of inflation minor crime increased and the lay judges trials were too slow.

30 01.09.1939 RGBl. I. p. 1658.

### d) *After the Second World War*

After the war the different states and zones enacted different laws regarding lay participation.[31]

In West Germany the Act of Unification of Law (Rechtsvereinheitlichungsgesetz) from 12.9.1950 re-established the legal situation from 1932 for the Federal Republic. In 1975 the Criminal Law Amendment Act (Strafrechtsänderunsgsgesetz) reduced the Emminger'sche Schwurgericht even further.[32] Now in the criminal division of the Regional Court only two lay persons sit with three professional judges. In contrast to 1924 this time the diminishment of lay participation was no longer criticised publicly. The question of lay participation was no longer a matter of public interest.[33]

Officially GDR and FRG had the same Criminal Procedure Code until 1968, i.e. the code from 1877. Whereas the FRG developed the Old Penal and Criminal Procedure Code, the GDR completely revolutionised criminal law and replaced the old law with a new system.[34] In the GDR there was no question of reintroducing the jury that was seen as fruit of the bourgeoisie. In 1949 the lay judges were re-introduced in East Germany. Besides, socialism found a number of different ways to let the citizens participate in the administration of criminal justice, as we will see later on.

Today German criminal law and criminal procedure law consist mainly of West German law, with some East German provisions and some transitional measures.

## A. Sense of Right and Wrong - Lay Participation in West

As we have seen there is no jury trial in Germany. Lay persons participate in today's German criminal justice process as lay judges or in arbitration bodies.[35]

### 1. Western Lay Judges

At the District Courts the Schöffengericht, (i.e. a bench consisting of two lay and one or two professional judges) hear cases for which a punishment higher than two years is expected.[36] Minor offences and procedures of Private Criminal Action are heard only by one professional judge. At the Regional Court, in first instance cases two lay and three professional judges decide about serious crime and crimes against the state. In appeal procedures two lay and one professional

---

31 Only Bavaria introduced a jury deciding only about the guilt and innocence.

32 Erstes Gesetz zur Reform des Strafverfahrensrecht vom 9.12.1974 BGBl. I, p. 3393.

33 This decreased public interest is mirrowed by the small ambition to become a lay judge: Vormbaum 1988, 148.

34 Renger 1990, 12.

35 By lay persons I mean not legally trained citizens who are not paid for their legal work.

36 Because of the limited space I leave out special regulations for juvenile cases.

judge sit. The Higher Regional Court and the Federal Court consist only of professional judges.

Every four years, the local councils have to produce a proposal list (§ 36 GVG). In practice the candidates are proposed by parties, churches, union etc. or the citizens themselves.

Nobody should be elected who did not agree to the election. After the election the position is an obligation.[37] From this list the lay judge election commission at every District Court elects the lay judges. Generally, every German citizen can become a judge. Between 1997 and 2000 there have been about 61 000 lay judges. That is about ten times as much as professional criminal law judges.[38]

According to § 42 II GVG the lay judges are supposed to display a representative cross section of the population regarding sex, age, profession, and social origin. However, empirical research has shown that women are highly underrepresented. The same is true for young male and older female citizens. The self-employed and members of the civil service are highly over-represented, whereas retired persons are gravely underrepresented.[39]

The lay judge who has administered an oath has to sit about 12 days per year. Her obligations are to take the oath, to appear for each hearing, to contribute to the bench discussion, and vote. Lay judges participate only in the main proceedings and do not sign the written sentence. What is often criticised is that lay judges are denied the right to read the case files and reports in order to prevent undue influence and to ensure that all evidence is brought orally and in public.[40]

The function of lay judges is the participation of the people in the administration of justice.[41] Besides the publicity of the public hearing the people shall have the opportunity to look into the court's conference room and understand the problems and inner conflicts that affect the deciding of a case.[42] The idea is not only that the citizens control the courts (which is the reason for the principle of public trial) but moreover that they understand the difficulties and inner conflicts of conscience in taking judicial decisions and share the responsibility of judicial decisions.[43] The aim is to maintain and strengthen the citizens' confidence in the justice system.[44]

---

37 Gerstein 2002, 2.
38 Gerstein 2002, 1.
39 Katholnigg/Bierstedt 1982, 267.
40 Rüping 1976, 272.
41 Kissel 1985, 490; BGH NStZ 1985, 512.
42 Rüping 1976, 273.
43 Rüping 1976, 273.
44 Kissel 2001, 681; That is why originally the lay judges were in the majority on the judges' bench (Kissel 1985, 490).

Another important function of lay judges is the promotion of modern popular justice.[45] The professional judge's reasoning shall be checked by an untrained sense of right and wrong.[46] The lay judges' common sense is supposed to guarantee popular administration of justice[47] including non legal values. The common criticism that court decisions are taken by remote judges without connection to real life shall be undermined. Besides, the judge should be prevented of being absorbed by routine decision making and instead consider each single case individually.[48]

Furthermore, the professional judge should be forced to express her argument in such a way that lay people can follow it (so called plausibility check).[49]

Another aim is to increase the citizen's legal knowledge as well as his understanding of the jurisdiction and the judges' problems.[50] Additionally, professionals increase their experience and general knowledge through the lay judges' technical expertise.[51]

## 2. Obligation of Peace - Conciliation Proceedings

Following the development of the French revolution and the rise of civil liberalism, settlement and conciliation institutions were established, often in the hands of lay people and most of all in the area of civil law. In 1851 Prussia introduced an obligatory Conciliation Proceeding for cases of libel and assault before criminal proceedings. After some controversial discussions, the Criminal Procedure Code of the Reich of 1877 also introduced these institutions[52] in order to relieve the District Courts and to open a forum for offender and victim to communicate with each other. There was a high number of such proceedings at the end of the 19$^{th}$ Century and in 1924 the number of offences was extended.[53]

Today a private criminal action (in cases of trespass, libel, breach of the secret of correspondence, assault, threat or criminal damage of property), - i.e. a criminal action brought by a private party instead of the public prosecutor - can only be brought about, if a previous arbitration proceeding was not successful. The idea is to avoid unnecessary private criminal actions and to conciliate interpersonal conflicts especially in the neighbourhood.[54] The arbitration boards are regulated in each German state independently.

45 Kissel 2001, 681.
46 Schäfer 1988, Einleitung, Rn. 8.
47 Schäfer 1988, Einleitung, Rn. 9 "Volkstümlichkeit der Rechtspflege".
48 Rüping 1976, 273.
49 Rüping 1976, 273.
50 Kissel 2001, 681.
51 Kissel 2001, 681.
52 But only for libel cases.
53 Trespass, breaching the secrecy of correspondence, assault, threat and criminal damage.
54 Luther 1991, 18.

The main function of a conciliation process is to prevent the stigmatisation of the offender yet still make her responsible for her behaviour. The Conciliation Proceedings can end in compensation, apologies, or payment to charity.[55] Besides, the proceedings are suppose to consider in particular the victim's interests social re-integration. Peaceful conflict management replaces punishment and retaliation, damage is compensated and relationships are re-established, which in the neighbourhood is usually easier to achieve than in a formal state court.[56]

The fact that obligatory conciliation proceedings work as a precondition for private criminal action, is proven by the statistics: there are three times as many conciliation proceeding than Private Criminal Action. 50% of the conciliation proceedings are successful, i.e. the case is settled. Surprisingly, 50% of the proceedings are initiated not as requirement for a later Private Criminal Action but informal private action and as the desire to mediate.[57] However, both Private Criminal Action and Conciliation Proceeding are initiated very rarely and numbers are even decreasing.

Obviously, the main advantage of arbitration proceedings is the private informal atmosphere. However, the comparison with the formal proceeding, i.e. application, proceeding, summon to appear, and taking of evidence might give the image of the arbitrator as judge and scares the parties. Often the settlement reflects the view of the arbitrator rather than that of the parties.[58]

Only in the new East German states the Arbitration Boards in Communities Act (Gesetz über Schiedsstellen in den Gemeinden) is valid.[59] The East German Parliament (Volkskammer) passed this law on the 13.09.1990.[60] Its function was to replace the GDR Social Courts[61] with conciliation boards. In accordance with this Act, each community or group of communities is supposed to establish an arbitration board (Schiedsstelle) for not more than 10 000 citizens. The bench consists of three arbitrators who are elected by the local council and confirmed by the head of the District Court for five years. The arbitration board is in charge of the conciliation proceedings as well as for the arbitration proceedings (as precondition for the private criminal action). Defence counsel can take part in the proceedings and whilst the proceedings are not public, witnesses or experts can nonetheless (voluntarily) appear.[62]

---

55 Rössner 1996, 457.
56 Rössner 1996, 456.
57 Rössner 1996, 457.
58 Rüssel NJW 2000, 2801.
59 On the discussion in the Volkskammer: Schönfeldt 2002, 416 ff.; Rössner (1996, 457) would like this law to be nation-wide.
60 GBl DDR I, p. 1527.
61 See below.
62 Luther 1991, 18.

Besides in cases of private criminal action, the prosecutor can hand over a criminal case to the arbitration board to extra-judicial settlement. The aim is to re-establish social peace as well as to find compensation between offender and victim. Condition is that the consequence of the offence is minor, that the offender has only minor guilt, and that he agrees to arbitrate proceeding, and finally that there is no public interest in state prosecution.

In the arbitration procedure the offender can voluntarily agree to one or more of the following obligations:

- apologise to the injured party
- compensate any damage
- pay a sum to charity or the state
- voluntary public work

The offender then has a time limit to carry out his obligation and to report to the prosecutor who is controlling it. After fulfilling of all the agreed duties the prosecutor will abandon the court proceeding. Otherwise the criminal case is continued at the formal court.[63] Unlike the Social Courts in the GDR, the arbitration boards require a fee.[64]

In 1997 there were 996 arbitration boards in the new German states.[65] But for reason of efficiency the prosecutors show a tendency to dismiss the charge of cases that were eligible to be transferred to arbitration boards.[66] Also defence lawyers do not encourage these procedures that are quite unprofitable for them.

### 3. Probe

As we have seen there are a number of aims that lay participation in West respectively reunified Germany is expected to serve. Now let us examine, whether these numerous expectations are in practice fulfilled.

#### *a) The expectation of democracy*

It is always claimed that lay persons involved in the administration of criminal justice is part of democracy. The people from whom all state power emanates[67] shall have a share of the jurisdiction in one of the three arms of state powers. This assumes that the group of people that participates in the jurisdiction is democratically elected. As illustrated above, lay judges are only elected indirectly by the citizens through several election levels, hence they can hardly

63 Luther 1991, 18, § 43 I.
64 Schönfeldt 2002, 423.
65 Schönfeldt 2002, 431.
66 Schönfeldt 2002, 433.
67 Art. 20 II 1 Basic Law.

be described as a democratic element.[68] Similarly, lay judges do not represent a representative cross section of the general population.

Secondly, the democracy argument presupposes that the lay judges have some influence on the court decisions. It is often complained that in practice the lay judges are acting rather passively on the bench. They seldom intervene and hardly ever outvote the professional judge, who de facto is the decision maker.[69] In addition the lay judges have quite restricted jurisdiction regarding the democratic importance that is ascribed to them. Crimes against the state, for instance, or the question whether a special case should be re-opened, are decided solely by professional judges.[70]

Of course the arbitrator boards have a more active role.[71] However their jurisdiction is limited to small cases when the offender has confessed and the damaged party is to some extent willing to conciliate. They come only into action when the question of guilt and innocence is undisputed. And as mentioned before, the number of cases they decide is extremely small. Hence their influence on the general jurisdiction is too small to speak of democratic involvement.

As well as having very little influence over the single court decision that the lay judges are supposed to control,[72] the lay judges themselves are easily influenced. Baur explains that originally lay judges were supposed to protect the court against undue influence exerted by the executive on the professionals who were highly dependent on the state. Today the risk of undue pressure comes not so much from the government[73] as from the mass media. All judges, but lay judges more than the professionals, are easily influenced by the mass media. The function of controlling the professional who is applying the law with his sense of justice is clearly undermined when this same sense is created by the media.[74] It is argued that the lay judge bears the risk that he puts too much weight on public opinion, whereas the professional judge is trained to distinguish between different arguments, interests and influences.[75] On the other side, the belief that professionals are more resistant to outside influences is an assumption that needs confirmation by empirical research.

Lay judges are also called an important democratic device, because in addition to the public audience, mixed benches "takes the public in the judge's conference chamber" and thus extend public control by the citizens. Kühne opposes

---

68 Volk 1982, 374.

69 Baur 1968, 52.

70 Volk 1982, 381.

71 I refer here expressively only to the participation in criminal law.

72 Gerstein 2002, 3.

73 For the undue influence from political parties see Schmidt-Hieber and Ekkehard Kiesewetter, Parteigeist und politischer Geist in der Justiz, NJW 1992, p. 1790.

74 Baur 1968, 53.

75 Baur 1968, 55.

this argument by pointing out that unlike the times when the judge was a profession exclusively for a special class, nowadays every citizen can become a professional judge. Thus it is assured that the judge is just a simple citizen as everybody. Besides, the discussion in the conference chambers are subject to professional confidentiality, so that public scrutiny is not extended to that part of the process.[76]

Another point is that lay participation was introduced, when today's procedural safeguards, i.e. the principle of immediacy, free evaluation of evidence and oral and public trial that were supposed to replace the inquisition process, were not yet introduced.[77] But today court hearings are public and oral and the judge is in theory and in practice highly independent. Further control is assured by the defence lawyer.[78]

*b) The expectation of extending legal knowledge*

Another expectation is that through the direct participation in court trials, the legal knowledge of the general population will be increased, deepened and internalised. Volk, however, reminds that in the courts only the lay judges themselves are trained, which is a comparatively small part of the population.[79] Contrary to the GDR, West German lay judges have no mission to spread their knowledge and experiences, so that there is no feedback to the society (only within the circle of acquaintance if at all).

On the other side it is hoped that the court will profit from lay judges' special knowledge. But in criminal cases, lay judges are elected for a fixed period of time, so they cannot be chosen according to their special knowledge.[80]

*c) The expectation of popular justice*

It is said that lay participation increases the quality of adjudication, because the citizens' sense of justice will bring the law closer to the people and make court decisions relevant to the present day. Antiquated values and academic dogmatics should be replaced by modern common sense.[81] It is claimed that jurisdictions with lay participation are becoming more popular due to the fact that legal gaps are filled with people's sense of justice, whereas the professionals are remote from reality and "professionally blinkered".[82] Gerstein argues that the criminal case not only consists of complicated judicial problems, but also of evaluation of witness statements, prognosis of future behaviour of the defendant

76 Kühne 1985, 238.
77 Vormbaum 1988, 135.
78 Kühne 1985, 237.
79 Volk 1982, 374.
80 Kühne 1985, 237; this was different in the GDR as we see later on.
81 Kühne 1985, 238.
82 Katholnigg/Bierstedt 1982, 267.

and finding the right sanction for offender and offence. A lay person can judge these issues as competently as a professional judge.[83] Kühne, on the other hand, argues that no explanation is given for the assumption that lay person are more able to identify and to express the people's sense than the professional. Since the legal profession is open to everybody, there is no risk of class distinction. It is true that statistically the lower classes are underrepresented in legal professions, but (as seen above) this is unfortunately true, for the lay judges, too.[84] But Kühne only considers class differences as an issue, whereas the proponents of lay participation state that it is the legal training and routine that makes the judges remote from the common citizen, not their social background.

Furthermore, the diversity of today's German society makes it for everybody difficult to speak about **the** people's wisdom and **the** common sense.[85]

In favour of lay participation it is often claimed that the people accept the court judgement better if it is taken not only by professionals but also by lay persons like themselves.[86] The question is whether the citizen has confidence in a lay person taking the right decision or whether he rather considers him as non-professional with too much emotional involvement and too little competence. Citizens also might feel that they have a right to a fully trained "expert".[87] Since neither of these has been addressed in empirical research, we have little to analyse aside from personal experiences and speculations.

The claim for a more popular justice is commendable but as Volk makes clear: if law steadily moves away from the people, moving people closer to the administration of criminal justice does not reverse or stop this development.[88]

One of the main functions of lay judges is the so called plausibility check. Because she shares the bench with lay persons the professional judge is forced to express herself in a way that her colleagues without legal training can understand her. But courtroom observations show that lay judges only rarely request explanations by the professionals. Moreover, I would suggest that the judges should be forced to express themselves in a way lay persons can understand it not just for the sake of the lay judges, but also for the defendant, injured party, public audience etc. Besides, the lay judges have no control over the reverse translation from their contributions into technical terms in which the final decision will be formulated.[89] Secondly, regarding sense of justice, one must not forget that precise legal language and interpretation has a justification in finding the

[83] Gerstein 2002, 3.
[84] Kühne 1985, 238.
[85] Kühne 1985, 238.
[86] Rüping 1976, 273.
[87] Baur 1968, 52.
[88] Likewise Kühne 1985, 238.
[89] Volk 1982, 387.

balance between stability of law and justice in the single case.[90] Lays might evaluate the defendant's life style and character more than the offence itself and let concerns about recidivism and danger for society prevail over common rules of evidence.[91]

Maybe I am biased due to my own German and English legal education, but I strongly hold that exact legal language and technical terms have a very strong justification in making law and its administration controllable, equal and foreseeable. Clearly, law needs to be expressed in such a way that it is understandable for lay persons, but language is a forceful tool and both sides have to be balanced carefully.

## B. Towards a better us - Lay Participation in East

The GDR assumed[92] that the many factors leading to crime have been eradicated by the establishment of the socialist society, guaranteeing full employment,[93] social security, equality, justice, free education, encouragement of collective consciences, and opportunities for political engagement.[94] Thus, it was assumed, socialism would replace individual envy and social interest differences with co-operation, mutual help and respect between the members of society.[95] In contrast to West Germany, the GDR believed that it was possible to overcome crime. The fact that there was still crime in socialist countries was explained with the theory of class struggle (the conquered resist the new order and foreign imperialists try to undermine the system) and the relic theory (crime is a remnant of bourgeoisie).[96]

Corresponding to that, criminals were classified in two categories:

On the one had there were those, who acted against the socialist society of the GDR. Everybody falling in this category was called a political criminal.[97] On the other hand, there was general crime, which was not directed against the state.[98] but damaging society and hence seen as failure to understand the benefits and the necessity of socialism. The punishments of "erring friend" serves special deterrence and education of the individual, where as the punishment of "enemies" serves general deterrence and repression.[99] Political crime was separated from general crime, investigated by the State Security, prosecuted by a special

---

90 Kühne 1985, 238.
91 Volk 1982, 376.
92 Engels argues that general crime is a form of workers to protest against their exploitation.
93 Laziness was considered as main condition for crime (Herzog/Wagner 1997, 81).
94 Kräupl/Reuter 1987, 24.
95 Herzog/Wagner 1997, 73.
96 Brunner 1975, 179.
97 For example persons who criticised the system or who tried to leave the country.
98 Herzog/Wagner 1997, 81.
99 Brunner 1975, 180.

state attorney and adjudicated by a special court, i.e. the IA,[100] all laying in the responsibility of the Ministry for Interior.[101] This feature is mirrored by the prison population. In 1988, the GDR had 24,305 prisoners. This ratio of 160 per 100,000 inhabitants was nearly twice as high as the one in the FRG with 85 per 100,000 citizens, but less than half of the USA ratio with 351 prisoners per 100,000 population.[102] Although only 27.5% of the convicted had committed offences against state security, they accurated for 47% of the prison population.[103] Whereas the perceived political criminals felt the whole range of the socialist state's strength, the "normal" criminal was treated as "the lost son", who was to be guided back to the right path.[104]

Within this system of criminal categories, the criminal courts demonstrated both repression and benevolence at the same time or as Markovits puts it:

> "Like a possessive parent, socialism could tolerate misbehaviour, but not rejection".[105]

Hence education of the criminal as well as of the general population was an essential task of the criminal justice system. This explains the active involvement of citizens in the administration of criminal law cases.

### 1. As many as possible

The belief in the necessity of large public participation is expressed in Art. 87 and 90 III of the GDR Constitution, whereas the West German Basic Law fails to mention any lay participation. Also the preamble of the Criminal Code and several provisions of the Criminal Procedure Code emphasise the importance of active involvement of lay persons. According to § 4 StPO-E[106] the citizens have a basic right to participate actively in matters of state and society and thus in the criminal procedure. The participation of the public is supposed to underpin the unbiased solving of cases, the mobilisation of the people, and contribute to the development of the citizens' conscience of state and law.[107] To involve as many members of the society as possible, but also to encompass leaders

---

100 Markovits 1992, 97.

101 Herzog/Wagner 1997, 70.

102 Markovits 1992, 97. The GDR prison population comprises 25% convicted who had refused to work, 10% who had attempted to flee and 6% who had resisted state organs.

103 Markovits 1992, 98. Some sentences were in the first place supposed to get Western money from the FRG who would buy the prisoners free (Roenne 1997, 110).

104 Herzog/Wagner 1997, 72.

105 Markovits 1992, 98.

106 StPO = Strafprozessordnung = Criminal Procedure Code. Since both German states used the same name, I chose the abbreviation StPO-E for the East German and StPO-W for the West German Code.

107 Ministerium der Justiz 1968, 30.

of economic entities was considered important[108] not only for the reintegration and education of the criminal, but also with regards to crime prevention.[109] It was the obligation of court, prosecution and the investigating organs to ensure citizens' participation (§ 4 III StPO-E).

According to § 4 II citizens acted as lay judges, representatives of the collectives, social prosecutors or defendants or give a surety for the convicted (§ 31 StGB). The function of lay judges was only in part the involvement of "general common sense and real-life experience of the citizens" in the state court adjudication. More important was the popularising[110] of law and the education of the general population through the communication of the lay judges with other people.[111]

## 2. Eastern Lay Judges

It is true that the term „judge" in the West German Basic Law also embraces the lay judges, but in the East German constitution the lay judges were expressively named in Art. 94 II, 95 and Art. 96 II. Every first instance procedure at the District Court and the Regional Court (not only criminal cases) was judged by one professional judge[112] and two lay judges.

### *a) Recruitment of Lay Judges*

In opposition to the members of the Social Courts,[113] finding people willing to work as lay judges was not a difficult task.

> "They would get their normal salary and it could be interesting to get for two weeks an insight at the court, some enjoyed this. It can be interesting to have a change from the every day's work".[114]

The selection of lay judges was quite different to the procedures in the FRG: The election took place every four years.[115] The enterprises were in charge of providing a certain number of lay judges.[116] The parties and mass organisations nominated their people according to a particular scheme and the whole enterprise would then discuss whether or not this person was worthy and appropriate

---

108 Kräupl/Reuter 1987, 24.

109 Herzog/Wagner 1997, 77.

110 Markovits 1992, 99.

111 Meador 1986, 143.

112 In exception two professional judges.

113 See below.

114 Interview with an former GDR judge. (All interviews mentioned in this paper have been semi-structured interviews conducted 2001/02 as part of my empirical research in Brandenburg.).

115 "Some of the lay judges were elected again and again and thus sitting there for years."

116 Interviews.

to sit as a lay judge. The nominees were then elected.[117] The list of the elected lay judges would be passed to the court which checked whether they had any previous convictions. Anybody previously convicted was usually excluded from sitting as a lay judge. Afterwards the list was passed to the State Security which would check whether there were any security problems, for example if they had contact to the West. In this case the State Security would speak directly (without consulting the court) with the parties, who nominated another person. Afterwards the confirmed list went back to court and in a formal event the lay judges would be appointed. The lay judges were regularly trained by the judges, but it is now hard to evaluate how much political training and even propaganda was involved.

Each lay judge would go to court for a fortnight. Every professional judge was accompanied by two lay judges, who then worked with him in all cases. In special cases, if the judge thought that lay judges with special knowledge and experience were needed, the lay judges could be chosen from the list, usually of the same profession as the offender. For example if a train accident was caused by a train driver, they would invite train drivers, "because they might be more adequate than housewives".[118]

### *b) Lay Judge Decisions*

The lay judges had equal voting rights as the professional judge and the presiding judge had to consult the lay judges for each decision, not only in the main hearing as in the FRG, but even in the opening proceeding (§ 188 StPO-E) deciding whether there was sufficient evidence. Literally every single court decision should be supported by lay people[119]. In the GDR, in contrast to today the lay judges had access to the files before the hearing and thus were able to check the prosecutor's evidence.

As "full judicial participants" the two lay judges could outvote the professional[120] like today. Outwardly, however, the sentence had to be unanimous. If one of the lay judges or the professional judge was outvoted, she could write down her opinion, put it in a sealed envelope and put this on file.[121] Only the next higher court would open it in case of an appeal or prosecutor's protest.[122] Lay judges would not only attend the trials but also control the probation afterwards (instead of today the professional probation officer). For example the lay

---

117 Interviews: Since 95 % of the workers were member of the union, the election could take place e.g. at a trade union meeting.

118 Interviews.

119 Interviews.

120 Meador 1986, 141.

121 Interviews.

122 Although the interviewee stresses how equal the lay judges were, he only wrote two such statements in an envelope during his whole working life.

judge had to get information from the work place of the accused, so as to ensure that he worked and fulfilled all obligations imposed upon him as part of the probation sentence.[123]

With regard to the question whether the role of the lay judges in East Germany differed from its function today, my respondents came to different conclusions.

One judge explained that the concept of lay judges was reasonable, and sometimes helped to discuss the sentence and to hear other opinions. However, he disapproved the quantity, i.e. having lay judges, every single case and not only in criminal law, but also in civil law, family law and labour law cases etc. The District Court in Nauen, for example, would get every 14 days 10 new lay judges, who would come to court every day.

Most of my respondents pointed out that the lay judges in the GDR were quite passive, very much like today. One judge told me that he was never outvoted but he admitted that he tried to influence his lay judges to get the right decision.

Many of my respondents claimed that lay judges used to be much more important than they are today, because they had more functions, were more involved in the proceedings and were better prepared, whereas today the lay judges do not know all the facts.[124]

> "Today the lay judges only come for the procedures without knowing the file and deciding only according to the expression they got in the oral trial. Today they work more like a jury rather than lay judges".[125]

The reason given for their more active role was that they were trained whereas today legal training is seen as a danger of undue influence. Moreover, they would have time to see the files before the trial, so they had more possibilities to put questions forward themselves rather than just listening all the time.[126]

### c) *Observations*

Through comparison of lay judges in the FRG and of those in the GDR many important differences are disclosed.

The selection process, for instance, was quite different, although formally they are both based on democratic elections. The election procedure in the GDR took place in the working place and each nominee was carefully checked and chosen, whereas the community based election in the FRG was often so formal and anonymous that cases are known in which the election was replaced by

---

123 Often the convicted was not allowed to change the working place for some time without the court's permission.

124 Interviews.

125 Interview.

126 Interview.

drawing lots.[127] Besides, in the GDR lay judges could be re-elected without restriction, whereas in West Germany lay judges can be re-elected only once (so that the period in office is limited to eight years).

In contrast to the GDR, in West Germany lay judges are not allowed to access the court files in order to avoid prejudice and preconception. In the GDR, on the contrary, greater store was set in informing and preparing lay judges for the proceedings. The West German reluctance to put the lay judges under any influence results not only in the denial of access to the judgement records, but also in very limited amount of training. In the GDR, on the contrary, regular and intensive legal training of the lay judges was considered necessary.

Also the lay judges' special knowledge was used by appointing them from special professions to special cases. Since the West German lay judges are elected for a fixed time period, this selection per case is not viable. Besides, as it was shown earlier, East German lay judges participated not only in the main hearing, but also in the preliminary procedure, and they even acted in the role of probation officers.

In sum, one can see that the lay judges in the GDR had a bigger role to play. In practice however, they seem not to have influenced the court decisions more than today, because their extended rights to participate on the one side were neutralised by extended political control and influence on the other.

## 3. Justice in the Community - Social Courts

The establishment of courts only staffed with lay persons, is unique in German legal history.

### *a) Organisation of lay judges*

In every residential area, community, enterprise, agricultural co-operative and so on there existed a so-called Social Court.[128] In opposition to other communist regimes, in the GDR these lay courts were recognised as part of the state court system.[129] A Social Court was either a Conflict Commission or an Arbitration Commission.[130] The Conflict Commission was a group of 5 to 15 volunteers that dealt with legal matters in the working place. Since in the GDR there was no unemployment, nearly the whole population was covered by such a Conflict Commission. For people who had no working place, for example pensioners, housewives etc. there was the equivalent in the neighbourhoods: the Arbitration Commissions.[131]

---

[127] BGH NJW 1984, 2839.
[128] Gesellschaftsgericht.
[129] Meador 1986, 145.
[130] Konfliktkommission and Schiedskommission.
[131] Interviews.

The Members of the Social Court would come together on a regular basis (approximately every fortnight[132]) and – among other things - settle petty offences that were committed by one of their workmates or neighbours. The interesting point is that the Social Courts would even decide cases that had nothing to do with the enterprise or the neighbourhood itself. Thus a Conflict Commission could hear a colleague that had stolen tools from the enterprise as well as, for example people, who took the train without paying for the ticket.

Although both kinds of Social Courts had similar functions and working mechanisms, they were formed and controlled differently. The Arbitration Commission was elected by the City Council and legally trained by professional judges. The members of the Conflict Commission however, were nominated by political parties and then elected by the colleagues. The training was provided by prosecutors.

*b) The Informal Procedures*

According to § 18 GGG[133] the Social Court could act upon requests from citizens, but usually it was the prosecutor who - after completing the police investigation - would hand the case over. Moreover, the police themselves could transfer a case to a Commission without asking (though reporting to) the prosecutor. The judge, too, had the right to pass on the case to the Social Court.

Only petty crime cases such as minor insult, libel, fraud, assault, falsification of documents small violations of property (until 1000 Mark) were allowed to be transferred to the Social Courts.[134] The simplicity of the case, low level of damage and minor guilt, lack of any previous conviction and an expectation of educational result constituted the prerequisites.[135] The evidence had to be complete and sufficient and the offender had to have confessed so that the Social Court needed not decide about guilt but only about the sentence. A further condition was that both the effects of the crime and the guilt of the offender were not too significant.

The Social Court would meet, at the latest, two weeks after the transfer of the case[136] and discuss the occurrence with the offender. There were no professionals present. Although the participants were allowed to receive judicial counsel before the process, the presence of professional defence counsels was not permitted at the Social Court. The reason for this was that defence should not be professionalised in this court of lay persons.[137] Instead the defendant could be

132 Herzog/Wagner 1997, 82.
133 Gesetz über die gesellschaftlichen Gerichte der DDR of 1982 = Code of Social Courts.
134 Herzog/Wagner 1997, 71.
135 § 28 I StGB-E.
136 Habermann 1996, 198.
137 Herzog/Wagner 1997, 82.

prosecuted and defended by lay persons.[138] The Social Courts procedure was not very legalistic, but rather informal. The aim was to find the underlying causes for the social problem and also to resolve the disharmony by removing the cause of the problem and educating the involved persons.[139] There were no fees to pay to the court.

If the Social Court found that the results of the crime and the offender's guilt was not overly harmful for society, and the social education of the criminal could be expected, it chose between the following measures:[140]

- Apologise to the injured person or the working collective
- Redress through money or work
- Obligation to work voluntarily at free time
- Fine between 10 and 500 Mark[141]
- Obligation to start working
- Duty of education by individual or collective
- Public withdrawal of insult in public
- Public reprimand [142]

In contrast to the state courts, a decision by the Social Court was not registered as a conviction against the offender.[143]

The accused could not choose whether to be tried at a State or a Social Court. In theory there was the possibility of not appearing at the hearing at the Social Court, because then the case was automatically sent back to the state court. However, there are no signs that this possibility was ever used (either because this option was not known or because it was feared that the state court might punish this tactic or other reasons). The prosecutor controlled the Social Court's decision. If it did not conform with the law or criminal justice policies, the prosecutor would annul the decision and the case was heard at the state court. The accused, too, could appeal against the Social Court decision. In this case, a state court with one professional judge and two lay judges would try him again, but only very rarely was an appeal brought about.[144]

One might be surprised that the Social Court decisions were supervised not by the judge but rather by the prosecutor. This demonstrates once more the comparatively powerful position of the prosecutor in the GDR. However, it protects the independence of the judge, who has an appeal function if the Social Court Decision is contested.

---

138 Herzog/Wagner 1997, 85.
139 Meador 1986, 144.
140 Schubel 1997, 136 ff.
141 Herzog/Wagner 1997, 83; Habermann 1996, 193.
142 Habermann 1996, 231; Interviews.
143 The offender in East Germany would not be sacked because of a conviction and every prisoner was guaranteed a working and a living place when he was released.
144 Schubel 1997, 152.

*c) Did it work?*

The main aim of the Social Courts was to "enforce socialist standards of behaviour through education"[145] of the party's "responsibility to socialist society".[146] The success of the Social Courts was measured by the future behaviour of the offender.[147] Herzog and Wagner hold that the Social Court has been used to establish moral education and scapegoats, to spread propaganda and general prevention, as well as to educate the members of the court.[148] The professionals in the GDR mostly favoured the Social Courts, because these commissions knew the offenders much better than the prosecutor or the judge did and came up with "sometimes extraordinary decisions".[149]

The Social Courts involved a huge number of citizens. In the mid Eighties nearly 300,000 people worked as judges in the about 26,000 Conflict Commissions and 5,200 Arbitration Commissions.[150] To provide you a comparison: there were only 215 District Courts staffed with 1111 professional and 2222 lay judges.[151]

One truly can say that the Social Courts formed

> "a countrywide network embracing all citizens, either in their residential areas or in their work places".[152]

Statistical data give different numbers, but the overall picture is clear: Social Courts played an essential role in administering criminal cases and hence engendered an enormous relief of the state courts. In 1988 the Social Court handled 78.2% of the falsifications of documents cases, and 46.4% of the intentional bodily harm cases. In 1989 about 40% of the intentional assaults and 35% of thefts and frauds were transferred to the Social Courts.[153] Overall, 24.4% of the defendants were adjudicated by Social Courts.[154] The Social Courts decided 26,084 cases and the State District Courts 44,256.[155] One prosecutor I have interviewed estimated that the Social Courts decided about 40% of all small criminal cases. Another judge held the view that few cases were brought to the

---

145 Meador 1986, 145.

146 Meador 1986, 144.

147 Bericht der zentralen Arbeitsgruppe Schiedskommissionen im Ministerium der Justiz über die Untersuchung im Bezirk Dreseden vom 25. Juli 1967, in: Habermann 1996, 243.

148 Herzog/Wagner 1997, 85; but they do not explain how the accused could and were used as escape goats.

149 Interview.

150 Herzog/Wagner 1997, 85; Meador (1986, 145) talks about ca. 1250 professional judges and 348,000 lay people (50% women) into adjudicating cases.

151 Habermann 1996, 191.

152 Meador 1986, 144.

153 Habermann 1996, 202; Statistisches Jahrbuch DDR 1990, 439.

154 Herzog/Wagner 1997, 82.

155 Blankenburg/Stock/Wolff 1996, 127.

Social Courts, because many Conflict Commissions existed only on paper, since it was so difficult to find volunteers. However, this opinion does not reflect the majority of my interviewees although it seems to be true, that because of the high number of voluntary social groups in each enterprise (trade union group, party group, cultural group etc[156]), it was sometimes difficult to get enough people.

The Social Courts were very effective, primarily because of the embarrassment caused as a result of the accused being judged by his working collective.[157] Even the Criminal Procedure Code itself equated the process of the Social Court with other punishments, such as a fine or imprisonment.[158] And indeed, the trial in front of the Social Court itself was perceived as punishment and the embarrassment in front of the working colleagues was feared.[159] Sometimes the case was even mentioned in the enterprise newspaper and of course, it was always subject to gossip. Certainly if the crime affected the enterprise and the colleagues themselves, the lay court was much more awkward for the defendant than an anonymous state court with an unknown judge. To have to account to his own colleagues for his offence had a big effect on the defendant. Another prosecutor I have spoken with told the story of a man who refused to pay maintenance for his children and was sent to the Conflict Commission of his working place. The commission consisted of 20-30 mainly female working colleagues and he had to give them explanations. He ran immediately to the bank, transferred the money and never delayed any payment again "I don't want to end up there ever again!". Indeed there were only very few recidivists. In Rathenow for example one judge and one prosecutor I spoke to estimate that only 2% returned to trial as offenders.[160]

Beside the effects on the convicted person, the Social Courts were also effective on socialist education. Not only did they guarantee active participation and legal training of a huge number of lay persons but also served as a demonstration that the GDR let their people take part in decision making.

*d) Observations*

*aa) Two sides of a coin*

Coming from a German and English legal education, an analysis of the institution of the Social Courts as an outsider shows many negative as well as positive sides.

---

156 Interview.

157 Interviews.

158 Habermann 1996, 201; § 23 StGB-E. This was a contradiction as such as the police and the prosecutor could transfer a case to the Social Courts. Besides, the Social courts were jurisdiction themselves according to the constitution.

159 Herzog/Wagner 1997, 85; The authors hold that this effect had diminished during time.

160 Interviews.

An important advantage of Social Courts is that the judging persons know the defendant and are able to include more personal information into the judgement. On the other hand the defendant is exposed to her colleagues or neighbours even if the case has nothing to do with the working place. There might be very personal matters to be discussed. This gives the colleagues and neighbours a huge and uncontrolled power over a person's private life. Neither is reconcilable with our current notion of privacy, even in its mildest form.[161]

Besides, excluding every professional interference at the Social Court holds the danger that law is not applied correctly and safeguards of the defendant are disregarded. One of my biggest criticisms of Social Courts is that the defendant could not insist on being tried by a state court.

The Social Court, of course, also realises the idea behind the principle of public trial, that it is open to public scrutiny. On the other hand, there are good reasons to limit the public and evaluate the public interest against the defendant's interest of privacy. In Social Courts this evaluation is too strongly in favour of public exposure.

It is very valuable for the criminal justice system, of course that the Social Courts show an extremely small number of recidivism. But the price to pay for this is stigmatisation in the closest circle of personal relationships. The embarrassment of being judged by one's own neighbours and colleagues can cause emotional stress that might not be justified by the crime committed. It is true that in opposition to a state court conviction by a Social Court does not lead to a criminal record, but the publicity of conviction might be more severe than a registration.

The active involvement of the citizens not only increases public interest and public involvement but also contributes to the legal knowledge and understanding of law. On the other hand, the free legal training includes the risk of state propaganda. Moreover, there is the risk, that lay persons make emotional decisions based on and according to personal interests and prejudices and following social pressure. One interviewee expressed his concerns that commissions used the Social Courts for their own interests. In theory professionals are trained to be more unbiased, but there is no empirical research data to confirm this.

Of course the extended work of Arbitration and Conflict Commissions meant an enormous advantage of relieving the state court of the high case load in small crime. But in the end this saving was paid for by unpaid volunteer work.

*bb) Power of the people?*

Herzog and Wagner criticise the Social Courts for disguising power. The delegation of deviance control to the society seems to be emancipating but in re-

[161] However, the publication of name and address in English newspaper of convicted offenders shows that there are systems who are less reluctant to make criminals public.

ality, - so the authors argue, - does the state hand over problem to the society, claiming that it itself holds the reason for the deficits of its members. The society is asked to look for the guilt in itself, not in the state, the party or the socialist ideology.[162]

I disagree with this argument. I strongly believe that only at the surface, the state handed deviance control back to the society. The fact that the Social Courts, free from any professional participation, decided such a huge number of criminal cases could suggest that the state draws back from a part of criminal justice and let the citizens handle this part. A closer look, however, shows that the Social Courts were but free from professional interference. The regular legal training sessions in particular made sure that the Social Courts would follow the state approved jurisdiction. Furthermore, it was the state that decided which case would end in the Social Courts, the state that could take the cases from the Social Court and the state that controlled the Social Court's decisions. Rather than diminishing the state's power over a part of its jurisdiction, the state enlarged its range by incorporating part of the society. The state employed part of the society for its own purpose and strengthened its own justification in a number of ways:

Firstly, apart from their legal training, the members of the Social Courts (remember this were about 300.000 in a country of only 16 million citizens) were exposed also to considerable propaganda.

Secondly, society was led to believe that the state would give them power in an essential part of the jurisdiction, and this bolstered its claim of democracy.

Thirdly, through the direct contact between judicial staff and population, the state could make its law more public and the citizens more aware of it, demonstrating the state's presence and observance power over the citizens, but at the same showing the closeness between state and society.

Criminal law is an integral part of the public law. A Social Court that offers the public such a big role in the administration of criminal justice signals a powerful tool of direct democracy. But there is the huge risk proven by the practice of the GDR that the state that can use this institution to penetrate and control communities and community values.

## 4. "Goody" or" Baddies" - Labour Collectives

Also in the formal state courts persons or groups who were not affected directly by the case were regularly involved in the litigation. In showing the collective consciousness about the right behaviour, this lay participation, too, educated the public.[163]

---

[162] Herzog/Wagner 1997, 86.
[163] Meador 1986, 121.

*a) Colleagues' verdict*

In every criminal case the working colleagues of the offender would be asked to come together and formulate a common statement about his personality.[164] Then a person was chosen who would come to the trial and present this colleague's evaluation.[165] According to my interview partners, in practice the question was often, whether this worker was needed or would the colleagues be glad to get rid of him, rather than his character or his expected future development etc. It was therefore very purpose oriented.

The collective's statement was used to evaluate a person and to find the right punishment, for example establish whether a sentence on probation was useful. Although in general the representative of the collective was not all that powerful, he could nonetheless tip the balance.[166]

*b) Defender and Accusers*

Beside the collective representative there could be a social defender or social accuser appearing at court. Usually this would be a member of the neighbourhood or working collectives,[167] but also local political representatives and the most important social organisations could take this part.[168]

They could support either the prosecution (for example claiming that the defendant did not support his family, or did not engage in the socialist society) or the defendant (for example witnessing her loyalty to the party or her good work).[169]

*c) A surety for the fallen colleague*

In addition to the collective's evaluation, it was also possible that the working collective would give a surety for the defendant. That meant that the colleagues agreed to control the person in future, regarding certain obligations, especially in case of a probation sentence, for example that he had to fulfil a particular amount of work. Or they would guarantee to make sure that he would pay maintenance.

One prosecutor admitted that there was a question of intruding into private lives, but she stressed that these procedures were very successful.

> "...especially the young guys who had a bad background and were in some way unstable. And then there was somebody at the working place who helped him to

164 Kollektiveinschätzung.
165 Interviews.
166 Interviews.
167 Meador 1986, 121.
168 Brunner 1975, 200.
169 Meador 1986, 121.

decorate his house and would bring him furniture and helped him to get a start. That had a big effect."[170]

## 5. And more legal education

The trial was used not only to educate the offender herself, but also the surrounding society. In general all criminal cases were public.[171] In addition the judge could decide to try in front of an extended public audience, for instance school classes or working collectives. If for example, a train engine driver caused an accident because he was drunk, the judge could invite a hundred engine drivers to attend the trial. Sometimes the whole case was moved in the enterprise instead of a courtroom. This happened, when the cases was closely related to the work place. Once, for example somebody was killed in a working place accident by a forklift truck. The judge, the lay judges and the prosecutor would then go directly into the enterprise. A judge told me that he did not favour this measure because it meant on the one hand more organisation and preparation and on the other hand more noise and disturbance during the trial, for instance when the case was held in an enterprise cantina. Once a judge had a trial in a cow stable![172]

In opposition to Western legal professionals, lawyers in the GDR, especially judges and prosecutors had a huge social role outside the courtroom, too. It was important not only to educate the people directly involved and persons present in the courtroom, but also to spread the findings. They had to hold seminars, discussions, and speeches in factories, and schools etc. about security, order, and law.[173]

Hence, the prosecutors had to go to the enterprises and organise sessions, where cases were discussed. The colleagues might be criticised of not foreseeing or preventing the crime. They also could be told what they had to take care now that the accused got a probation sentence with obligations concerning the working place.

Additionally, the prosecutor had to give talks in the different associations, societies or any commission in the village. Often the prosecutors were out two or three evenings per week to explain law to the people.

Another important connection between legal administration and citizens was free legal advice. Whereas today judges and prosecutors are not allowed to give legal advice, in the GDR courts, lawyer and prosecution offices were obliged to

170 Interview: "…hat eben doch etwas ausgeloest". On the other hand the disappointment if this unstable person fell back to crime, was of course very big.

171 However, it was easy to exclude the public, like it was done in nearly all the political crime procedures.

172 Interview: "The proceedings were very short this day...".

173 Herzog/Wagner 1997, 79.

spend one whole day a week providing free information on all points of law.[174] In the prosecution offices people would seek help against state authorities and institutions, because administration in the GDR was until the very end not subject to judicial review.

> "Tuesday it was always crowded, depending on the weather (more people when it was raining), sometimes 50 people were coming"[175]

## C. Some Conclusions

### 1. Lessons of the past

The different ways in which lay persons took an active part in the administration of criminal justice in the GDR outnumbers West German lay participation decisively. If we look at the different law texts, especially the constitutions of the GDR and of the FRG and see how often and in what ways lay participation is mentioned, we can get a clear picture about how much more importance lay persons were given in the socialist system. In West Germany, on the other side, the role which lay persons have in the criminal proceedings has decreased to a symbolic level. Lay judges have a long tradition and are acknowledged, but they are nowadays seldom the topic of academic discourse and even less the object of empirical research. They are not an issue of public discussion and it seems to be that, due to American movies and crime programs, there are more people who think that Germany has a jury than people who actually know of the existence of lay judges.

In the GDR the claims for more democracy, legal education, understandable law and language could be fulfilled and in part were fulfilled, because lay participation played a much bigger role both in quantity and quality. Moreover, one can assume that the law was much simpler and easier to understand and accessible to the general population in the GDR than in West Germany. The social gap between legal professionals and other citizens was minor and considered politically unacceptable. The laws were short, simple, and easy for lays to understand.[176]

But the primary claim for democracy was not fulfilled here either. Whereas in the FRG one cannot speak of the people sharing the state power of adjudication, because they have both in theory (seeing files, hearing appeal cases and less serious crime) and in practice (diminutive active participation) too little influence, the GDR gave the lay persons more power. But at the same time they

---

174 Interviews: Also the lawyers and the Social Courts would give free legal advice once a week.

175 Interview.

176 The extent to which simple legal provisions provide space for political interpretation shall not be considered at this point.

subjected them to so much state influence and propaganda that one cannot speak of democratic decision making process either. The GDR undermined free decision taking by lay persons by intensive political control, but the FRG decreased lay persons influence on the criminal justice system, too, if in different ways.

The analysis of lay participation in the West has shown that it is put forward as a response to criticism of the current criminal justice system. Lay participation is supposed to make the administration of law more democratic, more understandable, more people related and less dogmatic. Although I share these criticisms of the criminal justice system, I do not consider that just any kind of participation can be the appropriate solution.

If one wants to make court decisions more democratic, one could consider electing the judges as is done in the USA,[177] or making court decisions and related statistical data more open to public access. One could undertake empirical research on how the public would like to see the policy of court decisions in general[178] and take these findings into account when deciding cases.

Regarding the closer connection between law and people (in terms of legal language as well as the complexity of legal provisions), I believe that the professional judges should move to "the people" instead of the other way round. Judges have to be trained to express themselves precisely and understandably at the same time. Also they should be encouraged to take all their decisions not only according to the law but also bearing common sense in mind. Law should give space for taking common sense and sense a of justice into account. To some extent German law does these things, but there is still the correct criticism of German law being too complicated and remote from the people. However, to make law known and understood by the people is not the function of lay persons but rather of legislation.

On the other hand, legal education of the public would be much more increased by using the media rather than employing a small section of society at courts. We already have recently seen an enormous increase of TV dramas involving courts involving both criminal as well as civil law, and this demonstrates quite clearly public interest. Whether or not the quality of these programs is acknowledged, it is definitely a way to make the law and the criminal court system more public.

At the end of the day, I think that in both systems lay participation was used as a showpiece for the application of democracy, whereas there was none or just very little. Lay participation in different legal systems always shows what kind of picture a state has of its citizens. Whereas lay persons in the FRG, who are denied a look into the case files, do not seem to be considered to be able to de-

177 I personally do not support this way, because it holds the risk of deferring decisions based on fact and law to political considerations.

178 For example more severe sentences in sexual offences or white collar crime, or more lenient sentence in minor drug offences.

cide objectively, their counterparts in the former GDR with the continuous political influence seemed to be unable to decide in accordance with the party's wishes. In both systems we see the sad picture of a state which feels the need to involve lay persons in decision making without acknowledging their capability to actually do this. Accusing the other side of giving lay persons too little rights or influencing them too much, one could pretend to be much more democratic oneself, whereas in the end neither system seemed really to rely on its people enough to let them take court decisions free from professional and political influence.

Given the such different roles that lay judges had to play in West and East German courts the actual practice of both was quite similar, i.e. passively sitting at the side of the professional who leads and actually decides the trial. And laymen's passivity, disinterest, and reluctance to serve is reported in many legal systems.[179]

## 2. Lessons for the present

Lay participation in the forms which we could find in the former GDR, i.e. Social Courts and involvement of the working collectives is not possible any longer under the current liberal system. Such institutions would require not only full employment and a strong connection between employer and working place, but moreover a strong sense of social interests prevailing over the individual right to privacy (not to mention the willingness to do volunteer work). Besides, without centralised control (as by the party in the GDR) equal jurisdiction could not be guaranteed.

However, if we see how close the criminal administration used to be to the people, the present German legal system has to ask itself the following questions:

How simple do we want our criminal justice system to be? – In part the reason for the high complexity of German law is due to the aim of balancing criminal justice with the civil rights of the defendant and safeguards against state power. Do we want to give up this complex system of balance of interests in favour for a more understandable law? This question is particularly difficult, since comprehensibility of the law is part of the defendants' protection.

How important is our right to privacy? - Our sense of anonymous dealing with cases and the extended protection of rights bears the risk of removing social conflicts away from their contexts and the involved people. The often-criticised neglect of the victim's interests is just one aspect of this topic.

How much lay decision making do we want? – In our society with extended importance given to experts, do citizens really still look for the often praised common sense of the people or do we rather prefer the professional judge with

179 Richert 1983, 13.

her training and experience? How much confidence do people have in people's decision making?

## 3. Lessons for the future

One can observe that systems are very eager to establish many democratic institutions but only insofar as the outcome is controllable.[180] People are being influenced by the system rather than the other way around and that is true for the liberal FRG as well as for the socialist GDR.

A legal system should be clear about how much confidence it has in its citizens in order to establish how much lay participation it should allow.

First, if the system has confidence in its citizens, why not giving them a say in high jurisdiction, where not only important cases are decided, but moreover directions for future jurisdiction is set, which can be a highly political task.

Second, in the future Germany could think of combining its claim of democracy with its notorious overwork of the courts, by letting small criminal cases be decided by lay persons, like in the former GDR. As well as the mentioned confidence by the state, this change would require a population which is willing to participate in this work and moreover, which would accept such lay jurisdiction. Both requirements seem to be quite questionable in our present individualistic society. If such a model would find sufficient acceptance it would be indispensable to create a procedure that would guarantee the involved individuals, particularly the defendant the basic safeguards. The non-professional judges in such proceedings should be, to some extent, trained but guaranteed independence at the same time. If this is possible for professional judges, why not for lay judges?

How democratic a criminal justice system should be is subject to personal favours, political reasons and professional experience. In any case it is my belief that the most important thing, even outweighing any democratic claim, is transparency: it should be made public why the system does or does not allow lay participation.

## 4. Closing

This paper attempts to make the reader think about the important question: by whom do we want to be judged? Should there be only one judge or more than one? Should it be somebody who knows me (whether I am the defendant or the victim)? Should it be someone with legal training or somebody who lets common sense prevail over legal dogmas?

The question of what characteristics a judge should have goes directly to the core of justice as it implies the questions about what issues should be judged, i.e.

---

[180] One example is the big disappointment of nearly all political parties (except for the SED) when the people did not vote in favour for the unification of the states Brandenburg and Berlin, or the reluctance to let the British people vote about the introduction of the Euro.

what is part of the case? The question of the person of the judge is not only a political one but also always part of the question of justice itself.

## Bibliography

*Baur*, Fritz, 1968, Laienrichter – Heute? In Tübinger Festschrift für Eduard Kern, Mohr, Tübingen, 49-64

*Brunner*, Georg, 1975, Einführung in das Recht der DDR, München, C.H.Beck'sche Verlagsbuchhandlung

*Eser*, Albin, 1995, Laienrichter im Strafverfahren – Ein Vergleich zwischen inquisitorischem und adversatorischem System aus deutscher Sicht, in: Kroeschell, Karl, Cordes, Albrecht, Vom nationalen zum transnationalen Recht, Müller Verlag Heidelberg, 161-181

*Habermann*, Lothar, 1996, Schiedskommissionen in der DDR – eine Dokumentation, in: Renning, Christoph (ed.) et al., Justiz im Umbruch, Bundesanzeiger, Köln, p. 191-284

*Hartung*, Fritz, 1970, Um das Schwurgericht, Zeitschrift für die gesamte Strafrechtswissenschaft, Vol. 82, 601-609

*Herzog*, Felix and *Wagner*, Heike, Gesellschaftliche Präventation und Sanktionierung von Alltagskriminalität in der DDR – Ideologie und Praxis der Gesellschaftsgerichte, 69-87 in: Dilcher, Gerhard (ed.), 1997, Rechtserfahrung DDR: Sozialistische Modernisierung oder Entrechtlichung der Gesellschaft?, Berlin, Berlin Verlag A. Spitz

*Gerstein*, Hartmut, Laien teilen Verantwortung und Macht mit den Profis – Schöffen - Richter ohne Roben, Das Parlament, 10. August 2002. http://www.bundestag.de/cgi-bin/druck.pl?N=parlament

*Katholnigg*, Oskar, *Bierstedt*, Hinrich, Sind bei den Schöffen alle Gruppen der Bevölkerung angemessen berücksichtigt? ZRP 1982, 267-269

*Kissel*, Otto Rudolf, Das Frankfurter "Schöffenroulette" ist vorbei – Gedanken zur Entscheidung des BGH vom 19.6.1985, NStZ 1985, 490-492

*Kissel*, Otto Rudolf, Gerichtsverfassungsgesetz – Kommentar, 3rd ed. Beck Verlag, München 2001

*Kühne*, Hans-Heiner, Laienrichter im Strafprozess?, ZRP 1985, 237-239

*Lilie*, Hans, Deutsches Strafrecht? Über die Unvereinbarkeit der Strafrechtsnormen in der Bundesrepublik Deutschland und in der DDR, NStZ 1990, 153-159

*Luther*, Horst, Schiedsstellen in den Gemeinden als Möglichkeit für eine außergerichtliche Konfliktlösung in den neuen Bundesländern, DtZ 1991, 17-19

*Markovits*, Inga, Last Days, January 1992, California Law Review, 55

*Markovits*, Inga, Selective Memory: How the Law Affects What We remember and Forget about the Past – The Case of East Germany, 35 Law & Society Review 513 (2001)

*Meador*, Daniel John, Impressions of law in East Germany, 1986, The University Press of Virginia

*Ministerium der Justiz* (ed.), 1968, Strafprozessrecht der DDR – Lehrkommentar, Berlin, Staatsverlag der Deutschen Demokratischen Republik

*Renger*, Reinhard, Rechtspflege in der DDR, ROW 1990, 12-18

*Richert*, John P., West German Lay Judges: Recruitment and Representativeness, University Presses of Florida, 1983, Gainesville

*Rössner*, Dieter, 1996, § 380 in: Achenbach, Hans et. al., 1996, Kommentar zur Strafprozessordnung, Vol. 3, Luchterhand Verlag, Berlin

*Roxin*, Claus, 1998, Strafverfahrensrecht, 25th ed., C.H. Beck Verlag, München

*Rüping*, Hinrich, Funktionen der Laienrichter im Strafverfahren, JR 1976, 269-274

*Rüssel*, Ulrike, Das Gesetz zur Förderung der aussergerichtlichen Streitbeilegung – der Weg zu einer neuen Streitkultur?, NJW 2000, 2800-2802

*Schäfer*, Karl, 1988, Mitwirkung des Volkes in der Rechtsprechung, in: Riess, Peter (ed.) Die Strafprozessordnung und das Gerichtsverfassungsgesetz, 24th ed., Vol. 1, Walter de Gruyter, Berlin

*Schönfeldt*, Hans-Andreas, 2002, Vom Schiedsmann zur Schiedskommission – Normdurchsetzung durch territoriale gesellschaftliche Gerichte in der DDR, Vittorio Klostermann, Frankfurt am Main

*Schubel*, Britta, 1997, Geschichte und Gegenwart außergerichtlicher Erledigung von Strafsachen durch ehrenamtliche Schiedsinstanzen in den neuen Bundesländern, Duncker und Humblot, Berlin

*Staatliche Zentralverwaltung für Statistik* (ed.), Statistisches Jahrbuch der Deutschen Demokratischen Republik, Staatsverlag der DDR Berlin 1990

*Volk*, Klaus, 1982, Der Laie als Strafrichter in: Hanack, Walter (ed.), Festschrift für Hanns Dünnebier zum 75. Geburtstag, de Gruyter, Berlin, 373-389

*Vormbaum*, Thomas, 1988, Die Lex Emminger vom 4. Januar 1924: Vorgeschichte, Inhalte und Auswirkungen; ein Beitrag zur deutschen Strafrechtsgeschichte des 20. Jahrhundert, Duncker und Humblot, Berlin

*Wasmuth*, Johannes, Straf- und Strafverfahrensrecht nach dem Einigungsvertrag, NStZ 1991, 160-165

# Tort Law and International Jurisdiction under European Law Recent Developments in England

*Dr. Martina Schulz, Universität Gießen*

## I. Introduction

The paper deals with jurisdiction in tort or, to be more precise, with one aspect of jurisdiction in tort which is the location of the place where a harmful event occurred. Purpose of the paper is on the one hand to present recent case law concerning this issue in English law and then to compare it with the German point of view, and on the other hand to describe the changes the law of international jurisdiction in general has undergone in Europe in the last months.

So the starting point are two English decisions. In both judgments, it is a tort which forms the basis of the proceedings. However, the cases deal with different situations, i.e. with the question of liability because of a road accident on the one hand and with liability for negligent misstatement on the other hand. But the crucial point of both cases (and the issue of the paper) is the jurisdiction of English courts. And although the cases cover rather different situations, it is the same legal rule which is in the centre of both decisions.

The decisions are *Henderson v. Jaouen and Another*[1] and *Domicrest Ltd. v. Swiss Bank Corp.*[2] They date from 1998 and from 2002, i.e. February 2002. So even the more recent case *Henderson v. Jaouen and Another* was decided by applying the Brussels Convention on Jurisdiction and the Enforcement of Judgments in Civil and Commercial Matters, the so-called Brussels Convention, namely its article 5(3). The second case, *Domicrest Ltd. v. Swiss Bank Corp.,* was decided by applying the same article, i.e. 5(3), but of the so-called Lugano Convention which, while containing the same rules like the Brussels Convention, is the Convention ruling jurisdiction and enforcement of judgments for European states not necessarily Member States of the European Union. In both Conventions, article 5(3) rules jurisdiction in tort. The discussion of the problems arising out of this article of the Brussels Convention respectively the Lugano Convention in relation with these recent cases will be one part of the paper.

But the aspect of Article 5(3) and the two decisions just mentioned cannot be the only topic of the paper. Discussing this recent case law makes it necessary also to show the development of the legal basis in the law of jurisdiction in Europe. So it is not correct anymore, to mention simply the Brussels or the Lugano Conventions. By 1st March 2002 the Brussels Convention has been, for

1 (2002) Times, 8 March; [2002] 1 W.L.R. 2971 (CA).
2 [1998] All E.R. 577, [1999] 2 W.L.R. 364.

most of the European Member States, replaced by a Council regulation, Regulation (EC) No 44/2001 of December 2000 on jurisdiction and the recognition and enforcement of judgments in civil and commercial matters.[3] This development is the second part of the paper.

Therefore, the paper begins with the description of the recent English cases as illustrations of situations which might fall into the scope of article 5(3). Then there will be an outline of the changes caused by the replacement of the Brussels Convention by the Regulation 44/2001. The third part of the paper will deal with the discussion of the problems linked with the relevant article 5(3) which leads at same time back to the two English decisions. And even if the paper has not a traditional comparative approach, this recent English case law is not only of interest for English lawyers but also for the German and European perspective because the Brussels Convention, the Lugano Convention, and even more the Regulation 44/2001, have to be applied by lawyers of the respective Member States. So there may be an influence by case law of one Member State of the European Union or Contracting State of the Lugano Convention to the comprehension of a certain problem of the Conventions – and now also the Regulation – in general.

## II. The English decisions

### 1. Henderson v. Jaouen and Another

The first case which will be discussed here is *Henderson v. Jaouen and Another*.[4] This is a judgment passed by the Court of Appeal on 1st February 2002. The facts of this case represent a rather well-known situation respectively a situation which seems to be rather frequent: a person injured in a road accident later suffers a deterioration of his/her condition. The special element in this case

---

[3] OJ L 12, 16.1.2001, p. 1. Also in this Regulation, the meaning of article 5(3) is the same as in the Brussels Convention or in the Lugano Convention. The wording of article 5(3) of the Regulation is: "A person domiciled in a Member State may, in another Member State, be sued in matters relating to tort, delict or quasi-delict, in the courts for the place where the harmful event occurred or may occur."
Article 5(1) of the Regulation 44/2001 is as follows: A person domiciled in a Member State may, in another Member State, be sued:
(a) in matters relating to contract, in the courts for the place of performance of the obligations in question;
(b) for the purpose of this provision and unless otherwise agreed, the place of performance of the obligations in question shall be: - in the case of the sale of goods, the place in a Member State where, under the contract, the goods were delivered or should have been delivered, - in the case of the provision of services, the place in a Member State where, under the contract, the services were provided or should have been provided,
(c) if subparagraph (b) does not apply then subparagraph (a) applies.

[4] (2002) Times, 8 March; [2002] 1 W.L.R. 2971 (CA).

is the change of domicile of the victim, Mr Henderson, several years after the accident, from France to England. The facts of the case, in brief, are as follows: In 1978, Mr Henderson was injured in a road accident in France. The accident had been caused by M Jaouen. The judgment does not give any other information about the accident but that M Jaouen was found wholly responsible by a French Criminal Court for the accident and that special damages were ordered. This was in 1979.

Two years later, 1981, also in France, Mr Henderson issued civil proceedings against M Jaouen and the insurance company Mutuelle Assurance des Instituteurs de France (MAIF) which insured M Jaouen. In 1983, a tribunal awarded damages accordingly. They were based on the degree of disability at that date and these damages were final. But Mr Henderson was also given the right to seek a further award in the event of subsequent deterioration in his condition.

This right to seek further damages in the case of deterioration of the condition of the victim means in French law a fresh cause of action which gave Mr Henderson the opportunity to sue in the case of deterioration of the condition. In the same year, 1983, Mr Henderson returned to England. He made use of this opportunity in 1995 (he claimed "*aggravation en cause*") when he issued fresh proceedings in France while he was already living in England. In 1996 a provisional payment was made.

However, Mr Henderson did not pursue the proceedings before the French court, but issued a claim in England, in the Queen's Bench Division in May 2000, against M Jaouen and the insurance company (i.e., furthermore, about 4 years after the provisional payment was made). Mr Henderson asserted that the English court had jurisdiction under article 5(3) of the Brussels Convention of Judgments in Civil and Commercial Matters 1968, as incorporated by the Civil Jurisdiction and Judgments Act 1982. Basis of this assertion was that the deterioration of his condition occurred exclusively in England. The requisite harmful event, identified in article 5(3) would be the deterioration of his condition.

The judgment of the first instance in the Queen's Bench Division confirmed the jurisdiction of English courts. The defendants appealed against this decision and their appeal was successful. The Court of Appeal denied jurisdiction of English courts. Article 5(3) did not permit to issue a claim in England.

## 2. Domicrest Ltd. v. Swiss Bank Corporation

The second case which also gives an illustration of the different situations covered by article 5(3) is *Domicrest Ltd. v. Swiss Bank Corporation.*[5] This case was decided in 1998. The plaintiff is the English company Domicrest Ltd., a supplier of electronic consumer goods. Domicrest sued the Swiss Bank Corporation in England for damages because of the tort of negligent misstatement. The

5 [1998] 3 All E.R. 577; [1999] 2 W.L.R. 364.

background of this claim are the following facts: Domicrest sold electronic goods to a Swiss group of associated companies. Acting as banker for this group was a Swiss branch of Swiss Bank Corporation. They sent copy payment orders to relating to contracts of sale between Domicrest and the group of companies. So before delivering the goods to the buyer, Domicrest received several payment orders by fax from the defendant in respect of the respective invoiced prices. Domicrest doubted the security of those fax payment orders, but was informed that those faxes would not be sent if there were any doubts that the invoices would not be paid.

So Domicrest began to deliver goods from its stores in Switzerland and Italy. The defendant, Swiss Bank Corp., then paid according to the invoices and the payment orders. This procedure worked about a year but later, in October 1995, difficulties with the payments arose and in October 1995, three copy payment orders remained unpaid. As a result of the conversation with Swiss employees of the defendant – in the course of this conversation it was confirmed that those payment orders meant that the payments were "guaranteed" – Domicrest gave orders for the release of the goods covered by these last three payment orders. But they remained unpaid and led to the actual proceedings.

Domicrest pleaded that the Swiss Bank Corporation was liable in contract and in tort. It alleged that English courts had jurisdiction under the Lugano Convention, article 5(1) in respect of the claim in contract and article 5(3) in respect of the claim in tort – negligent mis-statement as the effect of the payment orders.

In respect to the claim in contract, the court decided that the place of performance (article 5[1]) is England so that Swiss Bank Corporation was properly sued in English courts as far as the contractual claim was concerned. But article 5(1) is not the topic of this paper. As far as article 5(3) was concerned, jurisdiction of English courts was denied.

So far to the facts of the two English decisions. Before discussing the results of the cases, I would like to describe the law of jurisdiction in Europe in general and the say some words on behalf of the rule which is in the centre of the two cases.

## III. The European law of jurisdiction

### 1. The Brussels Convention on jurisdiction and the enforcement of judgments in civil and commercial matters

The Brussels Convention on jurisdiction and the enforcement of judgments in civil and commercial matters entered into force on 1st February 1973. So since almost 30 years now, there is a common basis of European law ruling jurisdiction.

Originally, there were only six contracting states, namely the six original Member States of the European Community at this time. Afterwards there were several modifications, usually when new member States of the European Community signed the Brussels Convention.[6] So, for the Federal Republic of Germany the Brussels Convention entered originally into force already on 1st February 1973 in relation to Belgium, France, Italy, Luxemburg, and the Netherlands.

The United Kingdom incorporated the Brussels Convention directly into its domestic law by the Civil Jurisdiction and Judgments Act 1982.[7] It entered into force on 1st January 1987, at the same time as the coming into force of the 1978 Accession Convention to the Brussels Convention after its ratification by the United Kingdom on 7 October 1986.[8]

The Convention comprises in its first part a system of direct jurisdictions. The judge of the first instance is directly bound by those rules of international jurisdiction.

According to article 2 of the Brussels Convention,[9] there is a general jurisdiction of the courts where the defendant is domiciled. The following articles contain special or exclusive jurisdictions. Among the special jurisdictions is the jurisdiction in tort, article 5(3), which is in the centre of this paper.[10] If jurisdiction in tort according to article 5(3) will determine the forum of a case depends on the choice by the appellant.[11] As generally under the system of either Regulation or Convention, if there are several States having jurisdiction, the plaintiff may choose the forum.[12]

On behalf of the Brussels Convention, there was academic dispute about its character, i.e. either a contract concluded by the Member States of the European Union or the Convention being secondary Community Law.[13] But with the com-

---

6 Accession Conventions of 1978, OJ L 304, 30.10.1978, p. 1, of 1982, OJ L 388, 31.12.1982, p. 1, of 1989, OJ L 285, 3.10.1989, p. 1, and of 1997, OJ C 15, 15.1.1997, p. 1. For a consolidated text, see OJ C 27, 26.1.1998, p. 1.

7 Law Reports, Statutes, c. 27.

8 Cf. R. Geimer, European Law of Civil Procedure under the Brussels Convention, Festschrift Stiefel (1987), 219.

9 Article 2(1): Subject to this Regulation, persons domiciled in a Member State shall, whatever their nationality, be sued in the courts of that Member State.
Article 2(2): Persons who are not nationals of the Member State in which they are domiciled shall be governed by the rules of jurisdiction applicable to nationals of that State.

10 For Article 5(3) rules not only international but also jurisdiction of domestic courts, it replaces also the national rules on jurisdiction, e.g. § 32 of the German Civil Procedure Code, K. Kiethe, Internationale Tatortzuständigkeit bei unerlaubter Handlung – die Problematik des Vermögensschadens, NJW 1994, 222 (223, n. 16).

11 Case 68/93 *Shevill v. Presse Alliance S.A.* [1995] ECR 415.

12 R. Geimer, European Law of Civil Procedure under the Brussels Convention, Festschrift Stiefel (1987), 219 (233); J. Kropholler, Europäisches Zivilprozeßrecht (2002), Art. 5 Rn. 72.

13 For this discussion cf. M. Schwarz, Der Gerichtsstand der unerlaubten Handlung nach deutschem und europäischem Zivilrecht (1991), pp. 71 ff.

ing into force of the Regulation 44/2001, this dispute has lost its relevance almost completely. There is indeed now secondary Community Law.

Without qualifying the character of the Brussels Convention, it had been ruled by the Protocol on the interpretation of the 1968 Convention by the European Court of Justice (henceforth European Court), signed on 3rd June 1971,[14] that the European Court has to interpret the meaning of the rules of the Convention. By this transfer of competence on behalf of the interpretation of the Convention to the European Court, a splitting of interpretation between the Member States was prevented, and the success of the Convention was promoted by this transfer.[15]

## 2. The Lugano Convention

The Brussels Convention is accompanied by the so-called Lugano Convention.[16] It is indeed understood as a Convention parallel to the Brussels Convention.[17] The Lugano Convention is the instrument for European states not being member states of the European Union to adopt the harmonisation and even unification of the law of jurisdiction as created by the Brussels Convention.

The Lugano Convention was implemented into the domestic law of the United Kingdom by the Civil Jurisdiction and Judgments Act 1991, which came into force on 1st May 1992.[18] For Germany, the Lugano Convention entered into force on 1st March 1995.[19]

## 3. Replacement of the Brussels Convention by the Regulation 44/2001

As already mentioned, there has been a major change in spring 2002 in regard of the Brussels Convention. Basically, it has been replaced by the Council

---

14 The Protocol entered into force on 1st September 1975 (BGBl. 1975 II, p. 1138).

15 R. Wagner, Vom Brüsseler Übereinkommen über die Brüssel I-Verordnung zum Europäischen Vollstreckungstitel, IPRax 2002, 75 (78).

16 BGBl. 1994 II, p. 2660.

17 Originally, the Lugano Convention was a convention for the states of the EFTA (European Free Trade Association), Iceland, Liechtenstein, Norway, and Switzerland. However, Liechtenstein, although EFTA-Member State, did not adopt the Lugano Convention. But the accession to the Convention is open to other states. There are now 19 contracting states altogether. For a table of ratifications cf. http://www.civpro.unibe.ch/walter/pix/Ratifikationsstand.PDF. The state which last adopted the Lugano Convention was Poland in February 2000; cf. e.g. D. Martiny/U. Ernst, Der Beitritt Polens zum Luganer Übereinkommen, IPRax 2001, 29 ff.; R. Wagner, Zum Inkrafttreten des Lugano Übereinkommens für die Republik Polen, WiRO 2000, 47 ff.

18 The Civil Jurisdiction and Judgments Act 1991 (Commencement) Order 1992. The Lugano Convention is implemented as Schedule 3C of the Civil Jurisdiction and Judgments Act 1982.

19 BGBl. 1995 II, p. 221.

Regulation (EC) No 44/2001 of December 2000 on jurisdiction and the recognition and enforcement of judgments in civil and commercial matters.[20] The Regulation (EC) 44/2001 of 22 December 2000 entered into force on 1st March 2002.[21] According to its article 68, it replaces the Brussels Convention. So it is now the existing law for all European Member States, with the exception of Denmark.[22] Because of this exception, the coming into force of Regulation 44/2001 does not mean that the Brussels Convention does not exist any longer. It is still applicable law in relation to Denmark.

The changes of the contents of the rules of the Brussels Convention effected by the Regulation 44/2001 relate more to the issues of recognition and enforcement of judgments than the rules concerning jurisdiction.[23] On behalf of article 5(3), there has been no change in substance by the replacement of the Brussels Convention by the Regulation 44/2001. The wording of the article has only been adapted as a consequence of the different character of Convention and Regulation. So the term "Contracting State" has been replaced by "Member State".

More important is the addition of "may occur" to the text of article 5(3). Consequently, the new wording is expressly extended to actions in respect of threatened torts that are likely to occur. So this addition clarifies the scope of article 5(3). Under the Brussels Convention, there had been dispute if the cases of harmful events which were about to occur would fall into the scope of this article.[24]

## IV. Jurisdiction in Tort

Article 5(3) covers a large variety of situations when torts arise and damages have to be awarded. Road accidents like in the *Henderson* case have been one main situation which expressly should be covered by article 5(3).[25] But the scope

---

20 OJ L 12, 16.1.2001, p. 1.

21 According to its Article 76.

22 Legal acts on the basis of Title IV of the EC Treaty are not binding for Denmark (according to the Protocol on the position of Denmark). There would be a similar situation for the United Kingdom and the Republic of Ireland but these States participate voluntarily in the new legislation. However, there is now a splitting in the legal sources of jurisdiction in the European Union; cf. R. Geimer, Salut für die Verordnung (EG) Nr. 44/2001 (Brüssel I-VO), IPRax 2002, 69 (70).

23 R. Geimer, Salut für die Verordnung (EG) Nr. 44/2001 (Brüssel I-VO), IPRax 2002, 69 (72 f.).

24 Therefore the new wording removes any doubts which may have existed as to availability of jurisdiction in proceedings concerning threatened torts which are likely to occur. The European law has now clarified this problem and reached the same basis as did already the law of the United Kingdom after accessing the Brussels Convention on behalf of jurisdiction within the United Kingdom by Schedule 4, Article 5(3) of the Civil Jurisdiction and Judgments Act 1982.

25 This results from the Jenard Report, OJ C 59, 15.3.1979, p. 1 (26).

of article 5(3) goes beyond this as is demonstrated by the *Domicrest* case. The main problems in relation to article 5(3) are the ascertainment of the meanings of tort, delict and quasi-delict and secondly, the location of the place where the requisite harmful event occurred.

## 1. Tort

The main distinction to limit the scope of article 5(3) is that between tort and contract. So in an autonomous interpretation, laid down by the European Court in the *Kalfelis* judgment,[26] article 5(3) applies to all proceedings with a claim for tort liability. Excluded are claims for restitution.[27] But the concept of *Kalfelis* is extraordinarily wide in order to reduce the risk that different Contracting – now Member States – give article 5(3) a different scope in their domestic laws. Any action is therefore included which seeks to establish the liability of a defendant and which does not involve matters relating to a contract under article 5(1).[28]

## 2. „Place where the harmful event occurs“

### *a) Appropriate forum*

In this paper, however, the central problem concerning article 5(3) is that of the location of the place where the harmful event occurred.

The justification for the special jurisdiction in tort according to article 5(3) - and therefore the exception from article 2 - is the relationship which is especially close, between the issue of the claim and the courts of a member state different from those where the defendant is domiciled.[29]

The close relationship or the "particularly close connecting factor" between the dispute and courts other than those of the State of the defendant's domicile is the reason for the attribution of jurisdiction to those courts (i.e. the courts of the Member State where the defendant is not domiciled).[30] Reasons for this justification of a special jurisdiction because of the particularly close connecting factor are a sound administration of justice and the efficacious conduct of proceedings.[31]

---

26 Case 189/87 *Kalfelis v. Schröder, Münchmeyer, Hengst & Co.* [1988] ECR 5565.

27 P. Schlosser, EuGVÜ, Art. 5 Rn. 16.

28 Case 189/87 *Kalfelis v. Schröder, Münchmeyer, Hengst & Co.* [1988] ECR 5565.

29 Case 68/93 *Shevill v. Presse Alliance S.A.* [1995] ECR 415.

30 G. Hohloch, Erfolgsort und Schadensort – Abgrenzung bei Ansprüchen auf Ersatz von (primären und sonstigen) Vermögensschäden, IPRax 1997, 312 (313); K. Kiethe, Internationale Tatortzuständigkeit bei unerlaubter Handlung – die Problematik des Vermögensschadens, NJW 1994, 222 (225 f.).

31 This is a translation from "lien de rattachement particulièrement étroit », « bonne administration de la justice » and of « organisation utile du procès », cf. Case 21/76 *Handelswekerij G.J. Bier v. Mines de Potasse d'Alsace S.A.* [1976] ECR 1735 at para. 11; Case

These principles are e.g. laid down in the *Shevill* case and the *Marinari* case of the European Court which deal also with article 5(3).[32]

In the *Shevill* case,[33] the European Court extended its jurisprudence on behalf of economic loss to cases of non-pecuniary loss, especially here to damages caused by the tort of defamation (libel). The victim of the libel published by the French journal "France Soir" was not restricted to an action against the publisher in France where the publisher was established. However, it was possible to sue in each state in which the libellous publication had been distributed. This was even the case if only a small number of the journals was published in a certain state.[34] So in this case, a tort causes damages in several states and, because of the decision of the European Court, there is a splitting of jurisdictions in such a situation. For that reason, the *Shevill* case is indeed criticised.[35]

The *Marinari* case is also dealing with economic loss. Mr Marinari, domiciled in Italy, lodged promissory notes with an English branch of Lloyds Bank. It refused to return them to Mr Marinari who was afterwards arrested by the police. Furthermore, there was sequestration of the promissory notes. Mr Marinari sued Lloyds Bank in Italy seeking compensation for the damage he claimed to have suffered in Italy. Jurisdiction of Italian courts was denied. The meaning of place where the harmful event occurred in article 5(3) does not include the place "where the victim claims to have suffered financial damage following on initial damage arising and suffered by him in another contracting state."[36]

So these cases deal with further problems arising out of article 5(3). But nonetheless, they were also the basis for the development of rules which were also applied by domestic courts in the *Henderson* and *Domicrest* cases, even if their facts differ from those in *Shevill* and *Marinari*.

---

220/88 *Dumez France v. Hessische Landesbank (Helaba) and Others* [1990] ECR 49, at para. 17; Case 68/93 *Shevill v. Presse Alliance S.A.* [1995] ECR 415 at para. 19; Case 364/93 *Marinari v. Lloyds Bank plc (Zubaidi Trading Co., Intervener)* [1995] ECR 2719, at para. 10.

32 Case 68/93 *Shevill v. Presse Alliance S.A.* [1995] ECR 415; Case 364/93 *Marinari v. Lloyds Bank plc (Zubaidi Trading Co., Intervener)* [1995] ECR 2719.

33 Case 68/93 *Shevill v. Presse Alliance S.A.* [1995] ECR 415; see also K. Kreuzer/P. Klötgen, Die *Shevill*-Entscheidung des EuGH: Abschaffung des Deliktsortsgerichtsstands des Art. 5 Nr. 3 EuGVÜ für ehrverletzende Streudelikte, IPRax 1997, 90 (91).

34 In the *Shevill* case, the number of journals published in France was 237.000; in Europe altogether 15.500, among those: England/Wales 230 and Yorkshire, where the victim of the libel was domiciled, only 5.

35 K. Kreuzer/P. Klötgen, Die *Shevill*-Entscheidung des EuGH: Abschaffung des Deliktsortsgerichtsstands des Art. 5 Nr. 3 EuGVÜ für ehrverletzende Streudelikte, IPRax 1997, 90.

36 Case 364/93 *Marinari v. Lloyds Bank plc (Zubaidi Trading Co., Intervener)* [1995] ECR 2719, at para. 15.

Furthermore, in the line of judgments concerning article 5(3), they are not the first cases. At the beginning is the so called *Bier* ruling or *Rhine pollution case* of the European Court.[37] This case is a classic example of the situation in which the elements in a tort are split up amongst different states"[38] or of "torts committed at a distance" (*Distanzdelikt*).[39]

A French industrial company had discharged chlorides into the Rhine. Downstream, the salts caused serious damage to a Dutch gardening company. The Dutch market gardener brought an action in the Netherlands against the French company.

In *Bier*, it was outlined that the background of the special jurisdiction in tort like in article 5(3), is to find an appropriate forum for the proceedings. However, finding an appropriate forum which is closely connected respectively to the dispute and to the harmful event is no singularity of the Brussels Convention or the Regulation. It has also been the reason for the special jurisdiction in tort in German Civil Procedure law, and this not only in the existing Civil Procedure Code but this special jurisdiction was already known to its historic predecessors.[40]

In order to find an appropriate forum, the plaintiff is given the option of suing elsewhere than in the Contracting State (now: Member State, as far as the Regulation 44/2001 is concerned) where the defendant is domiciled like it would be the principle of article 2. Therefore, as the other special jurisdictions of the Convention or the Regulation, article 5(3) states an exception from the principle in article 2. But it is then still not clear which place is decisive. The *Jenard Report* expressly left open "whether reference should be made to the place of the event giving rise to the damage or to the place where the damage occurred".[41]

In the *Bier* ruling, the European Court now determined an autonomous interpretation of the term „place where the harmful event occurred".[42] It accepted the place of occurrence either being the place of the harmful event giving rise to the damage or the place of the damage itself.[43]

---

37 Case 21/76 *Handelswekerij G.J. Bier v. Mines de Potasse d'Alsace S.A.* [1976] ECR 1735.

38 Cheshire and North's Private International Law, p. 301.

39 K. Hertz, Jurisdiction in Contract and Tort under the Brussels Convention (1998), p. 238.

40 M. Schwarz, Der Gerichtsstand der unerlaubten Handlung nach deutschem und europäischen Zivilprozeßrecht (1991), p. 1 ff.

41 Jenard Report , OJ C 59, 5.3.1979, p. 1 (26).

42 Case 21/76 *Handelswekerij G.J. Bier v. Mines de Potasse d'Alsace S.A.* [1976] ECR 1735. The decision has been broadly supported, cf. inter alia M. Schwarz, Der Gerichtsstand der unerlaubten Handlung nach deutschem und europäischen Zivilprozessrecht (1991), p. 128, Fn. 51.

43 Case 21/76 *Handelswekerij G.J. Bier v. Mines de Potasse d'Alsace S.A.* [1976] ECR 1735, at para 15. See also P. Kaye, Civil Jurisdiction and Enforcement of Foreign Judgments (1987), p. 577; K. Hertz, Jurisdiction in Contract and Tort under the Brussels Convention, p. 241 ff.

The intention of the special jurisdiction in article 5(3) is the wish to make it easier for an appellant, at least to a certain extent, to seek justice.

For this reason also, it is more convenient to put the place of acting (the place of the event giving rise to the damage - *Handlungsort*) as well as the place of damage (the place where the damage occurred - *Erfolgsort*) under the notion of place where the harmful event occurred. This is the interpretation of article 5(3) developed by the European Court the *Bier* ruling. An additional aspect is the choice between the place of acting and the place of damage which was also the result of the *Bier* decision. This option to choose between two places in the scope of article 5(3) prevents from applying an artificial construction in concentrating on only one element (i.e. either place of acting or place of damage) in tort or delict and excluding the other elements of a case.

*b) Balance of interests of the parties*

On behalf of article 5(3), there is a balance of interests of the parties involved which has to be taken into consideration. At first, article 5(3) works in favour of the appellant. He/She does not have to "follow" the tortfeasor to his domicile by being forced to sue before the courts of the state where the defendant is domiciled.[44]

This seems to contradict the *Henderson* case, where Mr Henderson after the decision of the Court of Appeal has indeed to follow or to go back to the forum of the defendant. But this is only so because in the *Henderson* case there is the special situation of a later deterioration of the condition of the appellant together with the change of domicile of Mr Henderson from France to England.

On the other hand, the jurisdiction in favour of the appellant must not be overemphasized. The defendant has, at least, to be protected against jurisdictions which could not at all be expected. There has to be a certain degree of predictability for the defendant on behalf of the forum which may have jurisdiction.[45] Besides predictability, there are the aspects of certainty, appropriateness and avoiding fragmentation which should be the basis of jurisdictional rules.[46] So the choice for the appellant to issue proceedings either at the place of the event giving rise to the damage or at the place where the damage occurred is indeed in fa-

---

44 R. Geimer/R.A. Schütze, Europäisches Zivilverfahrensrecht (1997), Art. 5, Rn. 144; D. Coester-Waltjen, Internationale Zuständigkeit bei Persönlichkeitsrechtsverletzungen, in: Wege zur Globalisierung des Rechts, Festschrift Schütze (1999), p. 175 (182).

45 The aspect of predictability is also supported by other jurisdictions, cf. the judgment of the United States Supreme Court in *World-Wide Volkswagen v. Woodson 444 US 286 (1980)*: „The Due Process Clause ... gives a degree of predictability to the legal system which allows potential defendants to structure their primary conduct with some minimum assurance as to where that conduct will or will not render them liable to suit".

46 A. Reed, Special Jurisdiction and the Convention: The Case of Domicrest Ltd v. Swiss Bank Corporation [1999] 18 C.J.Q. 218 (237).

vour of finding an appropriate forum, and to reach a sound administration of justice and the efficacious conduct of proceedings.

### 3. Place of "further harmful event"

The *Henderson* case, however, concerns still another category of place of damage. The principles outlined above may not be suitable for these situations.

It is a sort of further or consequential harmful event, i.e. the deterioration of the condition of the appellant, Mr Henderson. It is not sufficient to distinguish between the place of the event giving rise to the damage and the place where the damage occurred. Both places would have been in France where the accident had happened and where Mr Henderson was injured. England as place of the harmful event in the meaning of article 5(3) would have had required to consider also the place of the deterioration of the condition of Mr Henderson as a separate place where a harmful event- and that would be the deterioration of the condition – occurred. Only this interpretation of article 5(3) could have resulted in the jurisdiction of English courts. But this interpretation was denied by the Court of Appeal.

The already above mentioned motivation for article 5(3) – to find the appropriate forum, a sound administration of justice, efficacious conduct of proceedings - is based on the considerations, that in special situations there may be a close relation between the case and the court which has to decide.[47] This close relation may exist either to the place of the event giving rise to the damage as to the place where the damage occurred. But there is indeed no close relation to a Court if the condition of the victim of a road accident deteriorates in the aftermath of the accident.

The choice which is otherwise given to the appellant has therefore no justification in the event of a later deterioration of the condition of the victim. Thus, there is no jurisdiction of the courts of a Member State where a consequential damage or a deterioration of the physical condition of the victim occurs.[48] Instead, the close relation with the place of the accident continues to exist. So, it is not the exception of article 5(3), but the general rule of article 2 which rules here the international jurisdiction of the courts.

Limit for the interpretation of article 5(3) should be that the principle of article 2 (jurisdiction where the defendant is domiciled) must not be completely abolished by extending the scope of article 5(3) in the sense of extending the jurisdiction to places other than the places of the event giving rise to the damage

47 J. Kropholler, Europäisches Zivilprozessrecht (7th ed. 2002), Art. 5 Rn. 73.

48 See also P. Schlosser, EuGVÜ, Art. 5 Rn. 19; R. Geimer/R.A. Schütze, Europäisches Zivilverfahrensrecht (1997), Art. 5, Rn. 192; J. Kropholler, Europäisches Zivilprozessrecht (7th ed. 2002), Art. 5 Rn. 77.

and eventually the place where the damage occurs.[49] So there may be the jurisdiction extended in favour of the plaintiff, but the result of case law is that article 5(3) is basically an exception from the principle of article 2 and that this principle must not completely be replaced by creating a jurisdiction of the courts where the plaintiff is domiciled. Neither the deterioration of the physical condition as in *Henderson* nor the principal place of business of the plaintiff as in *Domicrest* are therefore factors considered as particularly close or close enough to justify the application of the special jurisdiction of article 5(3).

The choice of jurisdictions must not be extended to those places of consequential damages. Otherwise, the jurisdiction in tort would be too much extended in favour of the appellant and the principle of article 2 (domicile of the defendant) would be too much restricted. This comprehension of article 5(3) and the term of "place where the harmful event occurs" considers that further damages often occur at the domicile of the appellant.[50] This is also the case concerning the deterioration of the condition of Mr Henderson.

Even if the above mentioned comprehension of article 5(3) has been developed in relation to pure economic loss in the *Marinari* decision, it is true also for the situation of deterioration of the physical condition.

The interpretation of the place where the harmful event occurred as "any place where the adverse consequences of an event which has already caused actual damage elsewhere"[51] is considered as too extensive.[52] Otherwise only the interests of the appellant would be taken into consideration which could also result in forum shopping. So the number of jurisdictions should not be multiplied by permitting to sue also at the place where only a consequential damage or further harmful event occurred. Neither the *Bier* ruling nor the wording of article 5(3) justify to consider as place where the harmful event occurred any place where a mere consequential damage has occurred. The German Federal Court, too, supports this approach. Only the place where the tort is completed could be interpreted as place where there harmful event occurred in the meaning of article 5(3).[53]

And in the *Henderson* case, it is indeed only by change of domicile to England that Mr Henderson is able to issue proceedings before an English court even if he did not succeed because jurisdiction of English courts was finally de-

---

49 M. Schwarz, Der Gerichtsstand der unerlaubten Handlung nach deutschem und europäischen Zivilprozeßrecht (1991), p. 160.

50 Collins, The Civil Jurisdiction and Judgments Act 1982 (1983), p. 60 Stoll, Gutachten im Verfahren EuGH 11.1.1990 – 220/88, Dumez France, Slg. 1990 I 53 f.

51 Case 364/93 Marinari v. Lloyds Bank plc (Zubaidi Trading Co., Intervener) [1995] ECR 2719, at para. 14.

52 *Henderson v. Jaouen and Another* (2002) Times, 8 March; [2002] 1 W.L.R. 2971 at p. 2980, para. 37 (CA).

53 BGH, 24.9.1986 –VIII ZR 320/85, NJW 1987, 592 (594).

nied. This demonstrates that jurisdiction could be determined by coincidence if the place of a consequential damage is considered as place where the harmful event occurred in the meaning of article 5(3). The appellant could have moved to any other state, therefore a close connection has to be denied if there is only consequential damage.[54] To allow the plaintiff to sue the defendant in a Member State other than where the defendant is domiciled because of considering a deterioration of the physical condition as place where the harmful event occurred would overemphasize the interests of the appellant, and even contradict to find an appropriate forum for the issue. Otherwise, the defendant would not be protected against fora not being appropriate.[55]

The facts of *Domicrest* differ from those of *Henderson* in the way that there are just several places which could be considered as place where the harmful event occurred. The places of sending and receiving the assurance about the payment because of the copy payment orders as well as the place of the delivery of the goods. Domicrest alleged that the place of harmful event was its principal place of business where the assurance of the payment was received so that jurisdiction of English courts should be allocated. However, this alone does not lead to the tort of negligent mis-statement.[56] Even if England is the place where Domicrest suffered economic loss, without the release of the goods in Switzerland and Italy there would be no economic loss at all. However, a disadvantageous aspect of the result in the *Domicrest* decision is also that the plaintiff is unable to issue proceedings comprising both the contract and tort claims altogether in England.[57] But here the solution is given in the *Domicrest* judgment itself. Of course, the plaintiff is entitled to pursue his action according to the general rule of article 2 before the courts of the defendant's domicile.[58]

---

54 This result is also supported by L. Uhl, Internationale Zuständigkeit gemäss Art. 5 Nr. 3 des Brüsseler und Lugano-Übereinkommens (2000), p. 219.

55 Staudinger/B. v. Hoffmann, 1998[13], Art. 38 EGBGB Rz. 257; OLG Stuttgart, 6.7.1998 – 5 U 22, RIW 1998, 809 = NJW-RR 1999, 138 = IPRspr. 1998/147.

56 *Domicrest Ltd. v. Swiss Bank Corp.* [1999] 2 W.L.R. 364 at 382 f. with reference to the *Marinari* ruling, Case 364/93 *Marinari v. Lloyds Bank plc (Zubaidi Trading Co., Intervener)* [1995] ECR 2719; cf. also G. Spindler, Die internationale deliktsrechtliche Zuständigkeit für Informationsdelikte (unrichtige Bankauskünfte), IPRax 2001, 153 (155).

57 G. Spindler, Die internationale deliktsrechtliche Zuständigkeit für Informationsdelikte (unrichtige Bankauskünfte), IPRax 2001, 153 (154); A. Reed, Special Jurisdiction and the Convention: The Case of Domicrest Ltd v. Swiss Bank Corporation [1999] 18 C.J.Q. 218 (237).

58 *Domicrest Ltd. v. Swiss Bank Corp.* [1999] 2 W.L.R. 364 at 382 f. with reference to Case 189/87 *Kalfelis v. Schröder, Münchmeyer, Hengst & Co.* [1988] ECR 5565, 5586, para. 20 and quoting Lord Goff of Chieveley in his speech in *Kleinwort Benson Ltd. v. Glasgow City Council* [1997] 3 W.L.R. 923, 930G.

Furthermore, a similar answer could be given Mr Henderson who is only prevented from pursuing his claim before English courts because of the decision of the Court of Appeal on behalf of the interpretation of article 5(3).

### 4. Australian cases

On behalf of consequential damages and jurisdiction, similar cases have been decided in Australia. Because of the Australian legal system with different jurisdictions of each state, there is also need to determine jurisdiction if several states are involved. The notion of "place where the harmful event occurs" is defined similar to the European solution. So there is no jurisdiction if the plaintiff is injured in an accident in Victoria, returns to New South Wales and gets most of the medical treatment there which means that the plaintiff suffers most of the after-effects of the accident not in the State where the accident itself happened. There is jurisdiction of the courts "where the whole or a material part of a cause of action "arose"", not of those courts where "a plaintiff … suffers consequential damage flowing from the injury inflicted by the defendant."[59]

## V. Conclusions

What is now the result of the changes in the legal sources of the law of jurisdiction and which is now the position of English case law considering the recent case law of *Henderson* and *Domicrest*?

Replacing the Brussels Convention by the Council Regulation has minor consequences relating to article 5(3). However, the splitting of legal sources because of the exception for Denmark must be kept in mind. But from a material point of view, there are no fundamental changes as far as the system of special jurisdictions is concerned. It is not the aim of the Regulation (formerly the Convention) to extend the special jurisdiction of article 5(3) by multiplying the place where a harmful event occurred. The special jurisdiction of article 5(3) works in favour of the plaintiff anyway. Therefore, the preferential treatment of the plaintiff has to be limited in order to protect also the interests of the defendant.

In other legal systems than English law, the development of the law concerning jurisdiction in tort in case of several possible places of damages had already come to the position that mere places of consequential damage or places of further harmful events do not lead to a jurisdiction of the courts of this state. This is the case, for example, in German law. But it is also demonstrated by the judg-

---

[59] *Thomas v. Penna* [1985] 2 NSWLR 171; *Stephen John Flaherty v. Laila Girgis* F.C. 87/017, High Court of Australia, 14 May 1987, http://www.austlii.edu.au/au/cases/cth/high_ct/unrep66.html; *Falls Creek Ski Lifts Pty Ltd. v. Leonie Fay Yee* Nos. CA 40532/94 and DC 737191, Supreme Court of New South Wales, 3rd October 1995, http://www.austlii.edu.au/cgi-bin/disp.pl/au/cases/nsw/supreme%5fct/unrep162.html?query=%22fall+creek%22.

ment of the United States Supreme Court mentioned above[60] or in the Australian cases. It was also the position the European Court had developed. So there is no jurisdiction of courts of a state because there is the place of a consequential damage or further harmful event but neither the place of the event giving rise to the damage nor the place where the damage occurred. To give the notion of place where the harmful event occurred in article 5(3) the meaning that would include these places of consequential damage would result in a jurisdiction only in favour of the plaintiff. Thus, the interests of the plaintiff would be overemphasized by this interpretation of article 5(3). This is now also the result of the *Henderson* case. So the *Henderson* case would not be decided differently when applying article 5(3) of the Regulation 44/2001 instead of the Convention. On behalf of the *Domicrest* case, this change does not have any effects, too, because it would still be the Lugano Convention which had to be applied.

As result of the *Henderson* decision, English law has therefore answered the question how the place where the harmful event occurred has to be determined and the Court of Appeal has described how European law (including the case law of the European Court, especially the *Bier*-decision) has to be understood. The case is decided in accordance with the existing European case law. It is also in accordance with, for example, the German point of view.[61] So, compared to the German position, *Henderson* does not mean a considerable development. Instead it confirms the position which elsewhere had already been reached.

However, the title of the Times publishing of *Henderson* is not exact – this title is "No power to use French law". The question if French law could be applied or not is not asked in the *Henderson* case. Before even asking this question, the Court of Appeal comes to the result that jurisdiction has to be denied. And this result is reached by applying European law (which, by the way, would be the same in France) not by French law. But the Court does not come to a point where it would have been necessary or at least possible to apply French law. Accepting jurisdiction of English courts would not have meant automatically that French law would have to be applied (even if this would have been probably the case). If there is jurisdiction in tort as result of the application of article 5(3), there would be the opportunity to use French law if this would be the applicable law. So, even if the Court would have decided otherwise, it could have applied French law. Article 5(3) does not require that jurisdiction and the applicable law are of the same legal system.[62]

In the *Domicrest* decision too, the Court followed the jurisprudence of the European Court, namely the *Marinari* ruling, and considered Switzerland as the

---

60 Cf. note 45.

61 For example BGH, 24.9.1986 - VIII ZR 320/85, BGHZ 98, 263; R. Geimer/R.A. Schütze, Europäisches Zivilverfahrensrecht (1997), Art. 5 Rn. 192; J. Kropholler, Europäisches Zivilprozeßrecht (2002), Art. 5 Rn. 77.

62 R. Geimer/R.A. Schütze, Europäisches Zivilverfahrensrecht (1997), Art. 5 Rn. 144, 175.

place where the harmful event occurred. The place of the event giving rise to the damage as well as the place where the damage occurred was Switzerland. The delivery of the sold goods was considered as the harmful event. The tort was not only committed by receiving the assurance that the invoices would be paid.[63] Therefore, there was no jurisdiction of English courts as the appellant had sought.

The result of both cases, *Henderson* and *Domicrest Ltd.*, is that there is now - without the necessity to have these questions decided by the European Court - a further common understanding of jurisdiction in tort according to article 5(3). In both cases, the courts follow the jurisprudence of the European Court, thereby denying the application of a "substance test", which was formerly suggested to determine the place where a harmful event occurred by considering the main emphasis of the tort.[64]

The main aspect is the close relationship between the dispute and the courts which have to decide a case. So this closeness is lacking if there is only the manifestation of a further or consequential damage.[65]

It would be discretionary if the victim could let a damage be manifest and therefore have opened jurisdiction in every state where such a further damage would happen by coincidence. Accepting the place of a consequential damage as place where the harmful event occurred would destroy the balance between the respective interests of plaintiff and defendant (this balance being, by the pure existence of article 5(3), already in favour of the plaintiff). In order to maintain this balance, the restriction of the meaning of place where the harmful event occurred in article 5(3) by excluding places of consequential damage or places of further harmful event is a necessary restriction.

---

63 G. Spindler, Die internationale deliktsrechtliche Zuständigkeit für Informationsdelikte (unrichtige Bankauskünfte), IPRax 2001, 153 (155).

64 Minster Investments Ltd. v. Hyundai Precision and Industry Co. Ltd. (1988) 2 Lloyd's Rep. 621.

65 See also G. Hohloch, Erfolgsort und Schadensort – Abgrenzung bei Ansprüchen auf Ersatz von (primären und sonstigen) Vermögensschäden, IPRax 1997, 312 (314).

# Conclusion

*Prof. Dr. Günter Weick, Universität Gießen*

First of all I would like to thank you and especially all the contributors to this colloquium. I am most grateful to those of my colleagues who had the marvellous idea to honour the anniversary of my 65th birthday and my "Emeritierung" with an international colloquium. I do not know exactly who the spiritual fathers of the idea were, but I know for certain that my colleagues *Thomas Groß* and *John McEldowney* took the burden of organisation, and that they did a great job. Thank you so much for everything. Many thanks also to all the other helping hands necessary for the success of such a conference.

During the colloquium I was privileged to listen to your inspiring and fascinating presentations of papers and contributions to the discussion. I learnt a lot. Even an almost emeritus is – to a certain extent – able to learn. But now I realise the difficulty of writing a resumé adequate to your profound thoughts and debate. I came to the conclusion that – at least today – I will not be able to acknowledge and appraise all of your papers. Instead I would like to make some final remarks related to the general subject of the colloquium and inspired by your contributions. I am deeply impressed by the many and diverse responses to the subject of the conference. It is a rich and colourful bouquet that you have presented to me – the most beautiful I have received on one of my anniversaries.

Our conference shows the broad spectrum and the fertility of an international approach to law, of comparison between laws and of transnational legal studies and dialogues. As part of the colloquium we have seen the classic comparative law that helps to understand the basic structures of law, the real problems underlying legal provisions, and their various legal solutions. It gives us a reservoir of ideas, methods and instruments, a fund of scholarly and practical experience. Last but not least it has an enormous practical importance in international transactions and in the everyday work of international lawyers.

However, today comparatists no longer restrict themselves to the description and analysis of existing national regulations and legal solutions. Increasingly, they are involved in creative and constructive work, particularly with regard to new problems, to modern phenomena such as electronic commerce and other internet facilities, intersexuality, genetic engineering, surrogate motherhood, cross border organised crime, money laundering, large scale migration or nuclear waste. No serious problem of modern societies can be solved by a single national legal system, but only by international cooperation.

Other fields of interest and activity for comparatists and internationalists are the harmonisation and unification of laws by means of international conventions, European directives, the jurisdiction of European courts, NGO rulemaking etc. Furthermore I wish to reiterate the importance of Human Rights as the basis of European constitutional principles, which was the subject of our colloquium in Warwick two years ago. I refer also to the development of an international legal order, to international jurisdiction and to private actors in Public International Law, some of the topics of our present conference.

A dynamic development is also apparent in Private International Law. Scholars in this field no longer concentrate on national conflict rules, but deal more and more with uniform substantive law, transnational law of international trade and other economic relations ( the so-called *lex mercatoria*), international dispute settlement and dispute resolution, and similar truly international aspects of Private Law.

Finally, comparative and international legal studies help in the understanding of one's own legal culture and the legal culture of other countries. We gain a deeper insight into the interrelationship between law and society. Comparative and international legal studies and research may even contribute to the development of a supranational legal culture (at least in certain areas), although I am far from dreaming of a uniform European law, as some of you know from our colloquium here in 1998.

So comparative and international law (in the sense of *"Völkerrecht"*) have grown far beyond the narrow limits indicated by their names. The notions have become too narrow and even misleading. We still lack an adequate comprehensive conception, but I am confident that it will be found in the near future.

Legal scholars have an important role to play in the transformation and internationalisation described above. They have to build theoretical and methodical foundations, to oversee the "value decisions" in a technology-oriented world, to develop suitable legal instruments for the new tasks, and to advise and criticize the often rushed and short-sighted lawmakers. There was a time when scholars interested in comparative and international law were seen as exotic and slightly eccentric people similar to an expert in foreign expensive wine, while an ordinary bread-and-butter-lawyer had to stick to water from the mains or the odd local beer. I don't say a word against the local beer, but I suggest that this point of view is outdated, and I hope that you will share my opinion.

In any case our students are keen on international and comparative studies, be it abroad or in their home universities, and on international experience. They prove that they realise the changes in the legal world. They accept in their hundreds the chances of ERASMUS exchange studies, of integrated programmes or of placements in foreign countries. If you asked me the question from the famous *Marcel Proust*-questionnaire "What gives you hope?" I would answer "that so many young colleagues and scholars are here." Comparative and international legal studies have become more and more natural in all fields of law. Academics and practising lawyers from different countries understand each other – in spite of significant differences between their legal systems – now much more than 40 years ago when I started my academic life. Better understanding, in turn, helps to demolish prejudice and to prevent distrust and rejection. If a jurist and a scholar makes a contribution to peace, understanding and cooperation, what else can he wish? I am happy to have had this opportunity, and in such a pleasant company as yours, and I hope to have it still into the future.

Jaakko Husa

# Nordic Reflections on Constitutional Law

## A Comparative Nordic Perspective

Frankfurt/M., Berlin, Bern, Bruxelles, New York, Oxford, Wien, 2002. 209 pp.
ISBN 3-631-39290-7 · pb. € 35.30* / US $ 33.95 / £ 22.-
US-ISBN 0-8204-5952-6

The author maintains that the Nordic constitutional legal-culture possesses some unique fundamental qualities if compared to common law or Romano-Germanic constitutional systems. The book offers a Nordic comparative perspective on the basic questions of comparative constitutional law. Also, the question of the relationship between judicial review and parliamentary system is explored in the light of Nordic experiences. The author analyses the discussion on the „Constitution of Europe" in its relation to the Nordic constitutional thinking, and evaluates the possible future of the Nordic tradition in the more tightly integrated Europe of tomorrow. Furthermore, Nordic constitutional thinking seems to be in a crossroads of judicial activism and self-restraint. *Nordic Reflections on Constitutional Law* brings together the latest development in Nordic constitutional law and highlights its possible role in Europe.

*Contents*: Valid law in comparative constitutional law · Methodology of constitutional comparison · Constitutional foundation of legal system · Separation of powers in Nordic systems · Judicial review in Nordic systems · Nordic family of constitutional law · Nordic constitutional tradition and the „Constitution ouf Europe"